GW00566464

Norman Foster
Foster Associates
Buildings and Projects
1982-1989

Volume 1
Norman Foster
Team 4 and Foster Associates
Buildings and Projects
1964-1973
Watermark 1991

Volume 2
Norman Foster
Foster Associates
Buildings and Projects
1971-1978
Watermark 1989

Volume 3
Norman Foster
Foster Associates
Buildings and Projects
1978-1985
Watermark 1989

Volume 4
Norman Foster
Foster Associates
Buildings and Projects
1982-1989
Birkhäuser/Watermark 1996

Volume 5
Norman Foster
Foster Associates
Buildings and Projects
1985-1991
Birkhäuser/Watermark 1997

Volume 6
Norman Foster
Foster Associates
Buildings and Projects
1987-1991
Birkhäuser/Watermark 1998

Volume 4
1982-1989

Norman Foster
Foster Associates

Buildings and Projects

with contributions by

Jean Bousquet
Deyan Sudjic
Colin Davies
Tim Ostler
Annette LeCuyer
Martin Pawley
Charlotte Ellis
Norman Foster
Graham Vickers
Piers Rogers
Kenneth Powell
and
Diana Periton

edited by
Ian Lambot

Watermark

Designed by Ian Lambot

First published in Great Britain in 1996 by
Watermark Publications (UK) Limited

Copyright © 1996 Watermark Publications (UK)
Limited, PO Box 92, Haslemere, Surrey GU27 2YQ

All rights reserved. No part of this publication
may be reproduced or transmitted in any form
or by any means, electronic or mechanical, including photocopy, recording or any other information storage or retrieval system, without
prior permission in writng from the publisher.

Typeset in Rotis Semisans 45 and 65
Colour separations by Evergreen Colour Separa-
tion (Scanning) Co Ltd, Hong Kong
Printed by Everbest Printing Co Ltd, Hong Kong

ISBN 1 873200 04 8

Contents

Foreword
by Jean Bousquet

Jean Bousquet is the founder and managing director of the Cacherel clothing empire. Between 1983 and 1995 he was mayor of the city of Nîmes, during which time he was closely involved with the commissioning of a number of contemporary building projects, including the Carré d'Art, the Nemausus 1 public housing development by Jean Nouvel and Jean-Marc Ibos, and the Grand Stade by Vittorio Gregotti and Marc Chausse. He also initiated numerous restoration projects of the city's historic fabric, not least the renovation of the seventeenth-century Town Hall to designs by Jean-Michel Wilmotte. Controversial at times, few would deny his 12-year tenure as mayor breathed new life back into the city.

In France, recent government decentralisation has given locally elected representatives the real power to organise and consider the growth of their cities. As a consequence, they have had to learn how best to reconcile the city's development with a respect for what already exists. This was a fundamental principle for any development in a city like Nîmes, a city remarkable for the quality and antiquity of its heritage.

At the centre of Nîmes stands the Maison Carrée, a little temple with a façade of six columns and astonishingly harmonious proportions. Facing it was a theatre based on the Italian model, which had been built between 1819 and 1827 in a late neo-Ionic style. It burnt down in 1952. All that remained was the main colonnade, perched on a flight of steps which gave on to no more than a piece of wasteland — a temporary car park in the middle of the city.

These two colonnades — the magical, voluptuous one of the Maison Carrée and the other rather graceless one of the theatre, as stiff as a poker — stood facing each other, forming a composition which no one dared touch.

Several projects had been envisaged for the theatre site over the years, but none had come to fruition. Then, in 1984, the city decided to commission a decidedly contemporary building to house various cultural and artistic activities.

Behind this decision lay the desire to make the heart of the city, once again, a place of lively topicality and cultural awareness. Across the ages, going back as far as the Roman forum or the Athenian Agora, city inhabitants have adapted the urban fabric to encompass a deeply felt need for a centre of social life. The predominant requirement has been either to preserve this forum or to rehabilitate it.

In Nîmes, our act of rehabilitation was to erect a building housing a children's library; a library for adults; a music department, complete with auditorium and record library; a newspaper stall; a bookshop; a reference centre for twentieth-century art; and a museum of contemporary art. Through networking and integration, we hoped this multi-disciplinary approach would encourage the spread of knowledge and improve education — one of the modern world's most important problems. To succeed, we needed a building that was neither over-bearing nor pompous. Instead, it needed to be attractive and welcoming, a place open to all.

Every century builds in its own style, and each has left its own imprint. That which is both beautiful and functional — that is to say perfectly adapted to the function for which it was designed — will never go out of fashion. Opposite the Maison Carrée, a symbol of 2000 years of history, we were going to build such a building. Imagine it!

What was the solution? An eighteenth-century pastiche? Such a choice would have been unpardonable. No, the Maison Carrée has been enhanced by an uncompromisingly contemporary building of absolute quality. It is always a question of quality.

The Carré d'Art, like the pyramid at the Louvre, was a challenge that has since met with outstanding success, even though, at times, the odds against this seemed impossible.

I condemn those who allow whole cities to die because no one is willing to touch them. (I think of the most prestigious, and of Venice in particular.) This is gambling of a quite different sort. Our architectural heritage must be modernised, adapted to the needs of contemporary life with care and respect. Not to touch it is to allow it to decay, to deteriorate, perhaps, to the point of extinction.

Norman Foster's Carré d'Art is a modern building. It is supported by a regular concrete frame. Like the Maison Carrée it faces, however, its main façade is a canopy that is largely open,

though supported here by five slender metal columns. The building as a whole lies on an axis which connects the ancient Roman Arena with the eighteenth-century Jardins de la Fontaine.

Though the public areas stretch over five floors, it is no higher than the surrounding roofs, whose pink tiles are allowed to dominate the view from the rooftop terrace. The materials used to complete the podium and refurbish the Place de la Maison Carrée include paving stones inspired by the Roman model.

One could say that, in Nîmes, a potential conflict has been avoided by considering and accommodating the element of time, bringing together the city's Roman roots and the modern world. This is probably how the Carré d'Art should be understood.

Introduction
by Deyan Sudjic

Deyan Sudjic trained as an architect at the University of Edinburgh, but chose not to practise after graduating. He has worked as a critic, journalist and curator. He is currently director of the Glasgow UK City of Architecture and Design programme for 1999, architecture critic for the Guardian and visiting professor at the Hochschüle für Angewandte Kunst in Vienna. He has curated a number of exhibitions, including the Foster, Rogers, Stirling show at the Royal Academy, and *Design as Identity* at the Louisiana Museum in Copenhagen. He was the founding editor of Blueprint magazine, and is the author of *The 100 Mile City, New British Architecture* and *Cult Objects*.

Ambitious young Brits abroad. Norman Foster, Richard Rogers and an American colleague, Carl Abbot, well wrapped up against the chill of a New Haven winter.

There is an almost infinite variety of Norman Fosters. Perhaps the earliest version to have made a mark on the world of architecture is the young student, who can be seen shyly peering out of the black-and-white snapshots taken of him in the company of the almost equally youthful Richard Rogers when they were both postgraduates at Yale. They huddle together in their overcoats against the winter chill of New Haven. They catch the train to Manhattan for bruisingly dry Martinis at the Four Seasons with James Stirling. They worked with Serge Chermayeff to explore the nature of the modern city. They collaborated on designing megastructures.

This was Foster as the personification of the ambitious Brit abroad, the bright young working-class Englishman from Manchester, for whom the spur of America and its uncomplicated social structure was an escape from the claustrophobia of post-war Britain. This was the brilliant student who reinvented himself in America, for whom design was an escape hatch from the bleaker aspects of British life.

Simply to have travelled to America at this period was enough to be different from his peers who had stayed at home. It was to have experienced at first hand what the builders of the California Case Study houses were up to, to have used commercially available colour film, to have seen Airstream trailers close up, to know about Charles Eames and Buckminster Fuller. It was enough to set yourself apart from the everyday reality of Britain, where such things were known only at third hand from blurry illustrations in magazines, and seemed like no more than colourful fairy tales from across an Atlantic that took three days to cross.

In America, it was taken for granted that architecture was about optimism and a sense of possibilities in a way that Britain, which had only just escaped from shortages and rationing, found impossible to comprehend. And Foster, apparently effortlessly, adopted those easy, optimistic assumptions. But as things were to turn out much later on, Foster's discovery of Fuller was not just to be confined to an enthusiasm

for the imagery of the geodesic dome. It was also about discovering a sweeping sense of scale, of not being afraid of making large plans. It helped prepare him to make the ambitious kind of statements that characterise his work, in a way that seemed uncomfortably out of place in the Britain of his student years.

Then there was the Norman Foster who emerged after the dissolution of Team Four — the practice that he and Rogers established together when they went home — still a young man, but by now in a hurry to reinvent the architectural profession. This was a moment when architects were divided between the large commercial firms who got most of the work, but none of the critical attention, the submerged nine-tenths of the profession as it were, and the charmed circle of small practices who built the art galleries and universities that accounted for a tiny fraction of Britain's buildings, but for almost all of what was conventionally understood as its contemporary architecture.

Foster, with his crew-cut and polo-neck, hardly fitted the conventional image of either architectural camp. The big firms offered nothing but business-like pragmatism, the small ones carried on as if they were country doctors or family solicitors. Or prima donnas. Exposure to America, and his own natural predispositions left Foster with an abiding impatience with each of these models. The turbo-charged, even ruthless quality of Foster's own work was instantly apparent.

He presented himself as a problem solver, he was refreshingly free of sentimentality, and as likely to ask a potential client, "is your new building really necessary?", as to offer heroic form-giving exercises involving tracing paper and soft pencil sketches. His favourite word at the time was 'systems'. He delighted in appropriating technology from industries more advanced than construction for use on the building site, or better yet, for prefabrication off site.

Even at this early stage, there was always an ambition to Foster's practice that seemed larger in scale than the material he was working with. Each project was always beautifully rendered — Helmut Jacoby was an early discovery: when it was completed, it was equally beautifully photographed. There was a sense

The Airstream trailer, that symbol of a bright, shiny future, cool and efficient, was a favoured image in the Foster office for many years, and was featured in numerous presentations and lectures.

Helmut Jacoby's inimitable drawing style captured many of Foster Associates' earliest projects — including this, the German Car Centre of 1972.

Efficiency and value for money at IBM Cosham — a temporary building still in use 25 years after its completion.

of keeping an eye on the future, and the place of the practice within it.

And yet, if Foster was enthusiastic to embrace the language of business-like technology, the reality was that he began his practice at a moment when there was a still unbridgeable gulf between those architects who treated the profession as a business, and those who were concerned with architecture for its own sake.

It wasn't just the architects on opposite sides of this great divide who saw themselves as belonging to different worlds, it was their clients too. The kind of people who commissioned office blocks and corporate headquarters in the 1960s tended to regard architecture that could be considered as art with an innate sense of scepticism. In their eyes this was a form of self-indulgence. To be seen to care about architectural quality at this period, was to be accused of spending too much tax-payer, or shareholder money. Bland, or banal building might actually be more expensive than a building of genuine architectural quality, but the very fact that it camouflaged its cost behind a slovenly exterior disarmed all criticism. Ugly buildings had — perversely — become synonymous with value for money.

Foster tackled this muddle-headed thinking head on. He talked about his work in terms of efficiency and value for money. He made his office, first in Fitzroy Street, then in Great Portland Street and finally in Battersea, look like a machine humming with efficiency. He had IBM as a major client, he looked for new methods of construction, he explored new development and contractual techniques with the intention of building well, but quickly.

Yet Foster was still essentially part of the architectural community. And there was still something of the poetic analogy in his work: it was often the dream of mechanisation rather than its substance that counted in the way he presented his work. Despite the visual clues offered by his office, he was anything but a businessman architect. To hire him was considered to represent an adventure by most of his

clients. He was anything but a conventional choice of architect. And he was anything but a conventional designer.

This was the Foster of the Willis Faber & Dumas building and the Foster of the Sainsbury Centre. The image that the office projected of itself was smooth, efficient, and technocratic. But it still used Rotring pens and tracing paper as its principal design tools, rather than computers. The staff numbers were still small, and the ethos of the practice was not so different from that of a score of similar bright young offices. Being small was still seen as a virtue, even if it might have been a virtue conjured up out of necessity.

But despite the air of quiet pragmatism, the office's output was anything but pragmatic. Each building that came out of the office was an event. Each seemed to be the product of entirely fresh thinking. A leap in a new direction, rather than the refinement of what had gone before. You could not say that this was an office that designed glass buildings. Nor that it specialised only in steel. It was ready to experiment with almost anything — though there was not, it is true, much in the way of brick.

It was a period when the practice was finding a voice. Certainly there was a clear attitude and vocabulary emerging. The early projects reflected Foster's discovery of Buckminster Fuller, in that there was a predisposition in favour of the lightweight, and making the most of the minimum of materials. But it still allowed for buildings of such individual genius and unpredictable inventiveness as the Willis Faber & Dumas building, with its black glass, grand piano superstructure, with its resonances of Mies van der Rohe's free-form glass towers from Berlin, as well as the pristine classical elegance of the Sainsbury Centre.

The pattern began to change with the building of the new headquarters for the Hong-kong and Shanghai Banking Corporation — itself another completely original solution, a reinvention of a familiar building type. Until they won the commission in an invited competition, Foster Associates had essentially followed the traditional pattern of the small creative British architectural office. Like many others it was based

[handwritten notes top of page: "1000s onwards start of NF Associates / similar to most other firms of the time / However it was driven by the willingness / of Foster and his associates to experiment / when all around saw Architecture / purely a business NF saw it as a ART. / NF wants to Reform profession" — marginal: "purpose for description of GPF?"]

The Hongkong Bank on display at the the Royal Academy's *New British Architecture* exhibition in 1986. The huge models and photographs first brought home to a popular British audience just how remarkable a project the Bank really was.

[handwritten right margin: "giving Architecture Icon / celebration"]

By 1982, with the Hongkong Bank project well under way, Foster Associates had outgrown its Fitzroy Street office. The near 50-strong staff was photographed there shortly before the move to Great Portland Street.

[handwritten margin notes: "only four tiers between the lot", "more/less business", "more related"; vertical: "Architectural Culture"]

The Hongkong Bank. The building's scale, ambition and sheer dynamism propelled Foster on to the world stage.

[handwritten bottom margin: "Attempts to / keep the original / lord or off creative / Lord foe / Sir NF"]

on the dedication of a band of slightly unworldly enthusiasts, living for architecture with no strategic sense of the wider world. It was important to share certain values and assumptions if you were to continue to belong to this world. To deviate from them was to risk ostracism, to be ejected from the club.

To be part of the architectural culture of the early 1970s, it was a given that the office would be managed by architects. And for such architects, running the practice, hiring, management, job-getting, financial planning and all the rest of it, were almost always treated as side issues. The only really important thing was to design buildings, and to maintain a structure that put the creative architect at the top of the tree, responsible for all decisions. This was still a time when the architectural profession continued to be tightly regulated: limited company structures were banned; unlimited liability partnerships were still a professional requirement. Fee cutting, advertising and building industry directorships were all taboo.

In this view of the architectural world, professional management was regarded as, at best, a distraction. A prerequisite to this approach was that the office stayed small. An office that followed this path could never rise much beyond about 30 people. But even after the Hongkong Bank came into the office, Foster deliberately maintained a practice with just such an ethos. For though the bank commission was one of the largest of its kind, it was mainly run from Hong Kong where a substantial team was established to build the project, employing upwards of 100.

Consciously or unconsciously, it was an arrangement which worked in such a way that the expansion needed to cope with a job of its complexity and scale never touched the London office, which continued to maintain the character of a small and intimate organisation. The infrastructure and the scale of operation needed to make Hong Kong a reality was kept at arm's length.

Thus it was that Norman Foster remained the quintessential English architect, even when he was first beginning to make a mark outside the narrow world of architecture. It was a caution that perhaps provided the reassuring sense of security that comes from familiarity. He

might have had a few unfamiliar characteristics, such as piloting his own aeroplane, but he still spoke the language of the architectural world, even as the Royal Academy's *New British Architecture* exhibition of 1986, bringing together Norman Foster, Richard Rogers and James Stirling, turned him into a national figure. So much so that his reputation has reached the point where Foster has joined the roster of celebrities promoting Rolex wristwatches, and he was part of Vanity Fair's recreation of the famous Beaux Arts Ball, which New York's most celebrated architects from the 1930s attended dressed as their own buildings.

It was the Mark Three Foster that really broke the mould: the post-Hong Kong Foster. The scale and complexity, the ambition and sheer dynamism of the Hongkong Bank moved Foster out of the purely British context, propelling him on to the world stage. And having crossed that threshold, he became an architect who was able to transcend the division within the profession between the critically acclaimed and the materially successful.

By the middle of the 1990s Foster was unique among British architects of the post-war generation in that he had become a dominant force both in the quality and the quantity of his work. This had not been seen in Britain since the days of Lutyens, who dominated the profession in a way that Foster has come to echo. And like Lutyens, Foster is now in demand to design both giant corporate buildings and individual houses.

But the transition was not immediately apparent. The shift in perceptions of Foster was almost covert at first. It seemed for a while — to the world outside the office at least — as if things had gone quiet for Foster Associates, as the practice was then called. For a variety of reasons — the accidents of cancelled commissions, and shifts in programmes, as well as the sheer length of time taken to complete large-scale projects — there was a gap between the opening of the Hongkong Bank and the completion of the next major Foster design. A gap that stretched almost to the end of the 1980s,

The BBC Radio Centre, at the time the most challenging urban problem the Foster office had ever addressed.

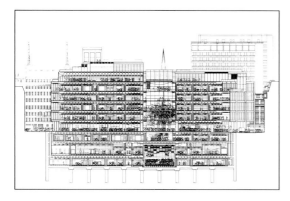

The BBC Radio Centre at the Royal Academy. What should have been the unveiling of Foster Associates' most significant project in Britain turned out to be a memorial for a cancelled design.

and was wide enough for it to seem as if the adventure into building on the scale of the Hongkong Bank was a one-off, rather than a settled new direction for the practice.

The exhibition at the Royal Academy was certainly a watershed for Foster — but it was not quite the immediate new beginning for his career that might have been expected, even though it attracted so much attention. The stunning photographic images of the Bank, and the huge models of it that dominated the Academy exhibition, brought home to a British audience just how remarkable a project the Bank was. It went a long way to overcome the tendency of the insular architectural community in Britain to discount the significance of buildings that were not within easy reach of central London. And it did much to change the sense that the architectural community in Britain lived in an embattled enclave.

For years there had been a feeling that architecture was cut off from the other visual arts, as well as from a wider public. The success of the Royal Academy show demonstrated that architecture could take its place alongside art in the Academy's galleries. And that it could attract a large audience as well. But the other scheme that Foster exhibited at the Royal Academy — the new headquarters building for BBC Radio in London, envisaged for the site of the former Langham Hotel, which should have been the triumphant unveiling of his most significant project in Britain and the natural next step in his career, consolidating the achievement of the Hongkong Bank — turned out to be a memorial for a dead design.

This was the most complex, and potentially the richest and most rewarding urban problem that Foster had yet addressed. But the building was cancelled while the exhibition was still being planned. Instead of building itself a contemporary civic monument, updating the inheritance of the Reith years, the Corporation opted for a banal metal box in suburban White City. It was a decision that said a lot about the state of contemporary culture.

The walls of the Royal Academy were crammed with countless study models that showed every twist and turn in the project's troubled history, betraying Foster's fondness for the model as a design tool, and also his way of exploring

every potential option to the full before finally committing himself to one approach rather than to another.

But it is hard not to interpret the display, not so much as an exposition of a design process in minute detail, but as a memorial for a great deal of futile effort. And as such, it sharply brought home the precarious nature of architectural practice. Critical success, and the successful completion of one giant project, is no guarantee that there will be a steady flow of similar work to follow. And in the end, the critical reputations of architects of Foster's kind are based not so much on ideas, as on completed buildings.

Nor are these fluctuations simple abstractions. They are fluctuations that can have painful consequences for individual careers and livelihoods. The period after the completion of the Bank certainly faced the firm's directors with some difficult decisions about the number of employees that their shifting workload could support. Teams and expertise that had been built up over several years had sometimes to be dispersed. The concomitant to this was that the Foster office by the 1980s had become one of the most important training grounds for young creative architects drawn in from around the world by the opportunity to work on what were widely seen as some of the most exciting projects available anywhere.

Until the BBC project, the majority of commissions that came Foster's way were of a nature that required pristine 'object' buildings, on out-of-the-way sites. The BBC, by contrast, would have been the centre-piece of one of London's great urban set pieces, the culmination of the eighteenth-century expansion of the capital north, toward Regent's Park. Thanks to its site it could not fail to engage in an intimate dialogue with Nash's bravura circular Church of All Souls, with its conical spire, just across the street.

The office had worked long and hard on the project, wrestling with the complexities of modern broadcasting technologies, as well as with the symbolic qualities of housing a national institution such as the BBC in a building that

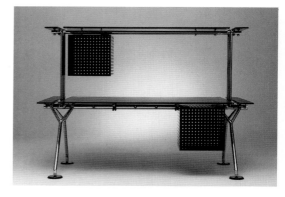

Foster Associates' Nomos office system, designed for, and in collaboration with, Tecno. During the 'designer decade' that was the 1980s, architecture and architects once more became part of the fashionable agenda.

Even the most Classical of Foster's buildings, the Sainsbury Centre, side-steps the issue of symmetry, with an entrance bridge that enters at an angle through the side of the building.

The Willis Faber & Dumas building, insinuates itself into the lanes of Ipswich with a constantly curving façade that reflects the city around it.

would be appropriately dignified, and yet democratically transparent. It had to deal with a site that required a building which simultaneously closed a vista, turned a corner and formed part of an urban block.

These were issues to which Foster, when he had previously had to address them, albeit on a much less demanding scale, had responded with ingenious sleights of hand. His formal buildings had denied the very existence of formality and symmetry. Think, for example, about the way in which the Sainsbury Centre's umbilical glass bridge uniting it with Denys Lasdun's concrete university megastructure had finessed the issue of a formal connection by approaching it at an oblique angle, rather than head on.

His contextual buildings had actually denied context. Think of the way that the Willis Faber building addressed its context by not addressing it at all, but by ingeniously adopting that black glass skin which insinuates itself into the lanes and pantiles of Ipswich with a plan that has no sharp edges, and a façade which literally reflects the city around it, rather than trying to look like it. Foster makes connections by stripping back the detail: two walls will meet at an oblique angle and appear not to touch at all. Ceilings do not touch walls, they stop short of them. Walls do not touch the ground, rather they are insulated from it.

But with the BBC, there could be no hiding behind this kind of sophistry. The Langham Place scheme was the first project for which Foster had to play the game of architecture according to rules that were not of his own making. Up until then, he had always been able to sidestep them, to pull a rabbit out of a hat. To find a new way of doing things. And the BBC was all the more impressive a design for the fact that it didn't try to beg any questions, but addressed the high game of architecture.

But it wasn't built, despite all the energy that had gone into it. The thinking that went into the BBC project helped to inform Foster's unsuccessful submission for the Paternoster Square competition to replan the setting of St Paul's, demolishing the crude structures of the 1950s, to renew both architecture and planning

concepts. Projects like this marked the rediscovery of masterplanning in the city context, an activity that had all but vanished after the 1970s, as planning became dominated by mathematical, rather than physical models.

The BBC and Paternoster Square marked a rediscovery of modern physical planning, not just by Foster, but by the architectural profession at large. But, in the event, neither was built. Nor was the spectacular plan for Televisa, the Mexican broadcasting company, which came into the Foster office at almost the same moment that the BBC project was cancelled. Televisa was characterised by a soaring roof that embraced the clarity of Stansted Airport, and prefigured the economy of means of the roof for the new Hong Kong airport.

There were a number of other schemes that came to nothing in this period. The projected athletics stadium in Frankfurt, for example, and the masterplan for the redevelopment of a massive 52-hectare site around the King's Cross railway terminal in London, which gave Foster the chance to work on the scale of a city and to draw in teams of other architects on a collaborative effort. And the other projects that the office was working on, in particular the scheme for London's third airport at Stansted, but also the Carré d'Art in Nîmes and the American Air Museum at Duxford, moved so slowly that there was nothing to be seen of them until well into the 1990s.

Meanwhile, London in the second half of the 1980s was going through one of the most feverish building booms that it had ever seen. Great tracts of the city were reconfigured, as Fleet Street was turned over from being the traditional preserve of the newspaper industry to an enclave dominated by the American banks. The docks were resurrected from derelict wasteland into a facsimile of the World Financial Center in Manhattan. In the process, architects grew prosperous and confident, and the profession shed the last traumatic memories of the collective nervous breakdown it had suffered in the 1970s when it had had to face society's disenchantment with the failed utopia that it had offered in the 1960s.

Architecture in the 1980s became part of the fashionable agenda again. It rediscovered the glamour that it once had. This was the design

Modernists.

Despite major projects all over the world, the relatively modest re-development of the old *Sunday Times* building on the Gray's Inn Road, for ITN, remains Foster Associates' largest project in London.

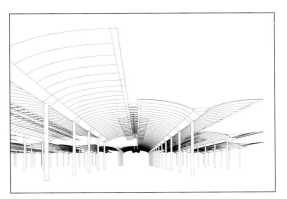

The Televisa project, in Mexico City, adopted a structural form that embraced the clarity of Stansted Airport, but transformed into pre-cast concrete.

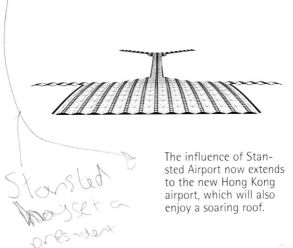

The influence of Stansted Airport now extends to the new Hong Kong airport, which will also enjoy a soaring roof.

Stansted project a president

decade; the Alessi kettle, the Eames chair — and Foster's Nomos table for that matter — became its essential props. The smart advertising agencies used them to establish their credentials as being in touch with the mood of the moment.

The decade saw the beginning of the revitalisation of the purist-influenced approach to architecture that is often called Modernism, in opposition to the decorative playfulness of Post-Modernism. And cool Modernism became the definitive image for a wave of smart galleries and boutiques. This phenomenon, with which Foster is often associated, is presented as a stylistic revival, a resurrection of the aesthetic of Modernism, and recycled, shorn of the original social content.

Certainly there are some examples of this. Richard Meier, for one, has played a limited set of variations on themes originally created by Le Corbusier. But this is not an interpretation that applies to Foster. His work is not so much a resurrection of the original Modern Movement pioneers, despite the resonances of Mies van der Rohe in the Willis Faber building in Ipswich or of the Le Corbusier of the Algiers period in the massing of the Hongkong Bank, but is part of a continuing tradition of lightweight, unrhetorical architecture that owes as much to the California of the post-war boom as to the radical Europe of the 1920s.

It is often claimed that the Modernists, for all their dreams of a machine age, in fact knew precious little about how machines actually worked. That they made buildings to look as if they had sprung from a production line, but which were actually made laboriously by hand. It is not a charge that is entirely justifiable: Jean Prouvé, Buckminster Fuller and Charles Eames knew what went on in factories and on production lines, and Foster learnt to understand the potential, as well as the limitations, of technology. His work is clearly influenced by the refined beauty of the components employed by the aerospace industry, but it is not simply a superstitious reproduction of its imagery. It takes those techniques and materials as its starting point, and applies some of the same concerns to architecture.

Foster is first and foremost an instinctive architect, rather than an intellectual. His architecture is informed by an optimistic embrace of the potential of technology, a spatial vision, but most of all by an aesthetic sense. In contrast to Richard Rogers, whose work is an elaboration and a celebration of structure and connection, Foster's is about refinement, the omission of the inessential, smooth skins and sparing palettes.

By the 1980s his work was already emerging from its original identification with High-Tech, a phenomenon given an important boost by the designs for the Royal Academy, and for the Carré d'Art in Nîmes. In both cases history and context took a leading role. Foster's office had seen so many bright young architects pass through it, that he had, if not exactly a school or a group of followers, at least a 'tail' of architects responsible for much of the wave of building in London during the 1980s who were putting his methods to good use.

But Foster found himself almost marginalised in all this activity. While Terry Farrell changed the face of central London, completing giant new structures at Alban Gate, Charing Cross and Vauxhall, and Richard Rogers beat him in the competition to design the new Lloyd's building which became the single most conspicuous architectural embodiment of the period, Foster was working — in the UK — on little more than a small speculative office development at Stockley Park, on the relatively modest redevelopment of the old Sunday Times building on Gray's Inn Road for ITN, and on the mixed-use building in Battersea to which he eventually moved his own offices.

Foster did, in fact, work on a design for a high-rise office tower at Canary Wharf, the archetypal 1980s building site, but it was just before the site's owners were forced into bankruptcy as the 1980s boom turned to the bust of the early 1990s, and it never saw the light of day. He did work on a couple of high fashion projects in the champagne-swilling 1980s — Katharine Hamnett's Knightsbridge store, a scheme for Esprit's headquarters in San Francisco and a shop for them in Sloane Street — but both of them ran out of steam.

And yet, despite all these apparent setbacks, the Foster operation in London was expanding rapidly. When the team that built the

An instinctive understanding of the potential of technology

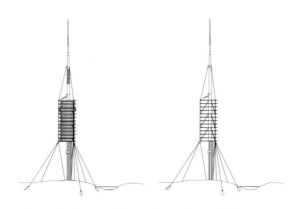

The Torre de Collserola, the telecommunications tower in Barcelona, was just one of a sequence of high-profile projects that established Foster Associates' reputation in Europe during the late 1980s.

Century Tower, Tokyo. The Foster office of the 1990s is one of very few British architectural practices working on a truly international scale.

Stansted Airport, every bit as elegant, cool and stylish as an Airstream trailer. To a large extent, the reputation of the Foster office is based on an unrivalled understanding of modern manufacturing methods.

Hongkong Bank came back to London, the office grew quickly. The new terminal for Stansted Airport eventually got the go-ahead; Century Tower, an office block in Tokyo, was built at breakneck speed; and the Carré d'Art in Nîmes eventually received the funds it needed to be built. At the same time, the office was doing all that it could to adjust itself to the increasingly global world of architecture.

The Hong Kong office closed in 1986, shortly after the completion of the Bank, but Foster quickly went back to Asia to pursue further projects in Japan. Mainland Europe was also an important place to be for Foster: first in France, then Spain and Germany. This was an acknowledgement of the realities of a global culture. American architects built Canary Wharf, just as British architects such as Foster now work throughout the world.

Foster's student days in America had opened his eyes to the world beyond Britain's sometimes narrow, and insular, view of the world. The experience of building the Hongkong Bank brought home the global nature of the building industry, to say nothing of the dynamic nature of the tiger economies of the Pacific Rim. It played an important part in shifting Foster's focus. And it did something to the nature of his approach to design. Foster was transformed from a purely English architect, into a designer with a global perspective. He became more than the product of English High-Tech, with its schoolboyish enthusiasms.

While the boom of the 1980s marked the high-tide of Post-Modernism, distinguished by heavy-handed playfulness and colour, Foster maintained a coherent belief in the architectural vocabulary which marked his mature approach. It was distinguished by a cool austerity that seemed to reflect the values particularly of European clients at the time, who felt uncomfortable with the element of fancy dress that Post-Modernism seemed to represent. And as the attractions of Post-Modernism faded, Foster's restraint has become, if not a uniform for confident corporations, then certainly an architectural benchmark.

It was a two-way process. Foster's exposure throughout Europe and Asia, and his confidence with large visions allowed him to adopt the aspirations of the cultures in which he worked. It is interesting to see how often Foster was able to build close personal relationships with his clients. It is no accident that he designed not only the Carré d'Art for the city of Nîmes, but a new house for the city's mayor. Just as he built not only Century Tower in Tokyo, but also a house for *its* owner.

It would not be an exaggeration to say that the rapid growth which characterised the nature of the Foster office in the 1990s, when it completely destroyed that old distinction between business architects and art architects to become one of the world's largest practices, was based on achieving an understanding of the nature of construction in the 1990s. The firm was big but, more to the point, it had found a way in which to impose some sense of order on the chaotic wave of building that was transforming the Pacific Rim.

That way included not just an aesthetic discipline which gave Foster's work a distinctive signature and, even more importantly, a coherence from one project to the next, but also an organisational structure which made the whole undertaking possible. The firm expanded in its ambitions, and in its size. It turned itself from a studio, into an office, and then into a series of offices around the world. It went from an intimate group of architects, to a highly organised structure, in which every creative architectural employee seemed to adopt, both literally and metaphorically, the handwriting of its founder.

These are all difficult achievements to pull off, and are just as much accomplishments as is the ability to design great works of architecture in isolation. And, in this sense, it is perhaps one of the greatest achievements of Foster's career that he was able to create an organisation that could be relied on, by the most demanding of worldwide clients, to produce architecture on demand of such distinction.

And yet it would have been hard to predict all this in the building that attracted the most attention that Foster completed in London after

A new headquarters for one of Korea's most successful corporations. It is perhaps one of Foster's greatest achievements that he has been able to create an organisation that can be relied on by the most demanding of worldwide clients to produce architecture of distinction on demand.

The Sackler Galleries at the Royal Academy. Though a relatively small project, it allowed Foster Associates to reflect deeply on their attitude to architecture in the broadest possible sense.

The Riverside office today, centre of operations for an organisation that now employs some 400 people worldwide.

the Bank. This was the creation of the new Sackler Galleries at the Royal Academy: a project that is all but invisible on the exterior, which exists only in the interstices of a complex web of historic layers of the old Academy building.

In comparison with the Hongkong Bank, or the terminal at Stansted Airport, it was a tiny project, and yet it allowed the practice to reflect deeply on its attitudes towards architecture; about the issues of spatial hierarchy and context; about the relationship of one historical period to another. And about the creation of spaces that can sympathetically accommodate great works of art. A reflection which could be seen as introducing a new richness to their work, and to their ambitions.

The project came at the time when the office was also thinking about the issue of context in Nîmes, where it was not only working on the Carré d'Art — a building which had as its immediate neighbour the Maison Carrée, the ancient Roman temple at the heart of the city — but was also looking at ways in which architecture could make sense of the shape of the city as a whole. Foster produced a strategy for linking the heart of the city with the airport on its periphery, for making sense of its existing public spaces, and for giving a presence and a dignity to the major boulevards.

As at the Royal Academy, Foster was interested in the creative tension that comes from juxtaposing new with old. But unlike what might have been expected from a younger Foster, the Royal Academy work takes care to respect the grain of the building as he found it. It is not confrontation for confrontation's sake. Foster searched for a way of unlocking extra space within a complex building. And he used the architectural detail of Modernism not to show off in an egotistical way, but to create a coherent and refined space.

But Foster wasn't only designing at the scale of the city and the individual building. This was also the time when he was working for the Italian furniture company, Tecno, at the scale of the desk, the drawer, and the work-station. This was a range of furniture that had its origins in prototypes developed for the office's own use.

The experience of working with Tecno brought direct experience of working at the scale of industrial design, an activity that is inevitably rather different from that of architecture. It was a chance to build up expertise in this area that the practice has gone on developing.

In the language of the pioneers of the Modern Movement, here was an architecture that truly went from the scale of the spoon to that of the entire city. And an architecture which had the coherence and internal logic to move effortlessly from one to the other.

The new headquarters
of The Hongkong and
Shanghai Banking Cor-
poration, photograph-
ed shortly after the
building's completion
in 1985.

The Hongkong Bank to-
day, photographed by
Norman Foster during
a recent trip to the city.
Over the years, the building has become a much-
loved landmark and a
popular meeting place.

1979-1985 Statue Square
Central
Hong Kong

Drawn during the competition stage for the Hongkong Bank's new headquarters, Norman Foster's sketch illustrates how, from the very beginning, he perceived the new building and Statue Square as a single urban composition.

In 1864 the Hongkong and Shanghai Banking Corporation opened its first offices in a building called Wardley House on the Hong Kong harbour front next to the old City Hall. The Bank has occupied the site ever since, but two land reclamation schemes in the intervening years — the first in the 1890s and the second in the 1950s — have moved the harbour front 250 metres to the north.

Despite this, the land between the Bank and the harbour has never been developed — a practically unique circumstance on this crowded island — but such remarkable restraint is no

accident. In 1896 a statue of Queen Victoria was erected on the land and, in 1901, the Government and the Bank agreed that Statue Square, as it became known, "should remain open space for all time and be preserved as a green oasis in the city centre".

When the Bank built an imposing new headquarters building in 1935, Statue Square provided it with a suitably grand setting. By 1947, however, the statue of Queen Victoria had disappeared, the railings around the gardens had been removed and car parking had begun to encroach on the green oasis. Then, in the 1950s, more land was reclaimed and the Star Ferry terminal was built, with a multi-storey car park to serve it, cutting off the visual connection between the square and the harbour.

What might have become a ceremonial civic space, on a scale somewhere between the Piazza San Marco in Venice and the forecourt

Never one to be constrained by a brief when better possibilities might exist outside it, Norman Foster submitted this photomontage as part of the office's entry for the Hongkong Bank competition. The gamble paid off and the Bank commissioned further studies as part of its appointment for the new headquarters.

A second montage that accompanied the office's Hongkong Bank competition entry shows how the redevelopment of Statue Square could be extended out into the harbour to include new piers for Star Ferry as well as other local craft.

Below: almost as soon as the Hongkong Bank competition was won, the office began preparing this sequence of drawings, showing the potential benefits that might be included in a new Statue Square.

of St Peter's in Rome, became a shabby and neglected strip of land carved up by busy roads. Small-scale improvements carried out in 1965 to mark the Bank's centenary hardly matched the potential of the space, flanked as it was by the Courts of Justice and the Cenotaph to the east and Princes Building and the Mandarin Hotel to the west.

This, then, was the situation in 1979 when Foster Associates set about preparing their competition entry for the new Hongkong Bank headquarters. Statue Square was not included in the competition brief, but it is clear from Norman Foster's sketches of that time that he conceived the new building and the square as a single urban entity.

As the design of the new headquarters developed during 1980, this concept was reinforced by the proposal to create an open public plaza beneath the building at ground level.

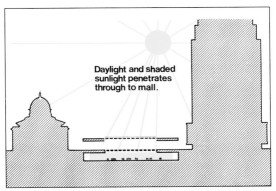

Daylight and shaded sunlight penetrates through to mall.

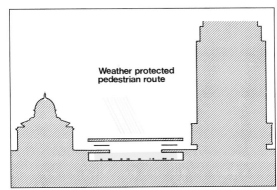

Weather protected pedestrian route

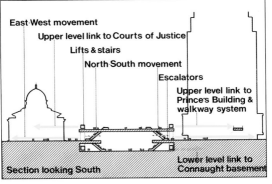

Courts of Justice

A continuous open air pedestrian route from Star Ferry to The Bank

Traffic at ground level

Lower level air conditioned pedestrian route from Star Ferry to The Bank

Upper level link to Central

Section looking South

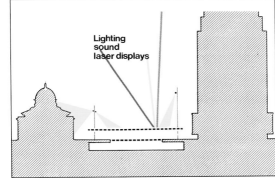

East-West movement
Upper level link to Courts of Justice
Lifts & stairs
North-South movement
Escalators
Upper level link to Prince's Building & walkway system
Lower level link to Connaught basement

Section looking South

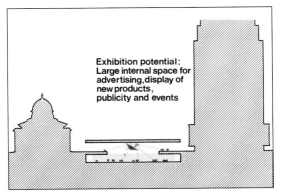

Lighting sound laser displays

Under local planning regulations this triggered an increase in the allowable plot ratio from 15:1 to 18:1, but it also added a new dimension to the possible remodelling of Statue Square.

The vision of a continuous public space stretching all the way from the ferry terminal to Battery Path, straddled by the multi-storey suspension bridge structure of the new building, was irresistible. Diagrammatic sections through the square were prepared to demonstrate its development potential to the Bank. They show a three-level structure with an open-air deck bridging over the busy roads and a continuous air-conditioned basement concourse passing beneath them. This structure could be adapted for many functions, including a shopping mall, a double-height enclosed exhibition space and an open-air auditorium for evening performances of various kinds.

Exhibition potential: Large internal space for advertising, display of new products, publicity and events

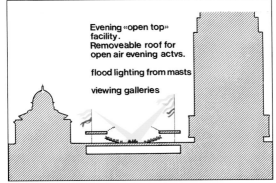

Evening «open top» facility.
Removeable roof for open air evening actvs.

flood lighting from masts

viewing galleries

Though superseded by later proposals, the simplicity of the first design provided an attractive counterpoint that was to recur in several forms as the design of the new headquarters evolved. This model dates from 1983.

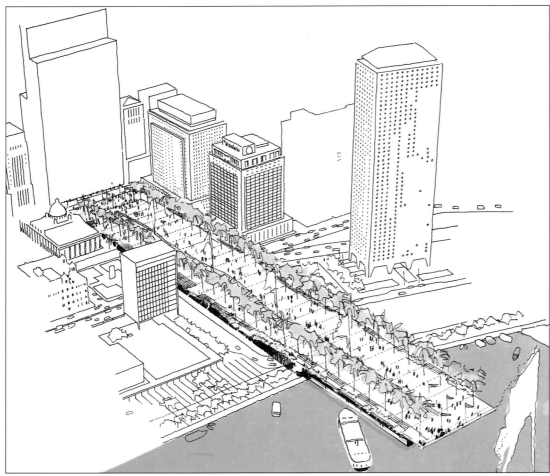

In 1982, even as the early designs were being evaluated, a major slump hit the Hong Kong property market and it soon became clear that a development on this scale, requiring deep excavations below the water level of the harbour, was not financially viable. A new, simpler proposal, requiring less excavation, was therefore prepared in the London office. This was known as the 'magic carpet' scheme.

The new design envisaged a continuous parallel-sided platform rolled out like a carpet from the Bank plaza, rising and falling in waves over the roads and other obstructions until it met the harbour front. It had an elegant lightweight structure of raking steel struts supporting cantilevered cross-beams which tapered to a feather edge. A shallow basement accommodated shops on either side of an air-conditioned mall rising between the struts to the underside of the deck.

Adorned only by an avenue of palm trees, the 'magic carpet' connected the Bank headquarters to the harbour in the simplest possible way, creating a processional route on a scale to rival the grand axes and boulevards of Paris or Rome.

But Hong Kong is a different kind of city, with a different culture and a different attitude to public space. Public investment on this scale was unthinkable, however simple and economical the scheme might be. Any comprehensive development of Statue Square would have to be self-financing, and that meant more commercial content than the magic carpet scheme could accommodate.

When a slump in property prices deemed basement excavations too expensive, a simpler — though in many ways far more radical — design was developed, that for obvious reasons was soon known by all concerned as the 'magic carpet' scheme.

The new proposal could hardly have been simpler: a raised platform extended the length of Statue Square over a single-storey shopping mall, rising gently to the necessary height over the intervening roads before sloping back to a lower level.

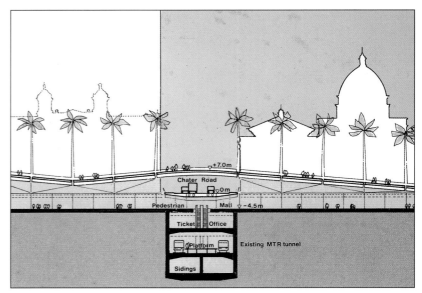

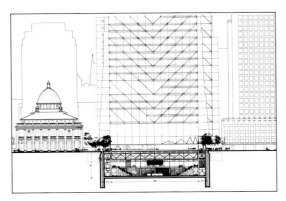

Yet another alternative, this time a public arena set below the section of Statue Square that runs between Des Voeux and Chater Roads. A retractable roof protects pavement-level public walkways that span the arena, allowing views of the events taking place below.

In many ways, the simplicity of the 'magic carpet' scheme also made it the most dramatic — a smooth rippling plane in counterpoint to the surrounding hustle and bustle of the city. Closing the vista from the Bank's new headquarters, a powerful fountain, similar to that in Lake Geneva, was proposed for the middle of the harbour.

Becoming attuned to Hong Kong's ways, the office soon realised that provision for the public good had to be paid for by commercial gain. Where conditions allowed, the shopping mall extended into a single-storey basement to maximise the lettable area.

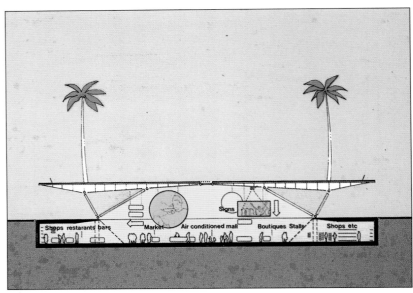

In the most advanced proposal for Statue Square's redevelopment, areas suitable for a variety of purposes were combined in a simple linear form that stepped up, or down, across the site from a ground-level walkway that ran alongside the old Supreme Court and the Cenotaph.

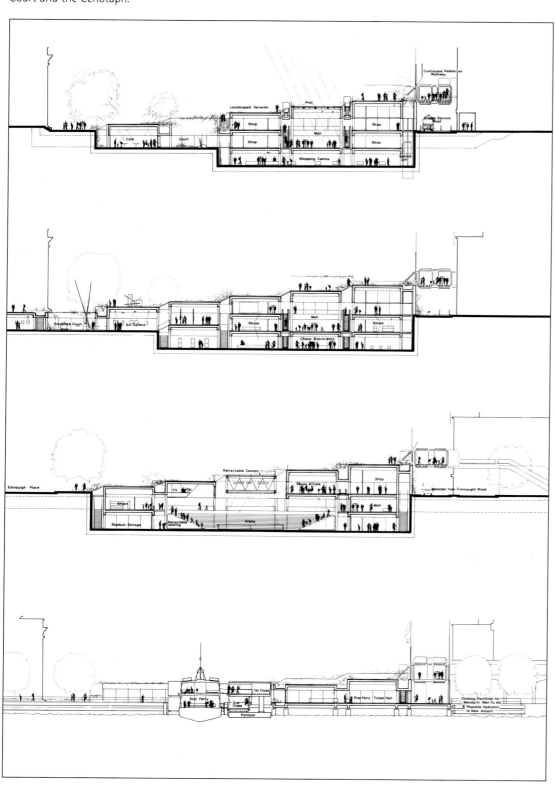

Below: Birkin Haward's elegant perspective of the view from the Hong-kong Bank's new head-quarters, the stepped form of the building reflected in the proposal for Statue Square.

In 1984 the Hong Kong property market revived and there was a steep rise in Central district shop rents. The relatively modest commercial content of the magic carpet scheme fell short of the site's development potential in the new economic conditions. While Foster's Hong Kong team struggled with the construction of the new headquarters building, the London office set about preparing a new scheme for Statue Square. The first objective was to include more commercial space. There would have to be a more realistic balance between public amenity and financial return.

The Foster office relishes the opportunity to rethink a design proposal. There is always another exciting possibility to be explored and when the brief changes the design also changes, often radically. Unsurprisingly, the new Statue Square scheme could hardly have been more different from its predecessor.

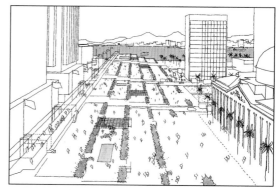

Rather than unify the site with a single undulating plane, the new proposal accepted its divided nature and even subdivided it further. Instead of a boulevard-like axial symmetry, an asymmetrical section was proposed, with terraces stepping down from west to east. And, instead of a full-width pedestrian deck, the roads were bridged only by a relatively narrow elevated spine along the western edge.

The deep basement of the original sketch scheme was reinstated and the height of the proposed new buildings varied from one to four storeys, including double-height spaces and a sunken arena on the largest section of the site, between Connaught Road and the harbour.

In fact, though it more than doubled the amount of commercial space, the new scheme was actually more responsive to its immediate

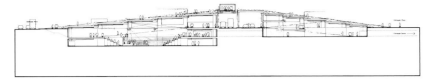

Learning from the 'magic carpet' scheme, a smaller mirror image of the stepped scheme was proposed for Connaught Place, beside Statue Square outside what is now Jardine House.

Only the public walkway at the very highest level of the stepped scheme ran the full length of Statue Square, allowing the sections between the intervening roads to be built in phases. The walkway extended along the side of the new headquarters to join Battery Path where it rose up the hillside beyond.

A model of the stepped scheme, set against the 'coat-hanger' proposal for the new headquarters, the penultimate stage in that building's design evolution.

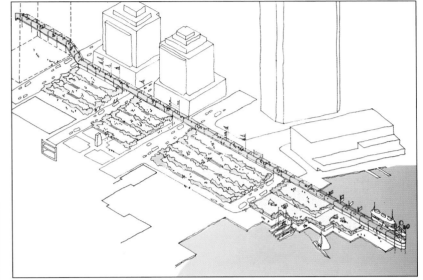

context. One possible criticism of the magic carpet scheme was that it cut across and partly obscured the Cenotaph and the Classical façade of the Courts of Justice to the east. The new scheme was more respectful of these symbolic structures, stepping down in broad terraces to ground level in front of them.

On the west side, the pedestrian spine was connected at first-floor level to the lobbies of the Mandarin Hotel and Princes Building, and was extended across Des Voeux Road to an entrance in the side of the new Hongkong Bank building that provided direct access to the main banking hall. From this entrance point, the spine then extended over Queen's Road to meet Battery Path, the original route connecting the waterfront with the government buildings further up the hill.

One curious feature of this, the most fully developed of the Statue Square schemes, is that it bears a remarkable formal resemblance to the new Bank tower. Though one is only four storeys high and the other 40, the two buildings share the same linear, additive and indeterminate form — a form that occurs in other Foster projects of this period, such as the Televisa headquarters in Mexico and Paternoster Square.

The tower is divided by its mast and suspension bridge structure and by its escalator circulation system into vertical 'slices' which rise to different heights. In a similar way, the Statue Square development is divided into slices by narrow, top-lit circulation and service strips.

The presentation model of the final 1985 proposal. Basements were rejected in order to save money. Instead, a new elevated plaza was created between Chater Road and the Star Ferry terminal, spanning Connaught Road and incorporating a three-storey shopping mall and a multi-storey car park.

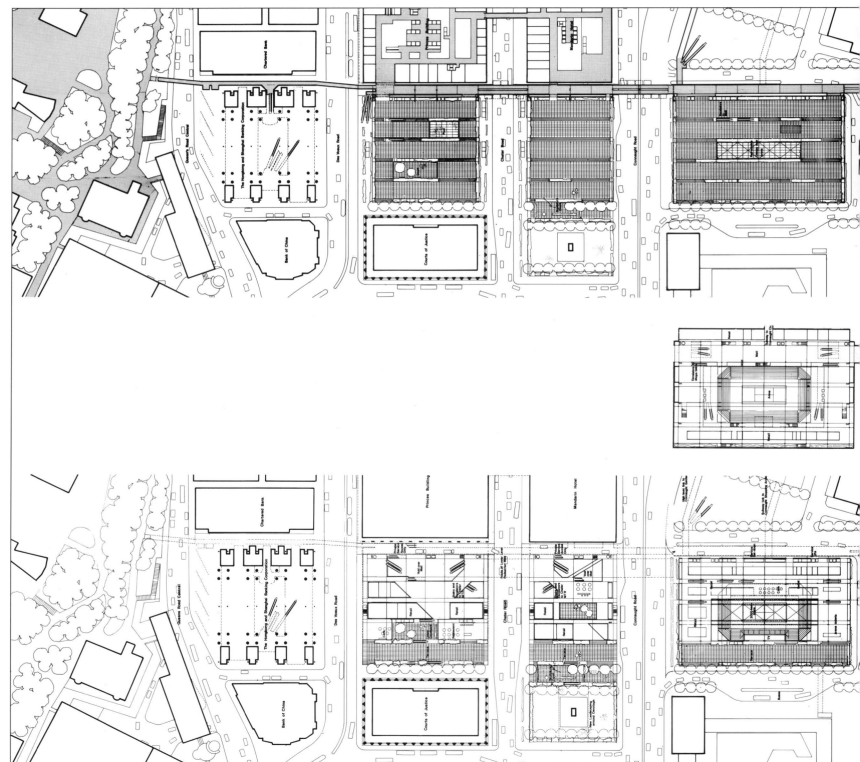

By far the largest of Foster Associates' proposals for Statue Square, the 1984 scheme was, in fact, specifically designed to be built in phases which might, or might not, have incorporated a new terminal for Star Ferry and other marine craft; this was shelved due to lack of financial interest. Property prices were to escalate rapidly before the end of the 1980s, but by then any further proposals had been made redundant by a major redevelopment which has since seen an extra 200 metres of reclaimed land added to this section of the Central waterfront.

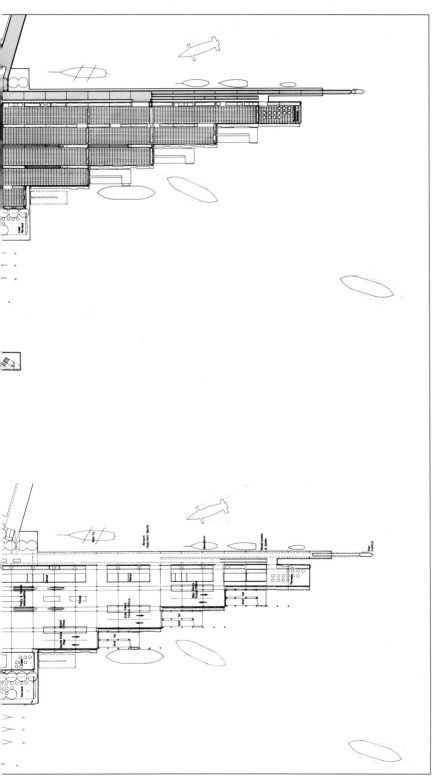

The slices rise to different heights to form the stepped section, but they also extend to different lengths, forming the stepped plan of the new ferry terminal. Thus the Statue Square scheme can be seen, almost literally, as the shadow cast by the tower. Even the double-height refuge floors which divide the tower horizontally into sections have their counterpart in the roads that pass through Statue Square and divide it into distinct zones.

In the event, even this more commercially orientated scheme for Statue Square failed to attract the necessary financial backing and was

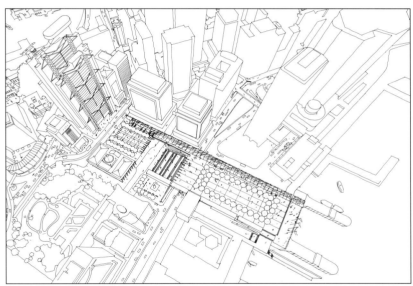

shelved. In 1985, a simpler and cheaper version was prepared in a final attempt to unify the urban space and connect the Bank to the harbour. The commercial component of the scheme was limited to a relatively modest three-level shopping centre, incorporating and extending the existing ferry terminal car park. Its roof took the form of a tree-framed pedestrian plaza, bridging over Connaught Road and reached via three flights of stone steps across the full width of the site.

Sadly, this scheme also foundered, and to this day the full commercial and civic potential of Hong Kong's biggest urban open space remains unfulfilled.

Colin Davies

Though a shadow of the 1984 proposal, the final scheme would have created a strong, single public space connecting the Bank to the existing Star Ferry terminal, the raised public plaza at that end offering spectacular views over the harbour beyond.

1980-1981 Hongkong Bank Annexe
1 Queen's Road Central
Hong Kong

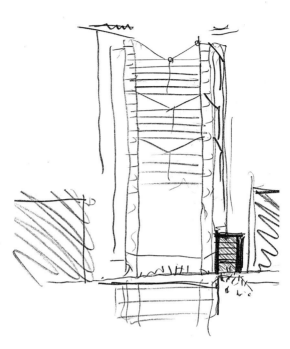

When the Hongkong Bank decided to build its new headquarters, it did so with some reluctance. It was not that the institution was unwilling to embark on a major new construction project, but that it was unwilling to demolish the much-loved 1935 building and, in particular, its magnificent mosaic-decorated public banking hall. Was there, perhaps, some way of preserving the banking hall? Foster Associates' competition entry demonstrated that there was. Indeed, the suspension bridge form of the competition-winning design, and the final built form, arose from the requirement to keep this option open.

It soon became clear, however, that keeping the old banking hall would be a time-wasting and expensive inconvenience. Nevertheless, the idea of maintaining a Bank presence on the site persisted. It made good commercial sense and, perhaps just as importantly, the Fung Shui consultant had advised that to abandon the site completely for a period might bring bad luck.

There was another way to achieve the necessary continuity. A long, narrow six-storey building between Des Voeux Road and Queen's Road, hard up against the west side of the site, had been built in the 1960s to accommodate the Bank's computers. Known as the annexe, this could be converted into a temporary banking hall which, when demolished, could be replaced by a downward extension of the suspended service modules on the side of the new building.

Foster Associates' Hong Kong office began preparing a design for a fast-track fit-out of this building, with tellers on the first three levels and offices above. As a replacement for the venerable old banking hall, and the public face of the Bank during the whole construction period, the fit-out was to be of the highest quality.

The annexe site sloped down about half a storey from south to north. The entrance from Queen's Road was therefore to the first floor, via a short flight of steps, and the entrance from Des Voeux Road on the ground floor. Two new hydraulic glass lifts were installed at the Des Voeux Road entrance, and the interiors of the three banking hall levels were lined with perforated metal panels.

Because of the narrowness of the site — only 8.5 metres — it was important not to constrict the space within by dividing it visually into public and private zones. The first proposal, therefore, envisaged open tellers' desks, but this was thought to be a security risk. There had to be a barrier of some kind.

As the final design for the new headquarters building evolved, it became apparent that the existing 1960s' annexe could be retained during the early stages by delaying the construction of the lower service modules and lift-shafts until later in the programme. As the construction sequence was refined, however, it became clear that the obstruction caused by the annexe's proximity to the basement excavations would be too great, and the refurbished annexe was closed after only 12 months and demolished before the main construction programme began.

To avoid a visual barrier between public and private areas, and yet retain an appropriate degree of security, the architects proposed the use of full-height, bullet-proof glass screens, off which the tellers' desks were cantilevered.

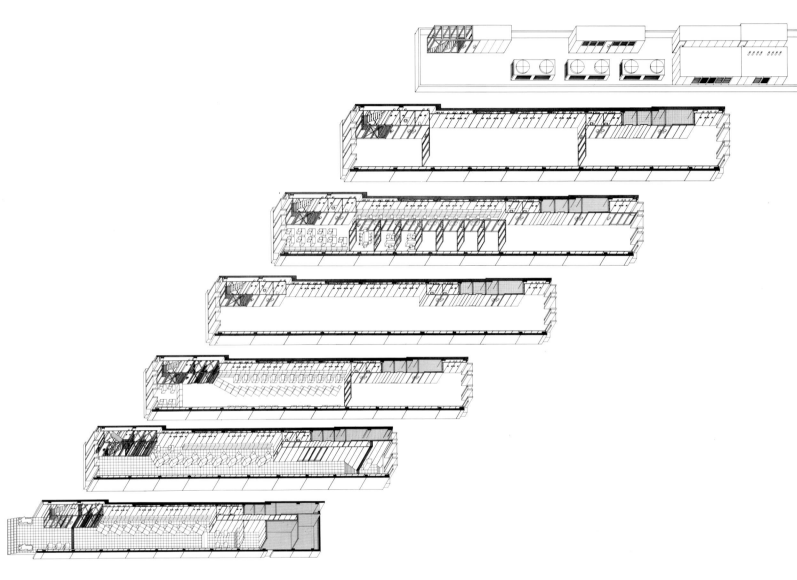

Designed as a test-bed for the raised floor and partition systems proposed for the new headquarters, the fit-out of the refurbished annexe was made up of self-supporting floor, wall and ceiling panels that touched the existing shell only through the supports for the raised floor. The three lowest floors were banking halls open to the public, with three floors of offices above. All six floors were connected by two new hydraulic lifts and a new escape stair that rose in glazed shafts at the Statue Square end of the building.

The solution was to build a free-standing, bullet-proof frameless glass wall, given stability by a zigzag plan form. To further increase the impression of openness at floor level, the individual tellers' desks took the form of thick horizontal planes, penetrating the glass panels and cantilevered from them.

But the most remarkable feature of the project was the lighting system, designed by Claude Engel. Luminaires mounted above the suspended ceiling shone through the fine perforations in the metal panels creating a delicate suffused glow. This provided the background lighting, which was supplemented by task lighting in the form of Tizio lamps on each desk.

Completed in 1981, as demolition work began on the old building, the annexe was open for only 12 months before the obstruction caused by its extreme proximity to the new basement excavations proved an expensive nuisance and it was demolished. The Bank's presence on the site was now maintained only by automatic tellers — enough, apparently, to satisfy the Fung Shui consultant.

Colin Davies

BBC Radio Centre
Portland Place
London

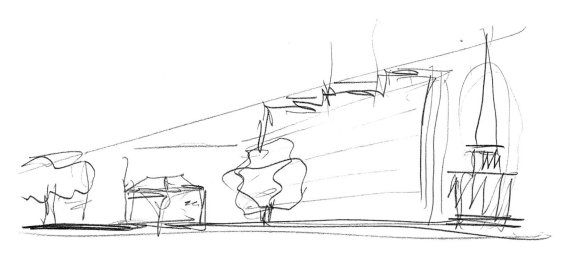

From the very beginning, it was the urban context that monopolised Norman Foster's thoughts, as this early sketch demonstrates. Intriguingly, the stepped form of the final design is already in evidence, as is the idea of linking Cavendish Square with All Souls'.

Birkin Haward's masterly ability to illustrate the spirit of a building, without necessarily showing what it looked like, was ideal for the BBC competition report, as the client had stipulated it was looking for ideas, not a final design.

In the words of Sir Richard Francis, formerly managing director of Radio at the BBC, it was "the Langham Saga". It is an apt description, giving as it does some flavour of the dramatic and, in the end, depressing sequence of events surrounding the design of the BBC Radio Centre. Metaphorically speaking, the three years between May 1982 — when Foster Associates were invited to compete for the commission — and May 1985 saw the architects undergoing a most exciting and challenging adventure in order to save a damsel in distress, only to have the damsel change her mind in the end and offer herself willingly to the dragon.

It can be argued that architects fall into two camps: those who design from the 'outside in', and those who design from the 'inside out'. With urban projects such as the Hongkong Bank and Willis Faber & Dumas already under their belt, Foster Associates had demonstrated their ability to balance both challenges. It is significant that the architects always prefaced their major presentations to the BBC with a sequence of three images.

The first showed the site of the Langham Hotel with the caption: "Is a building designed from the outside in?" The second showed a familiar image of BBC work areas inside Broadcasting House with the words: "or is it designed from the inside out?" The third presented both images combined with words to explain that it

had to be "both". The architects were keen to show that they were able to design a building to their normal standards of technical achievement, while still rising to the challenges of a sensitive central London site.

The BBC project was probably their first to pose questions of urban context as challenging as the functional brief itself. By the time of the final proposals, the BBC building had spread to occupy an entire city block. Its site, however, was not a traffic island, like other urban projects such as Willis Faber or Hammersmith, but a complex collection of buildings of varying scales and degrees of importance. In many ways, the closest comparison is with the later Carré d'Art in Nîmes.

Internally, pressure for space necessitated deep basements, in which acoustically sensitive studios and concert hall would be located only a few metres from the existing Underground railway lines. The final solution to the practical problems this presented was to be one of the project's triumphs.

Foster Associates' involvement with the BBC came about at what, with hindsight, can be seen to have been a watershed for the BBC itself, as the paternalistic tradition of an earlier era was forced to confront a newer, less gentlemanly climate. It was this shift in power between the old order and the new, coming at a

With an office in Great Portland Street, just a few minutes' walk away, Norman Foster was able to explore the site and its context to the full, producing a stream of sketches and photographs as he went.

Below: photographs of the site and surrounding buildings were to form a permanent backdrop in the office as the competition report evolved.

time when the licence fee was to be renegotiated, that was to lead to the project being a pawn in the power struggle and to its eventual demise.

The project came about after two decades of deliberation. BBC Radio had been growing in a more or less uncontrolled manner for a number of years. Like many organisations explicitly dedicated to public service, the question of how to accommodate this growth had long been frustrated by bureaucratic indecision. It had never been satisfactorily resolved beyond the acquisition of successive offices in a piecemeal fashion over the years.

As a result, the BBC had developed into something that was described at the time as "a loose collection of warring tribes". Although Broadcasting House was by far the most visible manifestation of the BBC's presence in the West End, in reality it was only one element in a veritable 'BBC village' that embraced a number of

buildings in the area. The Langham Hotel, acquired by the Corporation in 1946, was just one of a number of sites making up this community.

In its time, the onset of television had cast such doubt upon the future of radio that the 1961 extension to Broadcasting House had been designed as a speculative office block. In 1971, with Radio's future looking more assured, a move to Covent Garden was investigated and rejected. This was followed by the so-called 'Albino' project which envisaged a move to White City, to be near the Television Centre. This, too, was rejected: it was felt to be too massive and, BBC politics being what they are, Radio feared it would be overshadowed by Television.

Radio has a very different character from television and relies quite heavily on attracting interviewees and other people to come into

the studio; by 1978 it was decided that Radio should stay in central London. Nevertheless, in 1981, a short-list of sites was considered that included Bristol, Birmingham, Milton Keynes and, in London, Maida Vale, Gosfield Street, the South Bank and the Langham site.

Talks followed with Gordon Graham, a former president of the RIBA, about ways in which an architect might be selected, paying special attention to the process Lloyd's of London had employed a few years earlier. These discussions were abandoned when it was realised that it would not be possible to afford the new Radio Centre from licence fee income; but some months later, on 19 January 1981, the Board of Management considered a further note from Francis, seeking approval to restart the process.

A building on any site other than the Langham would have to be self-contained; while the choice of the Langham provided the opportunity of making continued use of Broadcasting House. So finally, on 8 May 1982, the Board concluded that there was no real alternative to the Langham site, and set about finding an architect.

The Board of Management at that time was headed by Lord Howard, whose attitude was that of an enlightened patron of the old school. This tradition went back many years; it was his family, after all, who had commissioned Sir John Vanbrugh to design Castle Howard. Not surprisingly, therefore, it was decided to hold a limited competition between 10 distinguished firms, two of whom were to withdraw without submitting. The BBC made it very clear that at this point it was looking to choose an architect, not a design.

Serious broadcasting was one of the few areas in which the British could still justifiably lay claim to world leadership, with extraordinary prestige accorded to the BBC. This pre-eminent position had been hard won over many years,

but perhaps owed its origins to the BBC's reputation for honesty during the war, when Broadcasting House was painted battleship grey and Europe fizzled and exploded all around it. Even as Britain's status in the world receded to that more normally due to a medium-sized industrialised country, the BBC had retained a disproportionate influence. BBC Television drama was admired and enjoyed all around the world. The World Service continued to provide a reliable and trusted source of accurate information, while many of its newscasters, with their clear patrician tones, still seemed to be speaking in dinner-jackets.

If myths take many years to develop, they take even longer to be brought up to date. BBC Radio was undoubtedly still a leader and was still the guardian of the soul of the Corporation. But it is also true to say that BBC Radio was being increasingly eclipsed in size and influence by BBC Television, and Foster Associates' commission came at a time when the BBC as a whole was feeling increasingly exposed.

The financial basis upon which its liberal tradition had been built was income from the licence fee, which has since been provided by Television alone. This means of finance, and the increase that had to be awarded annually by the Government, had become a source of extreme political sensitivity; a proposal to increase the fee by £10 a year would be greeted by howls

The 'phantom hammerer', tracked down from three floors away. The design team spent several days in Broadcasting House while preparing the competition report and were astonished by the cramped and often primitive conditions.

of anguish. Independent local radio stations had become established and had steadily drained the BBC's audiences. The situation was made worse by the fact that the Corporation's supposedly privileged position had come to be resented by the Government of the day.

The BBC remains a repository of an extraordinary range of talents. Journalists, musicians, actors, technicians, sound engineers, librarians, administrators and catering staff all worked within the walls of Broadcasting House, against a background which was continually developing, culturally, artistically and technologically. There

Margaret Thatcher and Robin Day, on the air in Broadcasting House. Easy access for politicians was considered of paramount importance.

was a major catering operation, as well as record and radio archives which serviced not only national and international radio, but also local radio stations across the country.

Within this organisation, there existed a fierce loyalty to the lofty ideals on which it was founded. It was a spirit with which the office found it easy to identify. Indeed, it might even be argued that Foster Associates hold an equivalent status in the architectural world to that of the BBC in the wider world.

But the BBC of the 1980s was far more populist in character than ever it was in the early, heroic days of Alvar Lidell. However, it was perhaps their joint belief in the importance of openness and accessibility that provided the greatest philosophical bond between the office and the BBC as it was when the commission was first announced. It is this aspect which was least adequately reflected in its existing accommodation, and in which the design team would take greatest pleasure in attempting to resolve.

For years, expansion had been carried out in an *ad hoc* manner, giving much of the building a ramshackle appearance at best.

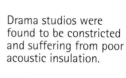

Drama studios were found to be constricted and suffering from poor acoustic insulation.

From disc jockeys to canteen staff, from librarians to sound engineers; all had to be accommodated in the new building.

32

The technology may have moved on but, in Broadcasting House, Foster Associates found a radio station that was still imbued with the spirit of a bygone age.

Central to BBC Radio was the newsroom, which operated 24 hours a day, every day of the year. Whatever happened, this had to remain on air.

Highly specialised studios, often with demanding technical requirements, had to be woven into a solution for the Corporation's social needs.

Building work was found to be proceeding on an almost continual basis, often in the same room as the most sensitive equipment, leading Norman Foster to record that the building was "quite literally strangling technology".

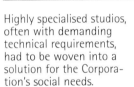

Broadcasting House was terribly overcrowded and many departments were spread across several locations, often in nearby buildings.

Norman Foster was aware that a successful solution to the project had to respond to the site and the BBC organisation in equal measure. Considerable thought was given to both in the competition report, starting with a detailed history of the site.

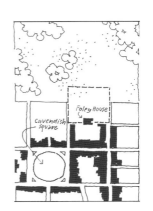

Foley House and Cavendish Square in the 1750s. In 1758, land for a new square, to the north of Foley House, was leased to Lord Foley by the Duke of Portland, who agreed that the view to the north should never be impeded.

Plans for Lord Foley's new square were transformed by the Adam brothers when they started work on what would become a new processional route into London. Later known as Portland Place, the width of the street was determined by the need for a clear view from Foley House.

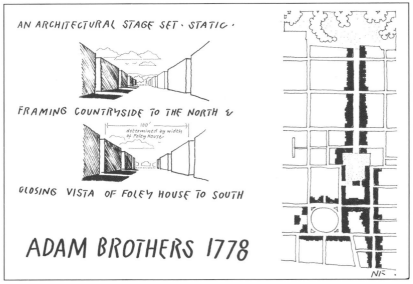

AN ARCHITECTURAL STAGE SET · STATIC ·

FRAMING COUNTRYSIDE TO THE NORTH &

100' determined by width of Foley House

CLOSING VISTA OF FOLEY HOUSE TO SOUTH

ADAM BROTHERS 1778

The full potential of Portland Place was only realised in 1812, when John Nash incorporated the street into his plan for a route from central London for the Prince Regent. Unable to drive the street due south, he was forced to step the street to the east to join his new Regent Street. This he resolved with a new church, All Souls'.

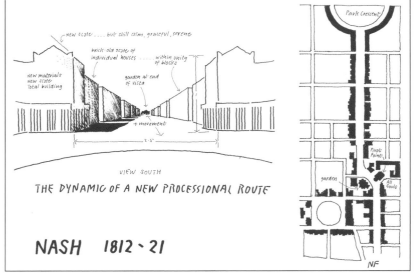

NEW SCALE ..... but still calm, graceful, serene

brick-old scale of individual houses ..... within unity of blocks

New materials new scale Total building

garden at end of vista

+ movement

VIEW SOUTH

THE DYNAMIC OF A NEW PROCESSIONAL ROUTE

NASH 1812 - 21

For a London street, Portland Place is uncharacteristically wide. It is not, as might be supposed, an early example of Beaux-Arts town planning, but instead a product of British property law. In 1757 Lord Foley built a house on a site at what is now the south end of the street. The site belonged to the Duke of Portland, but Lord Foley managed to negotiate a clause in the lease which stipulated that no building should be allowed to obscure the view northwards from the site towards Hampstead and Highgate.

The street was at that time enclosed by railings and garden walls at both ends, and was never intended as a thoroughfare. But when the brothers Robert and James Adam did lay it out as such, they were forced to take account of the lease and so made it 125 feet wide — the same width as Foley House. The house's powerful effect on the streetscape did not, however, save the house itself from being demolished in 1814, after John Nash had bought out Lord Foley to allow the construction of 'New Street' — later Regent Street. Sir James Langham secured the remainder of the site and built himself a house.

As the early views of Portland Place demonstrate, the northern end of the street was initially closed off from the Marylebone Road by railings, which were retained by Nash even after the completion of Park Crescent.

Below: Foley House began life as a country villa in the early 1700s, but was later transformed into a modest town house in keeping with its location at the end of the new Portland Place.

"The BBC does not expect to announce its choice until Christmas, and only then will work begin on an actual design. But already it is running into criticism from conservationists who object to the demolition that the new plans must entail. For the architect's task is not simply a question of solving the massive technical problems posed by a modern radio station. . . The site chosen is just across the street from Broadcasting House, at the focus of one of London's finest formal vistas, and could hardly be more conspicuous or difficult to build on."

Deyan Sudjic, *The Sunday Times*, 14 November 1982

Pressure from the residents of Cavendish Square prevented Nash from driving his new route directly southwards, forcing him to locate it 100 yards to the east. Thus originated the curved chicane of Langham Place — a crucial punctuation mark, accentuated by the extraordinary spire of All Souls', on one of London's great ceremonial routes.

Built by Nash in Bath stone between 1822 and 1824 as a terminal feature for the 'New Street' laid out southwards towards Piccadilly, All Souls' stands at an angle of approximately 45 degrees to Upper Regent Street. It is an in-

The house built by Nash to replace Foley House was bought by James Langham, who left his mark with the renaming of the southern end of Portland Place as Langham Place. In 1864, this house, too, was demolished, to be replaced by the Langham Hotel, considered on its opening "the greatest of the grand hotels".

THE LANGHAM 1864

As the competition report noted, the character of Portland Place has been seriously eroded during this century. A number of apartment buildings, built since the 1920s, have left only mutilated fragments of the Adam terraces. Broadcasting House dwarfed All Souls' Church on its completion in 1931, and several drab tower blocks have blighted the area since the early 1960s.

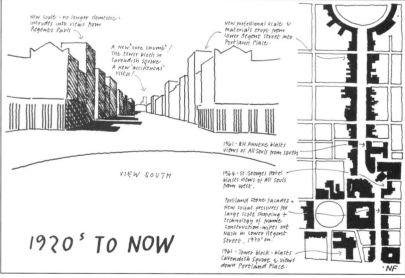

1920's TO NOW

genious design, closing the vista and turning the corner towards Portland Place. The angle between the church and Upper Regent Street is resolved by what John Summerson describes as Nash's 'circus principle' (in which a circus is used to resolve streets meeting at odd angles), adapted to the plan of a building. The spire has not been universally admired: in 1824 an MP said that he "would give a trifle" to have the newly-built steeple pulled down.

All Souls' shortly after its completion. In Nash's plan, Foley House was replaced by a new building in line with the west side of Portland Place, which now ended with a small park — thus giving the spire of the new church due prominence.

Uncontrolled development along Upper Regent Street during the 1840s had begun to cast a shadow over Nash's vision for a grand ceremonial route, even before the construction of the Langham Hotel.

By the late 1850s the area around Regent Street and Oxford Circus was already established as a thriving commercial district, placing ever greater pressure on development further north around Portland Place. Somewhat exaggerated in this view, All Souls' retained its importance, closing the vista along Regent Street with certainty and purpose.

As part of the competition presentation, a model of Portland Place and Upper Regent Street — stretching from Park Crescent to Oxford Circus — was prepared into which various solutions could be inserted.

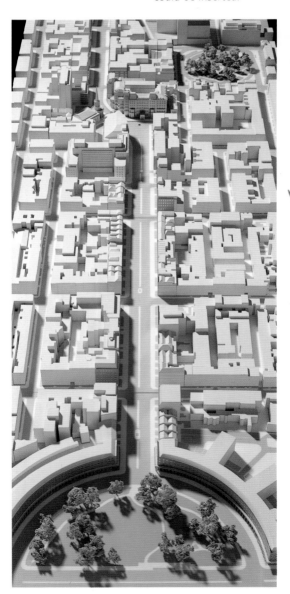

In 1864 James Langham's house was itself demolished, to make way for the Langham Hotel. This, "the greatest of the grand hotels", designed in 1864 by Giles & Murray and boasting a decorative scheme by Owen Jones, opened in 1865 in the presence of the Prince of Wales and 2000 guests. In its prime it had a glorious life. Guests included Napoleon III, Haile Selassie, Dvořák and Arnold Bennett. Along its corridors walked the ghost of a lovesick German prince who threw himself from a fourth-floor window. At the time of the competition, a pit for cockfighting still remained in the basement.

Despite this illustrious past, the Langham's effect on its immediate surroundings is bleak. Henry-Russell Hitchcock appreciated the "powerful, plastic composition" and carved animals on the window heads, but George Howard described it as "that dark cliff at the end of Portland Place". Nikolaus Pevsner's verdict, however, was even more damning: "The wilful destruction of [Portland Place], which was a monument of European importance, began with the erection

"Manipulating elements so that they *do* relate to the vertical aspect of All Souls', the dynamic corner position, the formal vista down Portland Place, the square on one side and the maze of small streets on the other. The scale leaps from huge to intimately domestic. We are making a response to all these varying scales and at the same time celebrating the things that our track record tells people, including the BBC, that we will always celebrate."

Norman Foster, quoted in 'Walking on Eggs', *The Architects' Journal*, 16 May 1984

Below: Giles & Murray's Langham Hotel, shortly after its completion in 1865.

of the Langham Hotel . . . a High Victorian monster, dark, big and grim, in a trecento style, with round-headed windows under pointed relieving arches, but ending at the top in French pavilion roofs. On the side towards All Souls' (which it crushes) . . ."

The construction of Broadcasting House in 1931 also dwarfed All Souls', depriving it of much of its subtle effect. Opinions about this building have changed with the years. For many years Pevsner's condemnation expressed a generally-held view. Today, this beached whale of a building is appreciated by some less for its lum-

pen form than for its sculpture 'Ariel' by Eric Gill and, more obscurely, for the extraordinary east façade overlooking Langham Street, where the roof slides precipitously downwards past ranks of inclined windows. Foster Associates' competition document quotes one observer who compares the building with a ship front. Appropriately enough, the building was painted battleship grey during the war and suffered very little damage despite being such an important target.

The Langham, on the other hand, was less indestructible than it appeared. In 1940 it was badly damaged by a land mine, probably intended for Broadcasting House. Its vast 38,000 gallon rooftop water tank was catastrophically damaged: 170 tons of water rained down upon the gilded pile, drenching it completely.

In defence of the building's size, it can be argued that Broadcasting House did, at least, come after much of the overscaled development immediately to the south, around Oxford Circus. Even these buildings, however, postdate the Langham Hotel, which must be considered to have set a poor precedent when just completed.

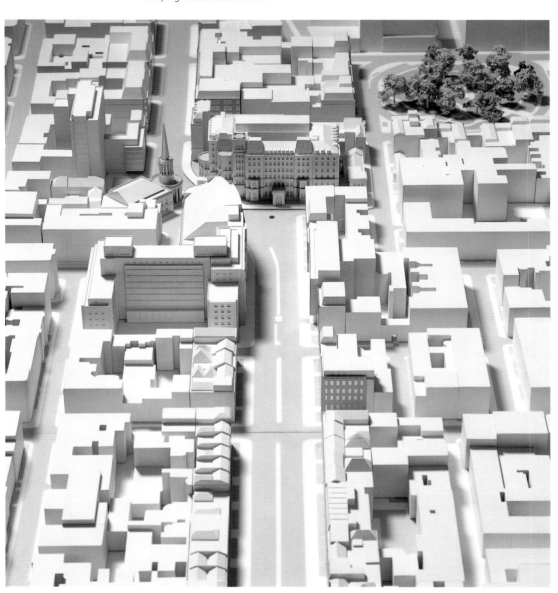

A detail view of the presentation model, looking down Portland Place. The curve in the street beside Broadcasting House — a coincidence of history — now marks a major shift in atmosphere from the wide empty spaces of Portland Place to the urban intensity of Oxford Circus and beyond. The new building would have to mediate between these two zones.

The importance of distant views was also considered. As this sketch of the view from Primrose Hill shows, there was an opportunity to let the building stand out on the skyline as a brightly lit beacon, a symbol, perhaps, of information being transmitted to the world.

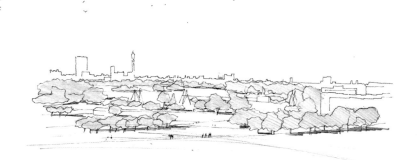

Norman Foster's sketches of Langham Place provide eloquent expression of his views on the problems of designing a new building for the Langham site. Surprisingly, they were not used in the competition report, being published instead in *The Architects' Journal* of 5 January 1983, in an article by Deyan Sudjic that announced the office's appointment. As the article concluded, "he took pleasure in the delicacy of Nash's All Souls' Church. He found people sitting in its peristyle even on the bitterest of cold mornings. He is aiming, he says, at a balance between people and space".

38

Inspired by an article by Gordon Cullen, published in *The Architects' Journal* on 10 November 1982, Norman Foster began a series of sketches that explored a variety of architectural responses to the corner and All Souls'. The idea of a central atrium first appeared at this very early stage.

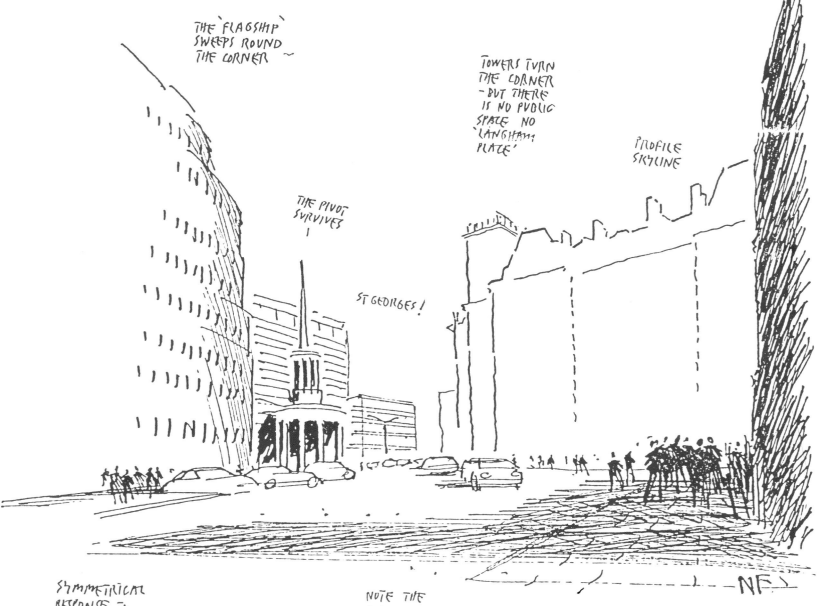

THE 'FLAGSHIP' SWEEPS ROUND THE CORNER ~

TOWERS TURN THE CORNER - BUT THERE IS NO PUBLIC SPACE NO 'LANGHAM PLAZE'

PROFILE SKYLINE

THE PIVOT SURVIVES !

ST GEORGES !

SYMMETRICAL RESPONSE TO PORTLAND PLACE - READS AS A CUL·DE·SAC FROM FURTHER NORTH - NO CLUE OR ADVANCE WARNING ABOUT WHICH WAY YOU ARE GOING TO BE TURNED.

NOTE THE SCALE OF ALL SOULS ! NOTHING TO DO WITH PHYSICAL SIZE SURVIVES DESPITE THE ATTACK OF ST. GEORGES ETC.

LARGE AREAS OF ROAD NOT USED BY EITHER TRAFFIC OR PEDESTRIANS CLUES? RE·ALIGNMENTS?

"The BBC looms over the area like a colossus, but it makes no impact on it, so forbidding are its two main buildings and so invisible is its presence in the various outbuildings. Even within the BBC complex, the sense of life and activity is deadened by the distances. The largest music library in the world is hidden away along Great Portland Street, surrounded by garment merchants. One of the most visible sights, the huge glazed wall of the central control room, . . . is ironically protected by the very anonymity of the area."

From the Competition Report, submitted to the BBC in December 1982

By 1982, Broadcasting House represented only the tip of the iceberg as far as the BBC's presence in the area was concerned, with somewhat more space being rented in a variety of nearby properties. One immediate concern was how many of these external departments should be accommodated in the new building.

While referring to what Gordon Cullen called the "fault line of change" that ran through the site, Norman Foster added his own observation that besides the axis along Portland Place, there was a secondary axis that ran across the site linking Cavendish Square, All Souls' and the Post Office Tower.

 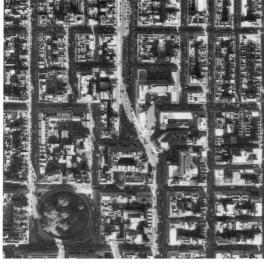

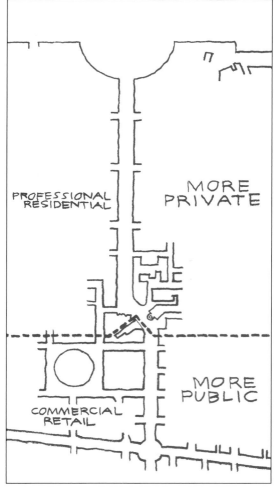

PROFESSIONAL RESIDENTIAL

MORE PRIVATE

COMMERCIAL RETAIL

MORE PUBLIC

Thanks partly to the way in which projects are conventionally organised, most custom-designed buildings are out of date before they are even completed. In their design report the architects contrasted this 'rigid' approach — characterised by the usual sequence of briefing, design, tender and construction — with the 'responsive' approach, in which briefing, design and construction are overlapped, and widespread use is made of mock-ups and research. As a building with complex functional demands, which would continue to change and develop not only after construction but throughout the briefing process, the BBC Radio Centre was ideally suited to this more fluid approach.

The BBC suffers from many of the same problems as other organisations that have grown in an uncontrolled way. The design team found that, while numerous centralised service facilities existed, the bureaucratic problems associated with using them had led to many departments maintaining their own dedicated facilities. One example was tape storage, where departmental libraries had led to the centralised library becoming more or less dedicated to those departments which found it most convenient or essential to use.

The current operation also lacked the opportunity to derive benefit from the management being housed with the production staff, with all the intangible benefits of random personal contact. There was a basic lack of conference meeting rooms, and a permanent sense of transience and makeshift adaptation.

As Norman Foster had noted in his sketches, Langham Place was not really a 'place' at all, rather an oppressive canyon that people passed through between one part of London and another. A new, more open building would make people want to linger.

If nothing else, the proximity of the Langham Hotel to All Souls' had created an obstruction to traffic that the new building could resolve.

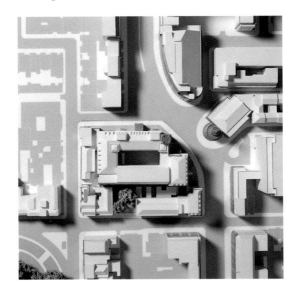

As might be expected, the staff's personal needs were no better served than their professional requirements. Eating facilities were split into centralised restaurants, which were seedy and institutional, and the more localised mobile food trolleys, which often seemed to end up in corridors, stacked up with stale food. The presence of tea-making facilities in the corner of many offices testified to the inadequacy of the trolley system in meeting staff needs. For those wishing to make their own arrangements, shopping was inconvenient: as one of them pointed out, "the closest place to buy an apple is British Home Stores".

The team developed a particularly close understanding of the workings of Broadcasting House. They identified three key considerations that would have to be incorporated in the programming of the project: it had to form part of

received, processed into products (edited) and then distributed far and wide (broadcast). For some services, however, there was a conflict between the need for proximity to the News Room and to studio facilities. The most prominent example was the Sports Room, which needed a large dedicated studio at weekends, but which could not justify it for the rest of the week.

In the new building it would therefore not be enough to group similar space types together, as each department was found to use many different kinds of space. These fell into three broad categories: cellular, for one, two or three people; group or team spaces, for between four and 20 people; and open spaces for between 20 and 200.

The new building would be primarily a mix of the first and second types. Meanwhile, the studios for different types of activity had differ-

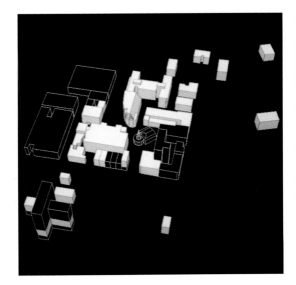

a larger accommodation strategy for the BBC; broadcasting to the full level of normal quality must be maintained throughout the project; and it must be closely co-ordinated with the ongoing programme of replacement of worn-out property.

News is one of the more important constituents of BBC Radio. Many programmes depend on it in some way, whether by making direct reference to it, or by using it as the source of features. The architects' design report, therefore, identified the News Room as the heart of Broadcasting House. In their briefing notes they compared the operations to those of a factory. In this analysis, the raw material (news) was

ent characteristics in terms of scale, proportion, insulation and reverberation times: talks studios, for instance, needed to be three metres high; drama studios, five metres: and music studios eight metres. For studios of the highest acoustical quality, it was necessary to create a box within a box by supporting the enclosure in flexible mountings. The studio thus became a structure independent of the building itself.

It was essential to retain the principle of flexibility in the case of the studio areas. In particular, it would be extremely advantageous to be able to move walls and to recreate acoustic

As these computer diagrams show, well over half the 120,000 square metres of space occupied by the BBC in the West End was in buildings other than Broadcasting House or the Langham. At maximum potential, the Langham site could accommodate only half of this, so the BBC village would inevitably remain.

Norman Foster used Russian dolls to explain "how buildings can happen within buildings, and private and public domains interact". This led to a plan-form concept that was concentrically responsive to the myriad small teams that make up the BBC.

Below: a lift capable of running both vertically and horizontally was proposed to provide a continuous link between every floor of both the new and old buildings.

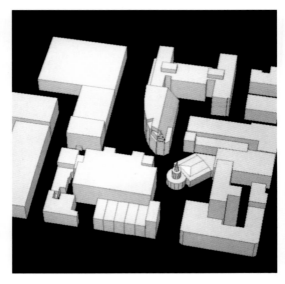

Computer models were developed that could readily demonstrate the relationship of the proposed building to its surroundings as well as the many hidden obstructions below ground — not least the Bakerloo Underground line.

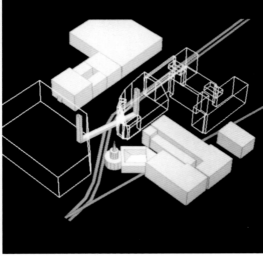

envelopes in each department wherever they were found to be necessary. The architects suggested ways in which this might be achieved without compromising acoustic criteria. The key to this, they felt, was a modular pre-engineered panel of high acoustic performance. Using such modular components, the necessary box-within-a-box could be achieved by means of panels inserted between floors — at this stage, it was still anticipated that the studio spaces might be slotted in between the same waffle slabs that accommodated the office area.

At the hub of the BBC village stood Val Myers' great edifice of Broadcasting House, steel-framed and clad in Portland stone: whatever its architectural quality, undoubtedly one of the great monuments to democratic ideals in the world. The affection in which the building is held, however, tends to obscure quite how impractical it has become as a base for the leading radio organisation in the world. The office found that approximately 40 per cent of the space was used for corridors and hallways. Many employees, especially on the technical side, worked all day long without daylight. Perhaps more to the point, not only the number but also the size of the radio studios was too small. This impracticality was by no means new, as it had been found to be too small within a few months of its construction.

By 1982 the Centre had become a continuous building site. It had resisted adaptation and yet the Corporation persevered. Studios needed

to be updated roughly every 10 years, but refurbishing just one of them took approximately six months, five of which were taken up in building work. This permanent state of inconvenience was made all the more expensive and time-consuming by the need to maintain continuity of broadcasting and to prevent noise from disturbing programmes. A system of 'no knocking chits' had been devised as a bureaucratic response to the problem.

The building's inner core of 22 soundproof studios was protected from the outside world by an outer buffer zone of offices. Yet, thanks to its steel structure, which proved to be an excellent sound transmitter, noise from the construction work permeated the building. During their research the design team tracked down a 'phantom hammerer' by following the sound from three floors away. In the studios, the sound of distant

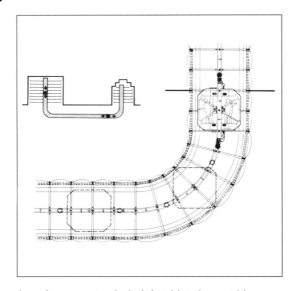

banging was regularly joined by the rumble from one of the two Underground railway lines passing nearby.

But even if Broadcasting House manifestly failed to work, it would have been unthinkable to have demolished it: not only because it was listed, but also because of its character, its role in the streetscape and — not least — its importance as a popular symbol of the ideals which were represented by the BBC .

But how could it be prevented from becoming a mere annexe to the new building? The architects' answer was to suggest that the 'BBC village' be retained, with All Souls' acting as the village church. Broadcasting House could be

To link the new and old buildings, a public subway was planned that combined hidden service zones with the proposed 'multi-directional lift' and active display panels explaining the work of the BBC.

So excited were the Foster team with their proposed multi-directional lift, that they applied for a provisional British Patent. Lift manufacturers, however, were more cautious and the idea died with the project.

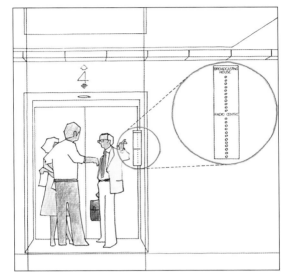

upgraded as a showpiece for the BBC's achievements, a repository for the BBC's 'greatness'. Some areas could be restored, others refitted to full contemporary standards.

A substantial underground concourse would be formed linking the new building to the old. This would contain not only a pedestrian route and major service runs, but also a novel form of lift which Norman Foster invented for the project and which was subsequently patented. This would run horizontally through the concourse and connect with a vertical shaft at each end so as to connect all floors on each site. The lifts would be suspended on gimbals running on continuous guides.

The existing building was quintessentially a closed building, belonging to an age when the broadcaster wore a dinner-jacket and never fraternised with the public. Even without modern

As Birkin Haward's competition drawing indicates, a new public entrance plaza, complete with an underground link to the old Broadcasting House, was planned from the very beginning.

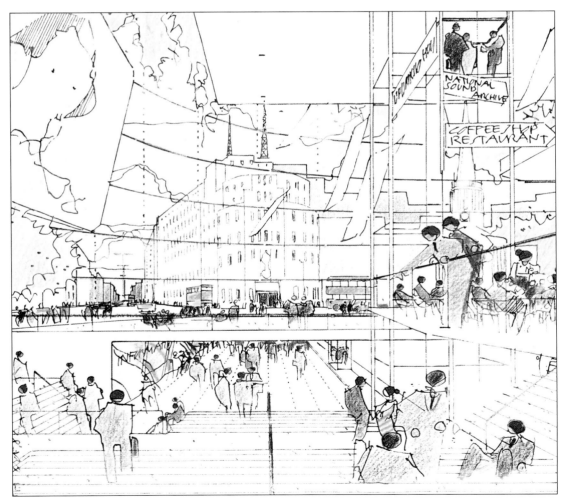

security precautions, the old building was not designed for more than a few members of the public to enter its hallowed portals.

The new building would be different — a symbol of a new age of open communications. Norman Foster extended the idea of the 'box-within-a-box' — as applied to the arrangement of the studios — to the entire new building. He used the idea of a traditional Russian doll to explain a conceptual model in which the outermost doll represented the public façade of the building. The space between this and the next doll was the public concourse, with the inner doll representing the operational areas. Inside these there were the studios, contained within a space representing control rooms and ancillary areas. While this layered quality achieved a functional shift from the public exterior to the private inner world of the BBC, Foster perceived the potential for expressing this in the design — for making visible this sequence of layers, and so achieving a glittering jewel-like complexity.

In Broadcasting House, the central studio block formed a 'holy of holies', surrounded by offices and connected by corridors. It was understandable in principle, as these offices and corridors formed a buffer zone protecting the studios from the noise of the outside world. But it allowed no possibility of re-organisation. Any relocation involving a change in space type tended to be constrained by servicing requirements, and the current difficulty of refitting technical facilities was one of the main reasons for moving out of the present building.

As part of the competition entry, a series of development options was considered, the most radical of which involved returning the Langham site to a park and redeveloping, instead, the H-block extension at the rear of Broadcasting House.

The presentation model, photographed as part of the competition entry, showing the site as it was *(top)* and with one of the many development options. Modelled in simple white blocks, Norman Foster emphasised that these were *not* ideas for a finished building, merely a means of explaining the bene-

fits of various structural forms — whether in terms of massing, modular growth, servicing strategies, or just turning the corner.

For the Radio Centre, Foster Associates took as their inspiration the standard electronic component rack, widely used throughout the technical departments of the BBC. Like the rack, the new building should be able to accept spaces of different shapes and sizes, as well as to accept the regular upgrading of engineering equipment and standards, and be able to adapt to new professional practices. In this analysis the new building would be equivalent to a modern hi-fi 'racking' system as opposed, perhaps, to Broadcasting House's sedate valve wireless. It is tempting to suggest that the new building would also not need to warm up before use.

The transparent building block model made to go with the architects' competition submission went some way towards showing what this idea might mean in terms of architectural form: the result is slightly reminiscent of Nicolaas John Habraken's 'Supports' proposals for flexible mass housing. But it was intentionally vague, showing only the potential for overall massing and the fact that things could go more or less anywhere. It did, however, serve to demonstrate the potential benefits to be gained from developing the entire site.

Typically, Foster Associates had expanded their brief to consider all radio elements, advocating what they called "the rich mix approach". All parts of the Corporation would benefit, they felt, from the increased social interaction that would result when management, production staff and technicians were thrown in together.

With this inclusive approach, it was difficult to see what could be left out. The design team rejected the idea of excluding drama and other long-timescale departments as being too forced, making the new centre too news-oriented. On the contrary, they suggested bringing in BBC Publications, BBC Information and Data and both parts of BBC Enterprises — then housed in offices a few hundred metres north of BBC Television Centre. Meanwhile, the Schools and Further Education departments could come in to occupy Broadcasting House.

They addressed the question of 'team spirit' — often lost when staff move into a new building. In the case of the BBC, it was a product of the insularity of individual work groups which was only accentuated by the existing building. But it was a creative force: how was it to be preserved in the new building?

The office hoped to be able to cultivate this individual identification within the context

Norman Foster strongly believed that the new BBC building should be as open to the public as the old Broadcasting House had been closed. Captions to Birkin Haward's drawings, however, suggested this need not be so; what was important was the spirit and sense of movement.

In the early months of 1983, immediately after the competition was won, a new series of models began to take shape — not so much as a means of explaining ideas to the client, but more as a way of allowing the design team itself to begin to understand the complexities of the project.

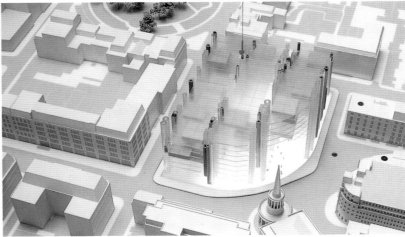

Early studies were based on a straightforward modular grid of service cores, orthogonal to the site, into which floor plates could be inserted at any height. Central to these considerations was the exact boundary of the site and whether extending it southwards, towards Cavendish Place, would not be more beneficial.

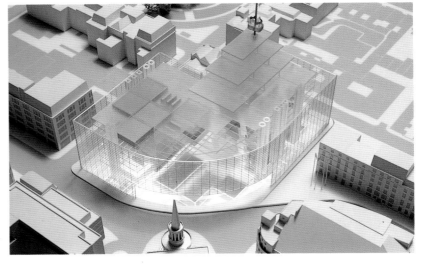

The BBC owned several, but not all of the buildings along the north side of Cavendish Place, and early designs had to assume only partial development on this side of the site. Independent studies had confirmed the benefits of developing the site as a whole, but the implications of such a decision had first to be agreed by the Board of Governors and with the planners.

of a greater 'souk' atmosphere, in which social interaction would take place at many levels in a general hierarchy of group sizes. The BBC was already a 'city-within-a-city', integrated in its surroundings, to some extent, by virtue of being fragmented into isolated buildings within the 'BBC village'. Once the constituent parts of this village were thrown together in a social condenser, the result should be an increased level of interaction and creative output.

The design report that the office presented in November 1982 was an attractively designed 120-page pamphlet, liberally sprinkled with Norman Foster's and Birkin Haward's characteristic sketches, as well as many 'handwritten' notes by Foster in the margins. It was more like a magazine than a grey technical tract; and, if anything, the informality of its layout belied the amount of technical research that had gone into the writing of it. The images it contained, while not overly specific, conveyed a sense of a busy, populated space. Like the contemporary report for the Humana competition, the tone was very much one that stressed partnership between client and architect and invited participation, rather than one which pronounced the required solution: here again was Foster's sketch of the note-pad, the pen and the question mark.

It did not attempt to provide a detailed architectural solution, but drew attention to certain areas of potential on the site. For instance, it mentioned three possible methods of handling that crucial curve opposite All Souls': the sweep, the step and the facet. Four possible forms of atrium were illustrated, and the idea of sunlight reflectors, as used at the Bank, also made an appearance. A diagonal link with Cavendish Square was already in evidence, although here it was orientated towards Broadcasting House rather than All Souls'. A succession of massing variations modelled on computer was also illustrated.

By the time of the presentation, the 10 consultants competing had dwindled to eight, after the two American firms had dropped out. The remaining architects presented their ideas in one frantic week in November.

It was Foster Associates' approach that evidently appealed most to George Howard and the other members of the committee. In December 1982 the BBC announced their choice of architects and the office learned that they had been successful in their submission.

Norman Foster had first proposed the idea of 'rooms within rooms' for the on-floor studios at the very beginning of the competition stage. The problem was determining how much space they might require.

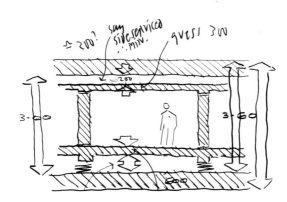

Foster Associates' characteristic approach starts with an emphasis on developing and refining the brief, and their design report had been based on just such an analysis. Nevertheless, once they had received the commission, the office was faced with an avalanche of conflicting requirements.

Soon after their engagement, Richard Francis, BBC Radio's managing director, arranged two weekend sessions for a team of approximately 40 senior staff to discuss the brief. The first, at Arundel, involved only Radio staff. It emerged that the BBC had very little idea about the size the building needed to be.

The design team began the task of building up the brief from first principles — the numbers of people, the size of work spaces they required, the groups that they worked in, the ancillary facilities they required — a process that occupied virtually the entire first year of the project.

At the time of its construction, the BBC Television Centre had been seen as something of a 'futuristic' building. Within the BBC, Radio might have appeared an increasingly marginal and out-dated medium. But Richard Francis — later Sir Richard — remembered feeling that now it was to have a building worthy of the twenty-first century, it was only a matter of time before the rest of the BBC decided to come in on the project. Sure enough, by the time of the second weekend at Selhurst Park, the brief had been expanded to encompass a new headquarters for the entire Corporation.

The office's perception of the BBC was less as a corporation than as a collection of individuals, bound by rules but following their own initiative. These were the inhabitants of the BBC's central London 'village', the members of the proverbial 'warring tribes'. The analysis of this community had formed an important part of the office's competition report. Accordingly, their first task after being commissioned was to take steps to understand the way the various parts of this community related to each other, and the precise status — legal and otherwise — of the 20 different buildings that it occupied.

Working closely with Dieter Jaeger and the Quickborner team from Hamburg, the architects acted as flies on the wall to chart the movement of staff during a programme's production process. The product of this research resembles the report of an O&M consultant, following, for instance, the lengthy journeys

Unlike television studios, which are designed for maximum flexibility, sound studios tend to be highly specialised, with different design criteria depending on what is being recorded.

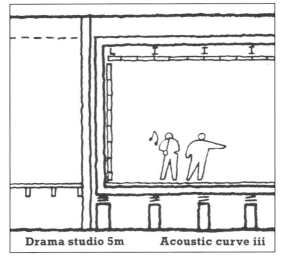

Drama studio 5m   **Acoustic curve iii**

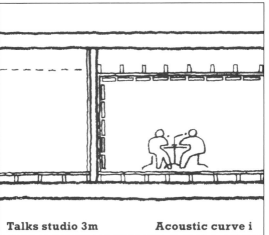

Talks studio 3m   **Acoustic curve i**

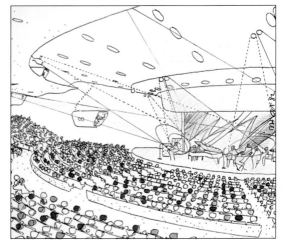

Orchestral or large-scale concerts were usually recorded in the BBC's Paris studios, elsewhere in the West End. Foster Associates suggested a new concert hall, possibly as large as the Royal Festival Hall, be incorporated on the Langham site, below ground level.

The original studios in Broadcasting House, though technically of a high standard, had been sealed in a protected area in the basement. Foster Associates preferred a simple range of standardised studios that could be located anywhere.

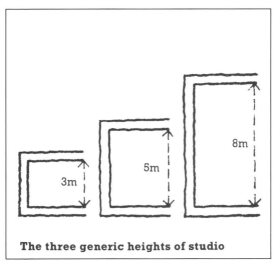

The three generic heights of studio

With only limited research data available on the problem of preventing the transmission of ground noise, acoustic consultant Tim Smith initiated his own tests in the basement of the Langham building, which culminated in this full-scale mock-up of a suspended studio floor.

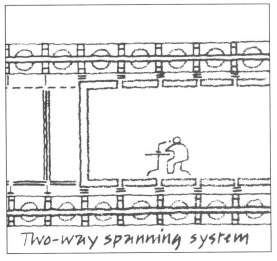

Two-way spanning system

Waffle slab

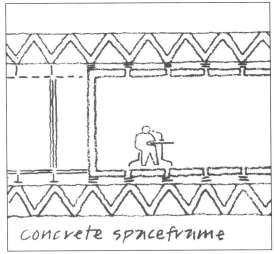

Concrete spaceframe

A variety of construction methods was considered for the primary structure of the new building, though all were based on concrete systems as simple mass remained one of the best forms of sound insulation.

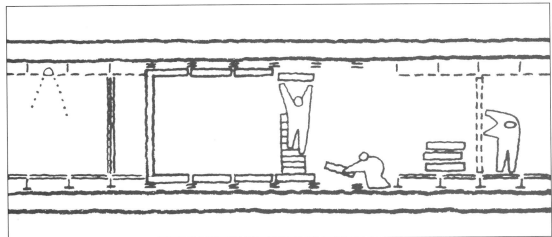

made by the producer of a Radio 1 programme, as he travelled from office to record library to studio and back.

Acoustic isolation is conventionally achieved by means of elaborate structures incorporating various combinations of resilient mounting and heavyweight construction involving wet trades. At the same time, the BBC's criteria for acoustic isolation, reinforced by the needs of modern digital recording technology, were the most exacting in the world. The challenge for the architects and their consultants was to satisfy these acoustic demands while allowing openness and flexibility for future change.

The demands of the larger studios for audience participation and for music studios were the most complex single issue to resolve. This

Given a sufficient floor height and effective flexible mounts, studios could be built just about anywhere from simple modular units that would allow them to be expanded or moved with the minimum of disruption.

While good sound insulation is essential if the studio is to be protected from external noise, it is equally important to establish the best possible acoustic characteristics within. The BBC demanded that the highest standards be maintained throughout.

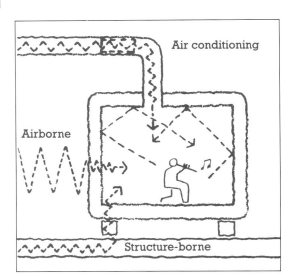

Solving the technical and organisational problems of the brief was not enough. Every development also had to be considered in terms of its impact on the urban context. It was a long, slow process.

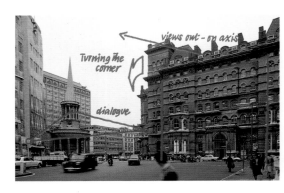

By April 1984, more than one year after the competition had been won, Foster Associates felt confident enough in their understanding of the brief and the site to start preparing more detailed floor plans.

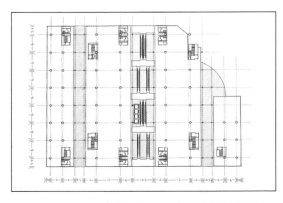

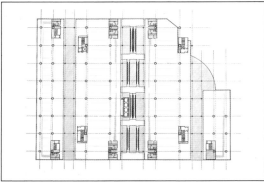

As proposed in the competition report, the floor plans combined a rich mixture of open-plan and cellular offices in clearly defined 'team' groupings.

was largely because of their fixed, finite nature, which was incompatible with the general level of flexibility that was required.

It is normal practice to locate acoustically sensitive rooms, such as studios, at the centre of buildings, surrounded by buffer zones; this was the strategy adopted in Broadcasting House. But the larger studios for audience participation and music, which did not need natural light, were difficult to justify in the precious space above ground. Placing them below ground not only created more space where it was required but also made it easier to achieve public access without compromising security in the working areas.

From the beginning Norman Foster, his partner Spencer de Grey and Richard Francis shared an ideal that the new Radio Centre should be a true public building. Interestingly, one of the sketches Foster had made when first exploring the site, only a few days after the invitation to compete, shows a public concourse opening on to the corner opposite All Souls' Church.

The cross-section that was now evolving was beginning to show public and service functions extending down from ground level, with only working areas above. To achieve the most demanding standards of acoustic isolation in

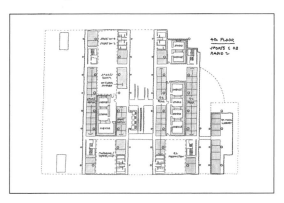

the very centre of a city, however, on a site seriously affected by noise from two Underground railway lines was a technical challenge. But the office's track record for solving similar problems in the past was good. Their acoustic consultant, Tim Smith, had previously been involved on the Willis Faber & Dumas building in Ipswich and the Hongkong Bank. More importantly he had also worked directly for the BBC in the past and was familiar with their established criteria for acoustic performance.

Nevertheless, he found that he had to start from scratch. Nobody had conducted any serious studies of the effects of Underground noise and how to protect against it. A prototype studio was set up in the basement of the Langham Hotel, not far from where the new studios would be located. This was carefully monitored with a series of studies which tested the feasibility of what was proposed. More importantly, the experiments helped to determine the kinds of springs which would be required to isolate the individual studios.

While design studies of the internal demands of the building continued, the architects found themselves having to come to grips with the implications of having to design 'from the outside in' at the same time. Around 100 massing options were modelled over the next few months, and though a few proved to be design cul-de-sacs, the majority show a steady evolution towards the final detailed proposal.

The most pressing question to resolve was how much accommodation should be provided on the site: what could be afforded, how many people — and which departments — should work in the building, and what the site could reasonably be expected to accommodate without being hopelessly out of scale with its surroundings.

A number of the models were to do with the process of 'honing down' the brief and reducing the scale of the building work within the site context. At Hammersmith and Willis Faber, the office's task had been made easier by the fact that the quality of the surrounding buildings could accommodate a uniform elevation without difficulty. The problem in designing for the BBC lay in the variety of conditions that existed in its surroundings: the scale varied from an almost domestic scale to the south-west, to the far grander proportions of Broadcasting House to the north-east.

Other models were developed as conceptual 'shapes', intended to explore basic strategies for responding to the site. Fortunately, the architects were well placed to observe 'outside' influences in some depth, as the Langham was only a few hundred yards from their then offices in Great Portland Street.

It was always evident that some kind of grand gesture would be required at the south end of Portland Place. Thanks to Lord Foley, no building in London — other than Buckingham Palace, at the end of the Mall — could boast a comparable axial location. But it would not be

"We prepared a breakdown of accommodation which indicated that some 75 to 80 per cent of this building will be concerned with the making of programmes, with all that that means in terms of studios and support facilities. This is no ordinary office building, neither in terms of its floor loadings, which will be about three times those of a traditional office, nor in terms of its floor-to-floor height, which will be nearly twice the minimum standard."

Norman Foster, presentation to the Royal Fine Arts Commission, 13 February 1985

The orthogonal grid had its merits, but as the design developed it became clear that it could not resolve the full demands of the brief *and* sit comfortably on the site. Almost out of frustration, a number of alternative forms were re-examined to see what clues they had to offer.

enough simply to close the vista: it was also necessary to find a way of turning the corner effectively into Langham Place.

In November 1982, Gordon Cullen, doyen of what might be called the 'outside' school, had published an influential article in *The Architects' Journal*. In it he suggested that an irregular roof line, and a tower on the north-east corner of the building, would help close the vista down Portland Place and at the same time steer the viewer deftly down Langham Place. Foster had long admired Cullen and has cited Cullen's writings as one of the influences that

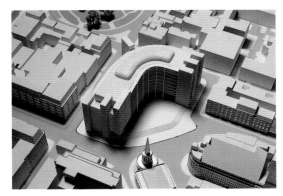

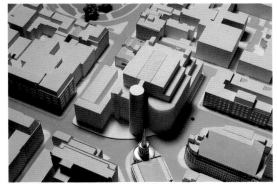

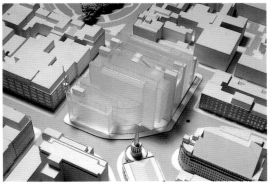

led him to study architecture. Given this background, it was perhaps not surprising that he now approached Cullen to discuss the project in more detail.

Cavendish Square, although it made contact with the building only at one corner, created a very special problem, as from here it was possible to step back from the building and sense its bulk. Some of the earlier models in which the building was low-set at this point on the perimeter, and then rose up in the middle, were found to have an oppressive effect. This placed a particular limitation on the shape of the building.

A further key factor was how to respond to All Souls' Church. To provide a sweeping curve on the north-east corner of the building or to seal this part of the building off in any other way tended to make All Souls' appear alienated and uncomfortable.

Continued on page 54

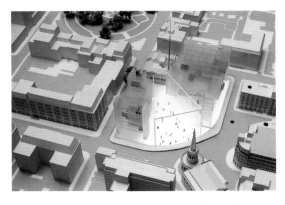

The breakthrough came with a model made a year before, showing a wedge-shaped atrium driven diagonally across the site from All Souls' to Cavendish Square. Was there an alternative geometry that offered better opportunities?

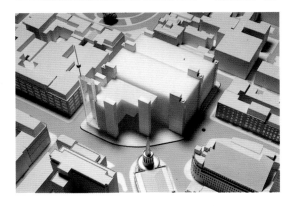

Building a Brief
by Annette LeCuyer

Annette LeCuyer is an architect who trained at the Architectural Association in London. She worked in practice in England for 13 years, initially for Foster Associates and subsequently with Allies & Morrison, where she was an associate. In 1994 she was appointed as an associate professor at the College of Architecture and Urban Planning of the University of Michigan. Annette LeCuyer has written for numerous international architectural publications, and her work has been published in journals both in Europe and the United States.

Foster Associates' winning submission for the BBC competition demonstrated both the vision which the practice would bring to the design of the proposed new radio headquarters and their rigour in addressing the problems and needs of a client. The competition brief, which had been prepared by the BBC, focused on the pressing problem of inadequate and outdated studios in Broadcasting House by calling for 22,000 square metres of accommodation for radio production departments on the Langham site. Foster Associates' competition submission broadened the scope of the enquiry by using the project as an opportunity to take a fresh look at BBC Radio in its entirety.

The stocktaking was long overdue. The Corporation had rapidly outgrown its headquarters in Broadcasting House and had expanded over the years in an *ad hoc* fashion. At the time of the competition, the BBC owned or leased

BBC RADIO PROGRAMME PRODUCTION PROCESS NEWS

PROGRAMME NEWS BULLETIN

INSERT RECORDING

OBSERVATIONS

The Foster team spent several days following various production units as they went about their work, logging the time taken on various tasks and the different departments involved, and noting the problems that were encountered.

23 buildings in central London in what Foster Associates romantically called the 'BBC village'. Apart from Broadcasting House, few of these buildings were purpose-designed for broadcasting, and many working environments were a tribute to Heath Robinson in their improvisation. The dispersal of facilities was inefficient and, in many ways, obstructive to the production and transmission of quality radio programmes. Foster Associates' contention was that, if the Langham site was developed to realise its full potential

and not just to satisfy the immediate needs of radio production, the BBC village could be consolidated largely within Broadcasting House and the new Langham Place building.

After the competition, the BBC quickly established its client structure, identifying responsibility for the day-to-day business of the project through to the ultimate authority vested in the Board of Governors. Sir Richard Francis, then Director of Radio, assembled the Arundel Group which comprised 40 heads of the key departments in BBC Radio. At a weekend retreat and numerous working sessions with this group during 1983, the Foster team participated in a lively debate about the aspirations of BBC Radio which would shape both the brief and the scheme for Langham Place.

However, following the appointment of Foster Associates in January 1982, the project did not follow the normal course of appointing consultants, being briefed by the client, and starting more or less immediately upon the design. Early meetings with the various client constituencies demonstrated that, while departments such as personnel and property services had information about the BBC's central London operation, it was neither comprehensive nor up-to-date. It became clear that the data necessary to formulate the brief for the Langham site would best be compiled from scratch. Consequently, during the first year of the project, an exhaustive — and exhausting — programme of investigation was undertaken.

Foster Associates' research included a departmental survey, work-station analysis, a technical audit and analysis of the programme-making process, a survey of central and support facilities, an area survey of all BBC central London properties and — last but not least — clarification of the parameters which would govern the capacity of the Langham site. To assist in structuring the analysis, several specialist consultants were engaged: Dieter Jaeger of the Quickborner team from Hamburg masterminded the surveys and space analyses, and Jolyon Drury took on the daunting task of predicting the movement of people, goods, and materials of all kinds for the proposed, as yet undefined new complex.

The departmental survey was effectively a census of the BBC, a comprehensive snapshot taken during the summer of 1983 to provide the database for the brief. A few statistics reflect the scope of the gruelling task. Interviews with every department head in W1 —106 in total —

Everything concerned with the making of a specific programme was assembled on a single display board. The size of the different departments and their location within Broadcasting House was noted, complete with photographs of every stage.

Brian Redhead, photographed in the studio during a broadcast of the *Today* programme. Understanding how individual programmes were made provided invaluable information on the intricate workings of Broadcasting House.

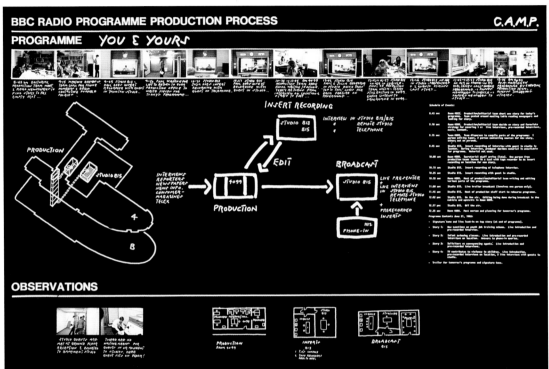

standard, which applied to nearly 80 per cent of the open plan work stations, was found to be too generous. Reduced area for work stations where proximity and eavesdropping were essential — in departments like News and Current Affairs — trimmed the brief by 1000 square metres. Even so, comparison of existing and proposed areas for a number of departments showed increases ranging from 30 to 100 per cent. While this underlined the inadequacy of existing facilities, it was also politically sensitive. The BBC, acutely aware of its public mandate, did not want to be accused of building luxury accommodation for itself. Through this exercise, Foster Associates learned that the rationale underpinning the brief had to be thoroughly and irrefutably documented.

Simultaneously, Foster Associates undertook a technical audit of studios and their support facilities. Because the BBC had shoehorned itself into existing buildings for so many years, the technical audit turned up enormous variations in sizes, even among studios of identical use. Visits to other broadcasting complexes in Paris, Cologne, Berlin, Copenhagen, Toronto and Minneapolis helped to provide a clearer picture of a range of desirable and workable purpose-built studio configurations and sizes.

The most fruitful line of enquiry in developing the studio brief was the analysis of the BBC's programme-making process. Generic programme types were identified, such as news bulletins, features, and popular music programmes. With forensic rigour, Foster Associates observed every detail of the production teams at work from initial concept through to production, transmission and post mortem evaluation. A photographic record of the process was compiled, together with notes and diagrams recording events, times, locations, the people and facilities involved, and the geographic relationship among the various facilities. The analysis led to a thorough understanding of the relationship between production departments, studios and support facilities such as tape libraries which would fundamentally influence proposals for studios in the new broadcasting centre.

Existing BBC studios were fixed in pools, the largest of which was in the basement of Broadcasting House, far from any production department. Furthermore, for news, current affairs and similar programmes which required

were conducted during a six-week period to collect data on nearly 6400 employees. An organisational diagram showing every member of each department was drawn. A staff list classified by job title was compiled, identifying full- and part-time workers, private and open plan work stations, and special requirements such as meeting space or listening facilities within offices.

Existing ancillary accommodation was scheduled and, because such facilities were generally woefully inadequate, unmet needs were catalogued. Hours and days of operation in this round-the-clock business were noted, together with numbers of outside visitors. Relationships with other departments, studios and central support facilities such as libraries were identified. Finally, a summary was prepared by each department head of problems, needs and future trends in the department. The working relationships among departments which emerged from the census were the basis of the first proposals about which departments might form the core of the new consolidated BBC village.

In parallel with the census, an analysis of work stations was undertaken. Because many

departments were making do in Dickensian facilities, existing areas could not be relied upon for the brief. Functions, furniture, equipment, and storage were recorded for a sample range of typical existing work areas. This data enabled Dieter Jaeger and the Foster team to identify work-station types for the future to which all staffing categories could be related. Eight such typical standards resulted, ranging from 7 to 54 square metres. Each standard had two permutations: for private offices, the area required was adjusted to fit into the nearest 1500mm planning grid, and for open plan work areas, circulation directly associated with the work station and within the team area was added. Primary circulation for the building as a whole was subsequently added as a separate factor. The application of the work-station standards to those departments which had been earmarked for the Langham Place development was the first ingredient in establishing the potential area of the new building.

Area standards were agreed for each job title identified in the census, and the four most commonly occurring standards were mocked up at the BBC for review and approval. One such

"We started with a number of preconceptions, some of which have since proved to be false and misleading. An example of this was that the BBC knew precisely what it wanted and that we would be off and running with a design after three months. Instead, we rapidly discovered that we would have to develop the brief with the BBC on every aspect from first principles."

Norman Foster, from the Whitworth Art Gallery catalogue, *Norman Foster: Architect — Selected Works 1962-84*

Below: once research of the existing building was completed, the design team sought to rationalise the information gathered — proposing a logical progression of standardised studios, perhaps, or individual work stations.

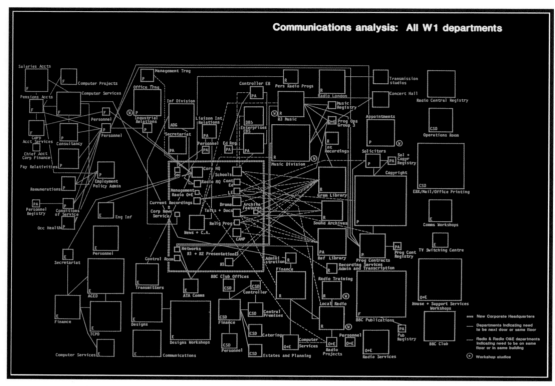

Similar rigorous processes of observation, analysis and interpretation were employed for support facilities including BBC Radio's many libraries and archives; ancillary spaces such as meeting rooms and filing; and common rooms, locker and shower rooms for the nearly 40 per cent of staff such as technical operators with no fixed address in the building, migrating from studio to studio.

In the department census, a high level of duplication and inefficiency was found in existing support facilities such as reception and waiting areas, post rooms and storage. Proposals were therefore made for rationalising such facilities on a floor-by-floor basis and, to clarify this concept for the client, a full-size mock-up was constructed. Finally, staff amenities including restaurants and a fitness centre were incorporated, as well as a range of public amenities including an auditorium studio, exhibition space,

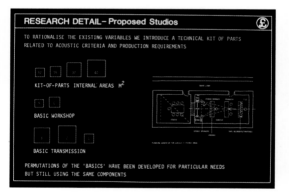

a BBC shop and other commercial outlets. A strategic proposal was made to use Broadcasting House — which was to be linked to the Langham site by a new tunnel — for support facilities such as libraries and archives, and for rationalised goods servicing, parking, and building services for the whole complex.

All of the data compiled for the components of the proposed brief were entered on the computer, which had just made its appearance in the Foster office. The database was structured so that it could be amended as the project progressed, with any change being tracked automatically through the entire brief. This was especially critical in terms of primary circulation which varied considerably among the many design options considered.

The first draft of the brief, presented to the BBC at the end of 1983, proposed approximately 42,000 square metres net accommodation for

The relative size of every department that made up the BBC village was shown on one display board, which also indicated the most important of the interdepartmental relationships. This, however, was only the start as each department then required its own study to determine whether changes would be necessary — either in response to current shortcomings or future developments. How this rich diversity of spaces could be brought together was to be one of the major challenges of the project.

a lot of recording, editing and compilation, producers block booked studios to ensure availability at pressured times. The result was congestion at peak periods coupled with general underuse.

Foster Associates' proposal was elegant in its simplicity, offering a new way of thinking about studios. Two basic studio types were proposed: workshop and transmission. Every production department was to have at least one dedicated workshop studio located in the department which could be used for interviews, recording, editing and compilation. Groups of transmission studios dispersed on production floors were to be shared among departments.

The transfer of production functions to the workshop studios solved both the problems of proximity and accessibility. Using modular components agreed with the BBC, three workshop and four transmission studio configurations were established. The types, sizes and numbers of studios formed the second ingredient of the brief for the proposed building. Acoustic criteria, the effects of digital technology, and the nature of studio construction would be explored more thoroughly as the design developed.

Study trips to other radio stations around the world were undertaken, to explore how similar problems — in planning or technical terms — had been resolved elsewhere.

Technical issues, too, required careful study, from the analysis of different construction methods to the identification of the problems posed by nearby mains services and Underground railway lines.

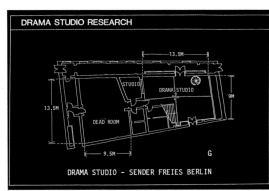

DRAMA STUDIO RESEARCH

DRAMA STUDIO - SENDER FREIES BERLIN

over 2000 staff in a new corporate and radio headquarters building on the Langham Place site. In order to understand the implications for the total BBC village, a net and gross area survey — on a floor-by-floor basis — of all central London properties occupied by the BBC was carried out. This enabled Foster Associates and the BBC to compare the proposed schedule of accommodation with the status quo and to develop a series of financial scenarios regarding the retention or disposal of buildings which would be made redundant by the new development.

The final strand of research, the exploration of the parameters which would govern the capacity of the site, was the most complex, and it was here that the emerging brief and design were most closely intertwined. The extent of the site itself had to be established. The need to secure Listed Building Consent for most of the existing buildings and the probability of a public enquiry led the design team to consider no less than nine site permutations, ranging from retention of all existing buildings to redevelopment of the total site.

In volumetric terms, the relative costs and benefits of shallow and deep basements were examined. Above ground, rights of light — which had figured so largely in the steeply raked roof of Broadcasting House — were investigated with the expert guidance of John Anstey. The area capacity within the volume thus defined proved a complex juggling act, related to floor heights which were, in turn, fundamentally influenced by the strategy for locating studios. A spectrum of possibilities was investigated for office and studio floor-to-floor height ratios including 1:1, 2:1 and 3:2. For each of these, span and cost analyses were carried out for a variety of structural grids. Finally, the availability of daylight on the deep plan site would affect both the area achievable and the quality of space provided.

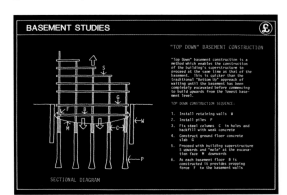

BASEMENT STUDIES

"TOP DOWN" BASEMENT CONSTRUCTION

SECTIONAL DIAGRAM

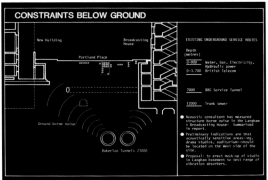

CONSTRAINTS BELOW GROUND

As work progressed, recurring themes of conversation cut across all areas of research and design. In addition to the studios, which comprised over 20 per cent of the proposed net area, nearly half of the work stations in the new building were required to be enclosed offices for acoustic reasons. The ramifications of a predominantly cellular plan were formidable in terms of daylighting. Although the status quo was challenged and the potential for using headphones was considered, Foster Associates' predilection for open, democratic space — as so convincingly realised at Willis Faber & Dumas — fell on stony ground. Most employees of BBC Radio listen to radio regularly as part of their work, and listening is often a group activity interspersed with discussion. The requirement for a large proportion of cellular space remained.

A second theme was the appropriate degree of flexibility required in the new building. Broadcasting House, with its masonry core of studios, was at the front of everyone's mind as the epitome of a building unable to adapt easily to changing requirements. However, because flexibility can be costly, there was much discus-

sion about just how much flexibility was really necessary to enable the new building to function efficiently and to adapt easily to changing requirements. Because studio loadings were two to five times office loads, their height was one and a half times office floor height, and their mechanical servicing was far more demanding than office services, the key to cost was the degree of flexibility provided in the construction and location of studios. Demountable studios with total freedom of location would increase building costs by 40 per cent over fixed studios with traditional masonry cavity walls. Many shades between these two extremes were to be explored as the design progressed.

Superficially, the outcome of the year's research was a schedule of areas for the proposed new building tailored to the capacity of the total site which formed a working brief to be revised and updated regularly as the design progressed. More importantly, the compilation of the brief from first principles enabled Foster Associates and the BBC jointly to develop a new conceptual framework about how BBC Radio might work. Although modest in size compared to the Hongkong Bank, the BBC was by far the most complex project which Foster Associates had yet tackled, with the urban considerations of the prominent central London site at one extreme and demanding brief at the other.

The brief and the design were developed hand-in-hand throughout the two-year life of the project. While the process was thorough and highly structured, it was not clear. There were so many unknowns at the outset that the definition of the brief was more akin to a sleuthing operation than to the scientific method. From the data gathered, hypotheses were tested and adjusted or discarded. In a manner worthy of Poirot, clues from the many threads of enquiry were painstakingly assembled and gradually combined until a total picture emerged. The final scheme, with its uniform structural grid, standard floor heights and flexible plan, was not a loose-fit speculative solution but highly tailored to the specific needs of the BBC. Its disarming simplicity was the result of a thorough consideration of the panoply of options, distillation and refinement — eloquent testimony to the Foster way of working.

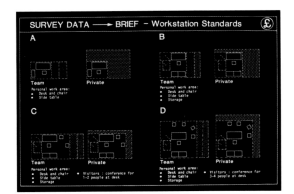

SURVEY DATA ⟶ BRIEF – Workstation Standards

Over the two years of design development, Foster Associates produced models of more than 100 proposals for the Langham site. Many were little more than conceptual, but more than a few were completed in some detail. Somewhat tongue in cheek, they were brought together as an 'ideal city' and displayed at the Royal Academy Summer Exhibition of 1985.

"Quite by chance, but to Foster Associates' immense good fortune, there is an axis which runs, more or less, from a diagonal across Cavendish Square, through the tower of All Souls' to the British Telecom tower half a mile away which, as luck would have it, is where the BBC's radio waves are *actually* broadcast from. This axis, intuited by the architects and grasped as a gift from above, bore rich fruit, providing the otherwise unexpected orientation for the entire scheme."

E. M. Farrelly, *The Architectural Review*, May 1987

One of the meetings of the Arundel group, held between 1982 and 1984. Chaired by Richard Francis (centre), this particular session was attended by Norman Foster, Spencer de Grey and Mark Sutcliffe from Foster Associates.

Discussions with the BBC had always assumed a split between operations and support areas. Foster Associates were unhappy with this idea, and the first studies had sought to create a universal space to be used either as offices or studios, which would form a 'mat' over the site. Further analysis, however, showed that separate office and ancillary zones would always exist, and it was wasteful, therefore, to provide studio standards across the whole floor. The space and weight of structure that this implied would have resulted in a building that was unnecessarily bulky and expensive.

The idea of an atrium was there from the start: as a deep, square site it was inevitable that some sort of space should be formed to open the building up to natural light. This space appeared at various points in the site during the design process: at first, it was formed by 'eating away' at the grid at the north-east corner.

The next sequence of models therefore provided two distinct zones: a high studio block and a low office block. In one option a large block in the centre housed the studios and went far higher than the perimeter block. This, in turn, changed in height to respond to the surroundings. In another, the perimeter block enclosed a 'U'-shaped studio block.

The idea of a 'U' enclosing the central atrium had certain advantages. In effect the 'U' was a linear block wrapped around the perimeter and, as at Hammersmith, it presented itself as one way in which the varying heights of the surrounding properties could be reflected. There were a number of permutations of what might happen on the corner. One version introduced a gap as a public route, forming a 'U' around the central block, but this was found to be wasteful of space.

The trouble was that the narrowness of the grid limited the range of spaces it could accommodate. In addition, pressure of space served to force the top of the building upwards, with oppressive effects in Cavendish Square. Internally there were also problems, as this approach disposed the studios in a more or less linear arrangement, quite inimical to the needs of networks which required the newsroom to form the hub for the studios. Nevertheless, the location of the lifts, at one end of the 'U' and at the south end of Portland Place, was a decision which remained the same in the final version of the plan.

A more sophisticated analysis of how to construct a flexible studio block economically

The diagonal axis, and the adoption of a diagonal structural grid to match it, opened up a whole new field of opportunities that responded, in equal measure, to the building's internal organisational needs *and* to the surrounding urban context. Almost immediately, a new planning diagram began to take shape around a narrow arcade that ran from Cavendish Square towards All Souls' Church, opening out as it reached the north-east corner into a grand, full-height atrium.

To explain the benefits of the diagonal axis, aerial photographs were prepared overlaid with the key lines of axis. One early idea was that the route through from Cavendish Square might fan out in the centre of the building to take in the view along Portland Place, as well as towards All Souls'.

The news floor, the most important and probably the most complex in planning terms, was chosen to show how well the new diagonal grid worked.

The new geometry was best explained by this image which overlaid the primary axis, which ran the length of Portland Place and — diverted — continued along Regent Street, with a new secondary axis that linked Cavendish Square to All Souls' and the British Telecom tower beyond.

The first proposal based on the new diagonal grid was worked up in some detail and employed certain ideas found in the final scheme. Other elements, however, such as the lifts, were timid in their response and required further refinement.

Though simply made, this early block model of an interim scheme clearly demonstrates how well the new diagonal grid sits on the site, both in terms of overall massing *(below)* and for the dynamic new view from Cavendish Square *(right)*.

produced a concept involving bands of heavy structure which provided sufficient space to construct studios in all their multiplicity of layout, and which were interspersed with service zones in a more lightweight structure and fixed zones for primary distribution. Parts could be slotted in and removed without affecting any of the rest of the functions of the building: here, indeed, was the flexible-racking system referred to in the office's design report.

In the series of models that followed, the building appears as a sequence of strips laid across the site in different orientations. A column spacing of 12 metres was found to allow almost any imaginable studio arrangement smaller than an auditorium — this was provided in the basement beneath the atrium.

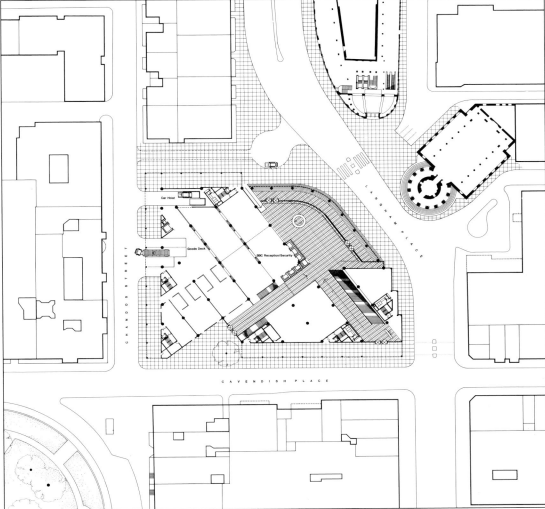

At this point the advantages of a diagonal grid began to emerge. An orthogonal grid, set out parallel to the neighbouring streets, was found to be less flexible in responding to the scale of the surroundings than one laid at an angle. So, instead, the strips were laid diagonally across the site. Some of the options were marked by a huge atrium on the north-east corner, with a glass wall and studios behind. From that came the idea of 'drilling a route through' on the diagonal towards Cavendish Square.

Now, the relationship between Cavendish Square and All Souls' Church was harnessed to provide the organisational heart of the building. Portland Place and the area north of Cavendish Square is very different in character from the

The ground floor plan of the preliminary diagonal scheme. The ability of the new plan to absorb departments of different sizes in a wholly rational sequence of bays allowed the internal organisation of the building to be resolved and refined with astonishing speed. Everyone was agreed, too, that the building sat more comfortably on the site. But this building more than most required an equilibrium between how it responded to influences from the 'outside in' and those from the 'inside out'. With the internal layout now under control, greater thought needed to be given to how the building might best respond to its surroundings.

57

As the design evolved, so the presentation material became more refined. Several photomontages were prepared, including this view from the peristyle of All Souls', overlooked now by the proposed entrance atrium of the new Radio Centre.

Better than any other drawing, Helmut Jacoby's perspective illustrates Norman Foster's aspirations for a truly open building. In fact, only the ground floor plaza would be open to the public, but even from here the full complexity of the BBC organisation would have been apparent.

hectic commercialism of Oxford Street. The design team realised that the 'seam' between these two zones actually occurred just to the south of the site. By connecting the building to the Square at one corner and creating a public route diagonally towards All Souls', they could subtly divert this boundary and bind the building to both areas at once. The new building would combine with All Souls' to form a gateway between the two zones, bringing new life to the area just in front of Broadcasting House. This was currently a social no-man's-land.

When Broadcasting House was built in 1931, the BBC's relationship with the public had been very different from that in 1983. Then, it had been a private company broadcasting on

only one channel. But in the intervening years the BBC had been through a war and attained a national role; following that it had gradually responded to a new, more pluralistic atmosphere by splitting its output into first two, then three, then four and now five channels; then developing a range of local radio stations.

None of this was reflected in the headquarters. The building was not only physically unworkable, it was also socially obsolete. It was quite impossible to bring in the public; visitors to the building were greeted by a small foyer and, in the absence of any other public facility, shepherded towards a tiny makeshift bookstall. Immediately before them stood metal doors protecting the inner sanctum as effectively as if it were the Crown Jewels.

It is interesting to compare the degree of public access at Broadcasting House with that of Charles Holden's London Transport headquarters, completed just two years earlier, in 1929. Here the ground floor was open to the public as a pedestrian street, reminiscent of certain Manhattan skyscrapers. Foster Associates saw this as something to be emulated in the new building. The public dimension had been a continuing preoccupation: the Renault Centre in Swindon, for instance, had had its own 'public areas'. But the BBC Radio Centre was not merely a company with a public relations interest: it was a public institution, and the public could claim to have a right to be involved in the process of broadcasting.

In the earliest stages of the project, the public dimension had not been fully integrated into the design. It involved only the corner facing Portland Place, and provided fairly limited access to the site. But as the design became more and more integrated with its site, so the scope for transparency and communication at street level grew.

The idea of public access meshed in perfectly with Foster Associates' desire for a large atrium facing All Souls', linked to a public route diagonally across the site from Cavendish Square. It also co-ordinated well with the decision to place an auditorium in the basement. Foster Associates envisaged shops and cafés, as well as a museum modelled on the Museum of Broadcasting in New York, where it would be possible to listen to archive recordings on demand. It was hoped that there would also be an exhibition of artefacts associated with historic

Various refinements were made as the design developed, not all of which lasted through to the final scheme. One such proposal suggested sloping the roof of the atrium in direct response to the line of sight to the British Telecom tower.

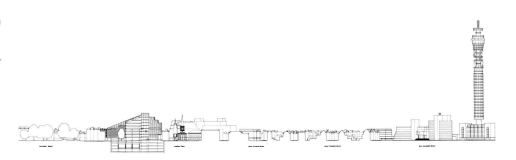

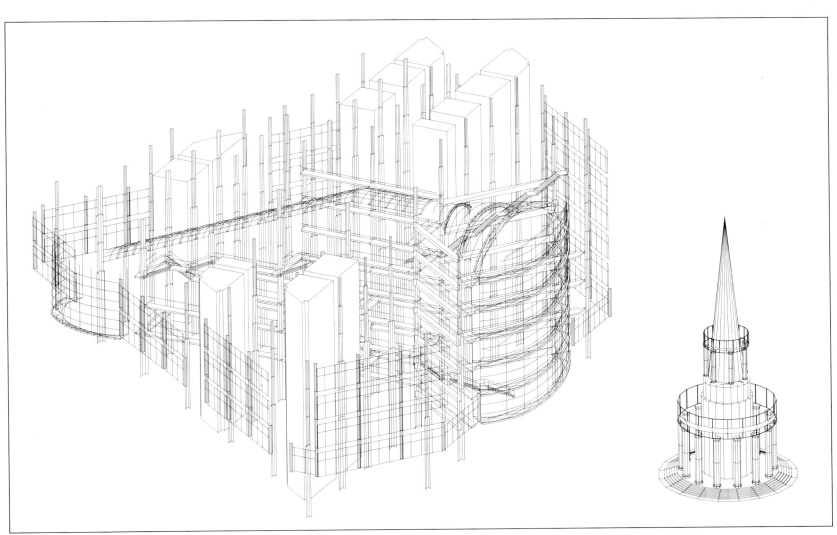

During the course of the development of the BBC project, Foster Associates took delivery of an Intergraph CAD system. Computer analysis had been used at the competition stage to try out basic massing variations, but the new system provided the opportunity of predicting the appearance of the building from a number of different viewpoints, allowing the quality of each space to be assessed. It also proved invaluable when Helmut Jacoby began to lay out his perspectives.

radio events. An area was designated on the west side of the site where Outside Broadcast vans would be able to back into the atrium on election nights, which would allow audience participation programmes such as the 'Radio 1 Roadshow' to take place.

It could be argued that the very openness of the building helped to mitigate the effects of its sheer size. A large building is far less oppressive if it allows passers-by inside to experience the space. The skyline and the building's relationship to Cavendish Square were undoubtedly helped by the architects' desire to see the roof spaces given over to gardens and terraces for people, and not allowed to become, in Norman Foster's words, "a battleground for engineers and their equipment". This was very much

in the tradition of their work for Willis Faber & Dumas in Ipswich, where the entire site was recreated in the sky, three storeys above the streets of the market town.

Fresh-air intakes would normally have been located on the roofs, in order to avoid traffic pollution. But Foster Associates questioned the conventional wisdom and, at their request, an air quality survey was carried out which showed that the air was satisfactory from level three upwards; at roof level it was, if anything, slightly worse. As a result it was decided to take in air at this level where the service bands of the tartan grid met the perimeter, and channel it downwards to the basement plant room.

The ground floor plan of an interim scheme, but displaying many of the features of the final proposal. Most importantly, the lifts — lost in the middle of the atrium in the preliminary scheme — have now been repositioned to the north elevation, on axis with Portland Place.

As with the lifts, so the escape stairs, too, are now brought to the edge of the building and boldly expressed, using the diagonal geometry of the plan to generate triangular niches within the façades.

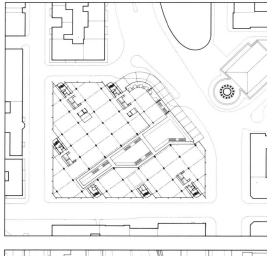

The floor plan is clearly articulated on the roof, where glazed strips, running perpendicular to the atrium, are used to identify the service and circulation zones below, grass terraces marking the open plan office and studio zones.

The interim scheme in model form. In an otherwise orthogonal grid of streets, the diagonal geometry of the new Radio Centre responds almost perfectly to the angled siting of All Souls' and to the curved sweep of Broadcasting House.

Gradually, the outline of the final design emerged and solidified. The new geometry neatly allowed the building to rise and fall in scale with its surroundings, and by the same means the varying floor-to-ceiling heights of the different studio areas could be accommodated. But this diagonal grid still had to meet the perimeter, and yet be divisible into a regular module that could be made up out of the same size cladding elements.

The 3:4:5 triangle is familiar to many from school geometry lessons as one of the few with a common factor which is an integer. By an extraordinary stroke of good fortune its acute angle of 37.8 degrees was very close to the angle of a line connecting the corner of Cavendish Square with All Souls'. By massaging the geometry and fine-tuning the boundary edges, the design team was able to establish a regular elevational grid which would mesh perfectly with the tartan grid of the internal structure. The alternating bands of the structural grid emerged at the perimeter in a rhythmic sequence, compatible in scale with that of the Georgian buildings to the south and west of the site.

Some observers at the time suggested that it was unusual to find Foster Associates — supposedly prime exponents of twentieth-century architecture — discussing a project with the Victorian Society. Perhaps of more significance, however, were the contributions from Ashley Barker, of the Greater London Council's Historic Buildings Division, and from the Royal Fine Arts Commission. In all these discussions, it was crucial that the office prove that what was being

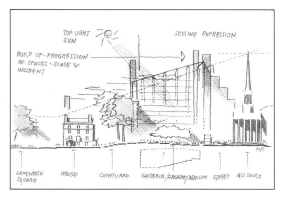

An early sketch by Norman Foster explores how the diagonal grid might be employed to regulate the massing of the building, rising across the site from the domestic scale of Cavendish Square to the urban dimension of All Souls'.

The Radio Centre in its final form, the sweep of lift shafts facing Portland Place now replaced by a distinctive tower matching the geometry of the whole building.

proposed was architecturally superior to what already existed. By the time of the project's cancellation, the Royal Fine Arts Commission was willing to recommend the design and the conversations with Barker were heading towards success. Considering that the proposals addressed site determinants at the most fundamental level, and made no superficial nods in the direction of earlier styles, this was quite an achievement. As the detail elevations of the models show, the new building effectively picked up the rhythms and nuances of the adjoining façades without any hint of pastiche.

The final location of the lifts and the tower they created on the bend is an example of the effect that the discussions had on the design. All of the conservation bodies were understandably preoccupied with how the transition around Langham Place might be effected. Although the design had always been higher on that corner, it was not marked with any particular emphasis until fairly late on in the design process. The addition of a cluster of towers at this point was seen as a very positive gain, creating a counterpoint to All Souls'.

These crystalline towers formed one of the areas in which 'outside' interests could coincide with those of the 'inside', as some sort of vertical element would be needed to house lift, stairs and service distribution elements. Putting it on the outside, to the north, would not only allow lift users to enjoy the view, it would also constantly communicate activity to the outside and so enhance the BBC Centre's relationship with the outside world.

In the final version the lifts were pushed into a cut between the structure and the service zone. David Morley saw this lift as a sort of animated obelisk at the end of Portland Place, in response to the obelisk-like quality of All Souls' in its own response to Regent Street. Mark Sutcliffe, by contrast, compared it to the flipper of a pin-ball machine, deflecting the observer round the Langham Place chicane.

The structure was cut away at the northeast, so as to form an open corner, revealing how the section worked. The building thus presented itself to its surroundings as a hive of communicative activity, like the workings of a calculator exposed to view. The building also opened up towards All Souls', creating a hub of activity in the space between them, so tying the church into a closer and more comfortable relationship with the new building.

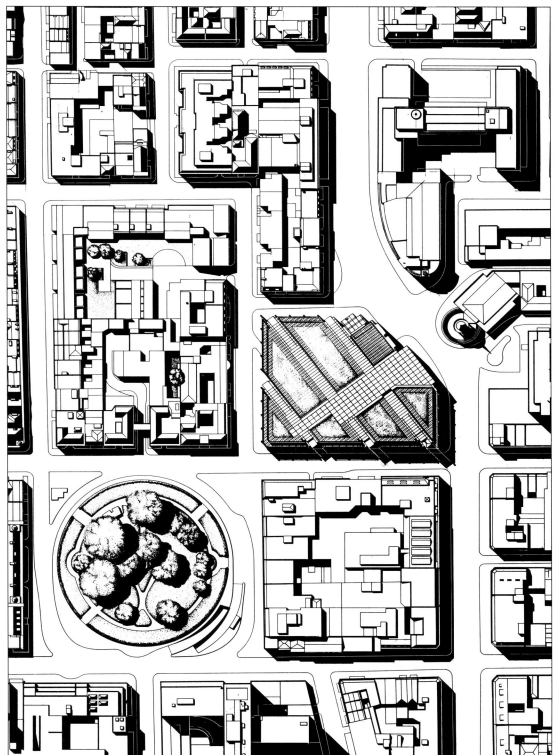

"Across the diagonal axis is laid a structural grid. It happens that the diagonal axis discovered in the context intersects with the given orthogonal geometry of the site in just such a way as to produce a 3, 4, 5 triangle, on which the geometry of the new building was then based. This gives a 12 x 9 metre structural grid which, when cut as specified by the triangular relationship, gives an even distribution of columns at 7.5 metre intervals around the perimeter. Very neat."

E. M. Farrelly, *The Architectural Review*, May 1987

In preparation for the expected planning process, a beautifully detailed model of the final scheme was prepared, showing the building in context. Matching the growing height of the building as it moves away from Cavendish Square, the atrium increases in width, allowing improved views of All Souls' as the visitor progresses through the building.

The overall form of the final BBC design is reasonably familiar to many. What is less appreciated is the design at the detail level, only a limited amount of which was possible before the project was cancelled.

The highlight, undoubtedly, would have been the glass wall across the external face of the atrium. A glazing structure was being developed, in association with Richard Howe and Peter Rice, with vertical supports in steel which would have been exceptionally thin, by virtue of being regularly supported by a series of catenary structures from top to bottom.

All Souls' Church would have dominated the view from the atrium. Seated at a café table beneath internal trees, it would have been possible to appreciate Nash's church in an entirely new light. Between this and the cluster of lift towers was a stack of studios, glazed and looking out northwards along Portland Place and towards Broadcasting House.

Beneath the public mall, which was sized in such a way as to allow the installation and removal of complete studio suites, would have been the BBC's own private mall, lit by the glass floor above. In the daytime natural light would filter down from above, while at night the public mall would have been lit from below. A similar proposal had been put forward at the Hongkong Bank, where a proposed glass floor at plaza level transferred light to the vaults in the basement below.

Leading on from this mall was the link to Broadcasting House, serviced not by a horizontal/vertical lift, but by a powered trolley system. The refurbishment of Broadcasting House was an essential part of the proposed development, and this main circulation route would lie at the centre of gravity of the whole complex.

The roof, stepping down towards Cavendish Square, would have allowed an open-air restaurant looking out over a spectacular series of cascading terraces.

The form of glazing being considered on the main elevations was a combination of transparent and translucent glass. The use of metal and glass was now so firmly associated with the work of the office that the materials themselves had become part of their aesthetic. The cylindrical perimeter columns, however, would have been clad in Portland stone — even solid Portland stone was considered. If the BBC Radio Centre had gone ahead, it would surely have caused a major reappraisal of the essential character of their architecture.

The design team's task had been to produce a building which was as flexible as an electronic component rack. However, a more exact metaphor might have been a rack that was designed to match a room crowded with antiques of varying quality and age, ranging from the eighteenth century to monolithic 1930s Classicism — without sacrificing any aspect of flexibility or functional attainment.

In the final model, the BBC Radio Centre appeared to fit into the surroundings very well. It also seemed to have found favour with the Royal Fine Arts Commission. It may be that this degree of harmony was helped by the fact that the building and its surroundings were all modelled in the same colour. On the other hand, in all the most elemental aspects of the plan, the building was rooted in its site, and in its environment. Without doubt, this was Foster Associates' most profoundly contextual building at that time.

"A further advantage of the diagonal geometry, in this particular context, is the way in which it allows the height of the building to respond to the varying degrees of urbanity and grandeur around it: stepping up in bands from its lowest point on the south-west, where the building juts into the private world of Cavendish Square, towards a triumphant culmination in the cluster of transparent, flag-bearing glass lift towers on the north-east."

E. M. Farrelly, *The Architectural Review*, May 1987

Proposals for the final scheme included a grass roof complete with roof-top restaurant, offering the Corporation's many employees unparalleled views over London.

A long section through the atrium of the final scheme. Situated directly beneath the atrium, the concert hall avoided the need to transfer floor loadings imposed from above and could enjoy public access at all times with the minimum of inconvenience.

"The building respects the historical divide. To the south, busy, commercial; to the north, embassies and institutions, much calmer, more formal. The atrium becomes the link between these two worlds, with a formal entrance to the north for the BBC, and a public entrance to the south. This is a tradition that can be traced back to the nineteenth century, whether in the domestic scale of London's Burlington or Piccadilly Arcades, or in the much larger scale of the Galleria in Milan. The atrium becomes a route that is also a meeting place — for people and for culture. Information displays, cafés, exhibitions; all are provided as a means of promoting communication. Behind glass screens, broadcasting is seen in action. The barriers have been taken down to create an open house, a place of welcome, a place where the Corporation and its public can strike up a dialogue."

Norman Foster, lecture at the UIA Congress, Brighton, 17 July 1987

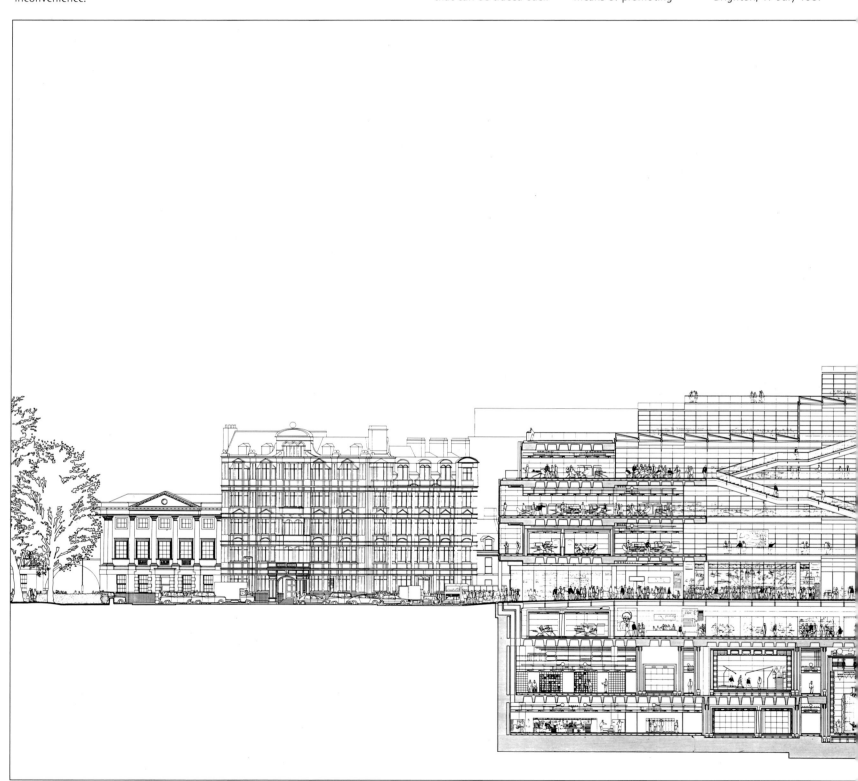

"The architects saw their client, the BBC, not as a huge unwieldy bureaucracy, but as an exciting, dynamic and essentially communicative organisation: both metaphorically and, because of the unusually high level of interdepartmental communication (running up and down stairs) that goes on within it, literally, too. Wishing therefore to present the organisation in this light to the public, the architects clung to an image of transparency, of revelation — of an apparently solid block whose one chamfered corner was carved away by a huge glazed gash, or atrium, to reveal, like complex microchip circuitry, the mass of blips and bleeps and humans and tiny flashing lights that constitutes the inner sacred workings of the BBC."

E. M. Farrelly, *The Architectural Review*, May 1987

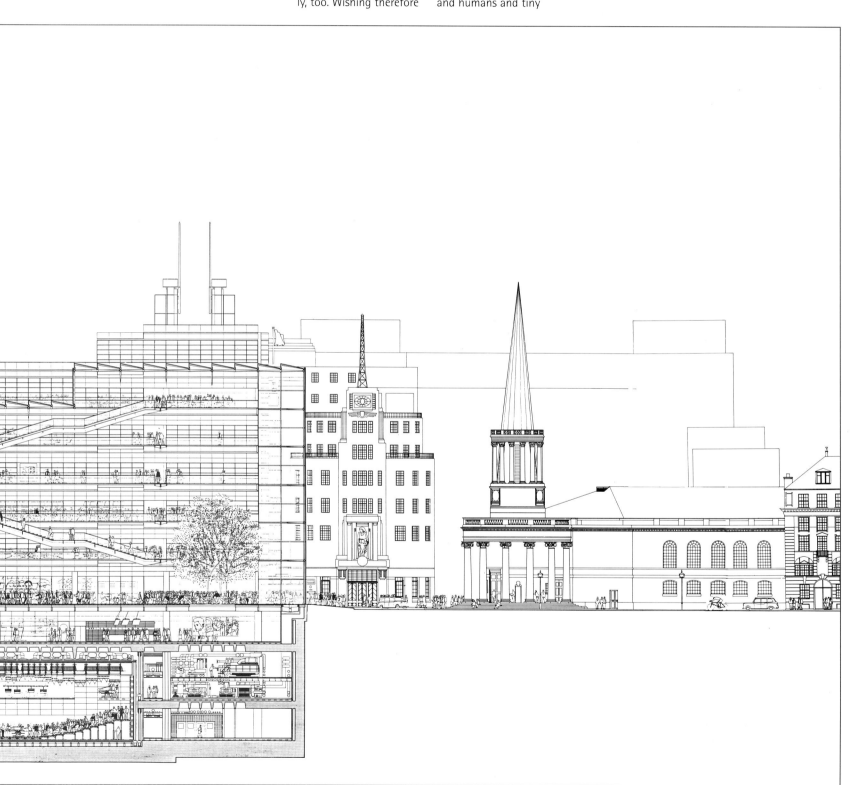

"The key to the design was flexibility: the flexibility to build, or rebuild at some future stage, acoustically secure studios in almost any part of the main core of the building; the flexibility to offer open-plan or cellular offices, for team activities or private concentration; the flexibility to change shapes and working practices as technology altered or networks were restructured."

Architectural Design
no 56, August 1986

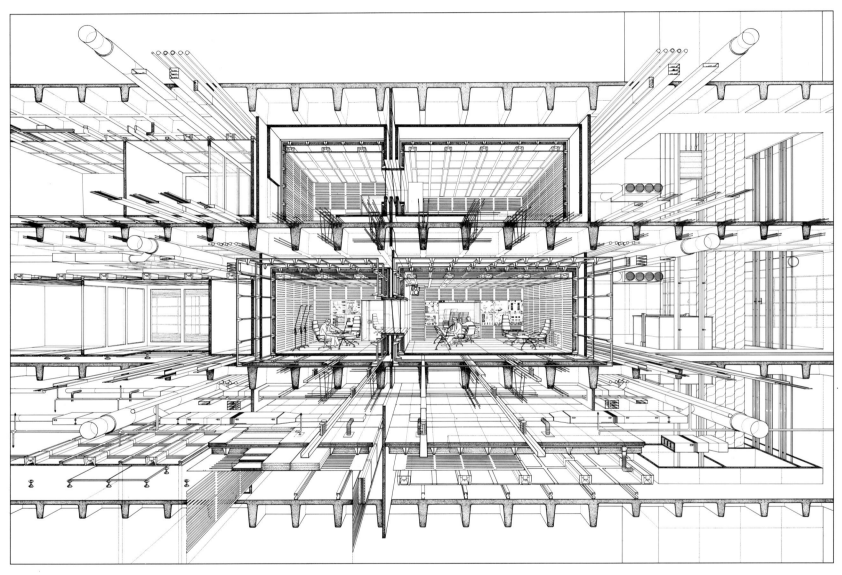

This perspective section through a typical group of studio suites graphically illustrates, in the most dynamic fashion, the working in practice of the 'box-within-a-box' principle. Based on a concrete waffle-slab floor structure, the concept required a higher floor-to-floor height than normally associated with offices, but this in turn allowed the introduction of far deeper suspended ceiling zones, capable of accommodating the most complex of servicing requirements. A raised floor handled local telephone and electrical needs.

Client links at the BBC, via Richard Francis and the layers of middle management, had gone from strength to strength. Budget, time and technical demands were identified as firm goals and had been unequivocally met. There were prototypes, detailed cost plans, space standards and voluminous programmes to demonstrate the viability of the project.

Unfortunately, at senior management level, the situation was anything but stable. George Howard, the BBC chairman who had commissioned the project, had been a patron of the old school. He felt that the Corporation, as a public institution, had a duty to excel. Strengthened by this conviction he had persuaded the Board of Governors that, in the Reithian tradition, the Corporation must invest wisely in its future and deserved the kind of building that would make this possible. There were also good economic and management arguments for consolidating on one central London site.

But by the time the project began in earnest, Howard had retired and his place had been taken by Stuart Young, an accountant by training. At the time there were those who suggested that the appointment had political overtones and was part of a move by Government to cut the BBC down to size — and not only financially.

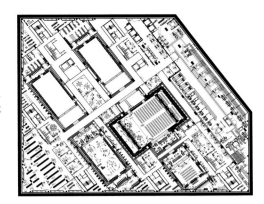

Conceived as intricately as the inside of a calculator, the deep basement floors accommodated the larger studios with their need for higher standards of sound insulation and more complex servicing requirements.

In December 1984 the project was well on course to be submitted for a detailed planning application at the beginning of the new year. But this was only three months before the licence fee increase was due to be settled. The Board considered that, in the middle of a recession and at a time when the Corporation would be seeking more money from the Government, it might not be prudent to announce proposals for a glittering new building, however well justified the proposal might be.

The Board decided to defer the application until after the new licence fee had been agreed. But the increase, when it came, was smaller than had been hoped. BBC Television was already short of cash to make programmes and was not enthusiastic about spending a large amount of money on a facility which, although part of a mixed-use complex, was viewed by some as purely for the benefit of BBC Radio.

About this time, the BBC became aware that the old dog-racing stadium at White City, next to the BBC Television Centre, was up for sale. The site was large enough to accommodate not only the Radio Centre and the new headquarters, but also several other television facilities then dotted about west London.

The Langham project had been ushered in as the vision of a chairman who saw the BBC as a national institution very much in the tradition of its founder, Lord Reith, which would continue to demand a metropolitan presence. He and others would advance strong cultural arguments to support this view.

However, when the power structure of the BBC changed, this perception of the Corporation and the viability of its key project were called into question. In this more hawkish view, it was suggested that studios and their offices were anonymous and could be located anywhere. More significantly, the Langham and its site could be sold off as a valuable piece of real estate. Soon after, the stadium was acquired and White City became the subject of a contractors' design-and-build package deal.

In hindsight, it is impossible to separate the demise of the project from the political atmosphere that predominated at the time — the time of the Falklands War and a recession — particularly when contrasted with the optimism that had prevailed when the architects had first been appointed, just two years before.

Timothy Ostler

A section through the main concert hall. Triple lined walls, the inner two leaves mounted on rubber blocks, and a fully suspended floor guaranteed total sound insulation from all external sources, while moveable ceiling panels allowed the internal acoustic performance to be adjusted to suit individual programmes exactly.

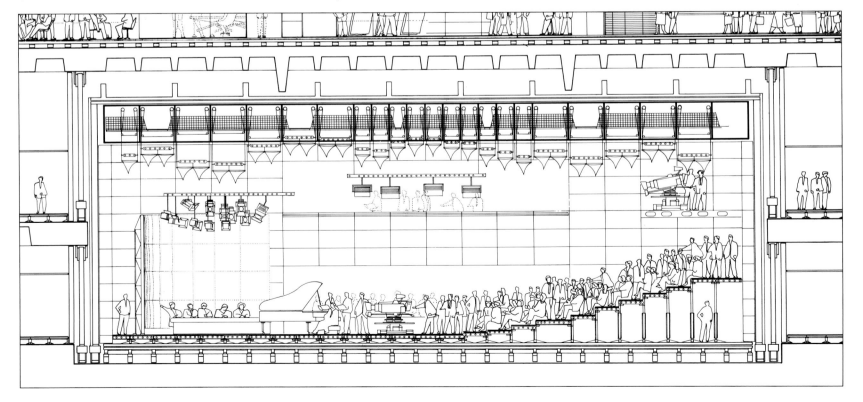

Adopting an idea first put forward for the plaza at the Hongkong Bank, Foster Associates proposed a translucent glass floor for the Radio Centre's new atrium, a glowing presence at night and transmitting daylight down into the basement during the day.

Unlike the earlier proposals, the atrium in the final scheme was hidden from Cavendish Square, a dramatic gesture that only became apparent when the visitor entered the building.

The highly detailed presentation model allowed an almost endless exploration of the final design and its relationship to the surrounding buildings. Far from being a fixed entity, the model was almost constantly adapted after completion, as lessons learnt from its study led to further refinements of the design.

The vertical rhythm of the exposed columns, the stone facing of all exposed structural elements, and an eaves height that matched that of the building's Edwardian neighbours were all specifically chosen to ensure that the new Radio Centre blended almost imperceptibly into the existing streetscape when approached from the south.

"The BBC, in its wisdom, has decided to buy 16 acres of land at White City. It is a site with room for expansion, where new buildings can be speedily erected — but it is a sub-urban site, something of a retreat from the metro-politan presence now enjoyed by BBC Radio at the hub of the capital.

There is an awful irony in the decision for Foster Associates. They have been analysing the BBC's needs in some detail and were naturally critical of the Corporation's occu-pation of some one mil-lion square feet of off-ices and studio space at some 20 different loca-tions. The Langham site had its problems, but Fos-ter Associates had shown they were not insoluble. In their final scheme they had demonstrated that in the sensitive heart of London a new building could be built which would have been an elegant and exciting addition to the capital, though a tight squeeze."

Colin Amery, *Financial Times*, 24 June 1985

Drawing on contempo-rary studies for the Carré d'Art in Nîmes, the ele-vations of the new Radio Centre combined clear and translucent glass with natural stone, though further articula-tion was introduced here by exposing the service cores and their escape stairs.

The breakdown of scale from service cores to exposed structure and then mullion grid was refined through a series of detail studies, the best of which were incorpo-rated in the presentation model. This is the view of Cavendish Place from Regent Street.

As part of the competition entry, Birkin Haward had imagined a clear-glazed lift, rising in a glass shaft that overlooked Portland Place. Three years on, the idea had turned full circle and become a key element in the final design.

The ground floor plan in its final form. Far from being considered a self-contained building, the new Radio Centre was intended as the new heart of a revised and much condensed BBC village, which would include a fully renovated Broadcasting House.

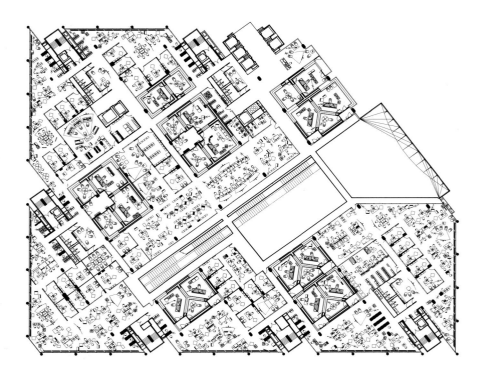

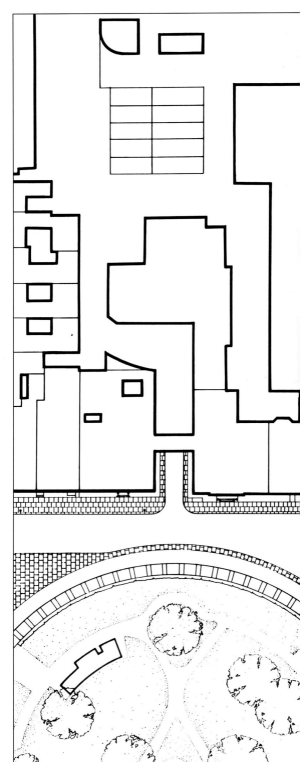

Though still in the final stages of design development when the project was stopped, many of the floor layouts had been worked through in considerable detail. One of the benefits of the diagonal planning grid was the natural gradation of different sized office zones it created at each floor level. This made it far easier to assign different departments an appropriately sized space which was not only easily accessible to other departments but which also established its own identity.

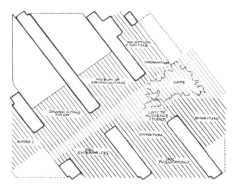

As with all the best Foster buildings, the new Radio Centre had the simplest of planning diagrams. This is the ground floor which, furthering the concept of accessibility, is almost entirely open to the public.

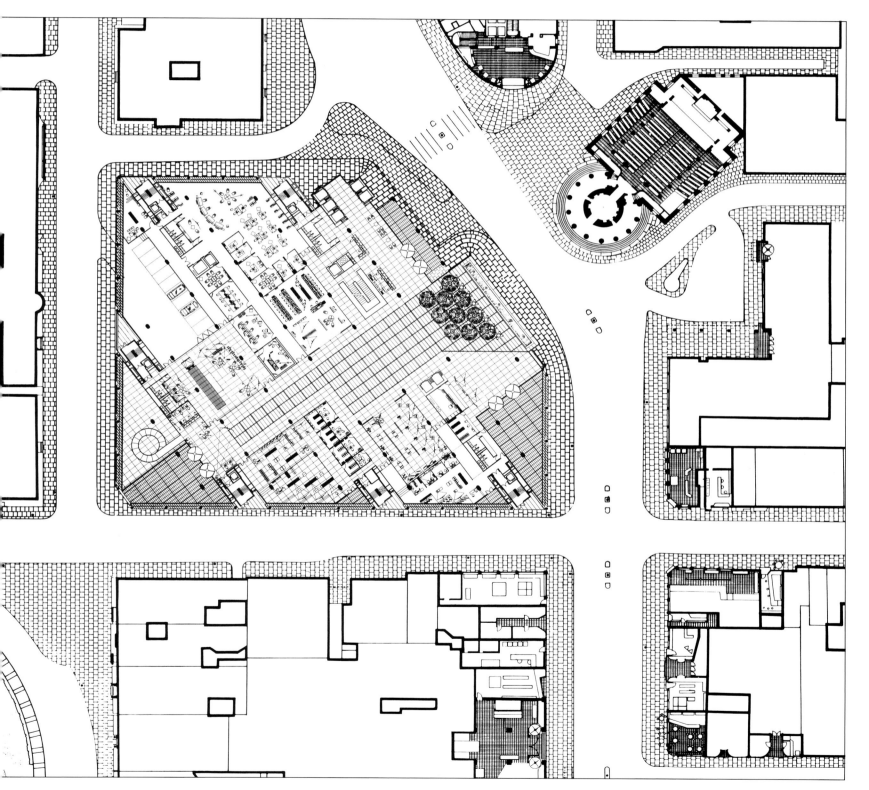

"Staggeringly bold in concept and fully in the Foster manner, with no overt concessions to conventional contextualism, the design (when finally unveiled in 1984) was greeted with almost universal approbation. It seemed that Foster . . . had managed to pull off one of the most difficult jobs of the decade . . .

Unfortunately, the two-year gestation period was to prove the scheme's undoing. No sooner was the scheme unveiled than the BBC decided to move its radio broadcasting head-quarters from Portland Place to White City and Foster's client and pat-ron, George Howard, re-tired as chairman. Fos-ter's mighty scheme was dead at birth. As the AR lamented in May 1987: 'in June 1985 the job was cancelled, and with it was lost one of the most elegant and assur-ed new buildings that Londoners have had within their grasp for some time.'"

Architects' Journal, 11 & 18 December 1991

Reflecting an idea first expressed by Gordon Cullen during his analy-sis of the Langham site for the *AJ* in November 1982, and explored in some of Foster Asso-ciates' earliest designs, the towering lift-shafts of the new Radio Centre actively echoed the ver-tical thrust of All Souls' Church across the street, to create a new gateway to the heart of London's West End. Unlike the elevations on the other sides of the building, the Portland Place façade made "no overt conces-sions to conventional contextualism", other than matching the eaves height of the two near-est buildings.

In the final design, a pair of glazed lift-shafts, sep-arated by glass-walled lift lobbies, had been carefully aligned with the central axis of Port-land Place, providing a fitting close to the vista from Regent's Park, but at an angle determined by the building's diago-nal grid which naturally deflected traffic round the corner towards Upper Regent Street.

"The real architect of the BBC building was the then chairman, George Howard. It was *he* who had the vision of what the BBC was, and it was he who had found a group of people who shared that vision and were sympathetic to it."

Norman Foster, lecture at the UIA Congress, Brighton, 17 July 1987

A photomontage of the view from Park Crescent, along the whole length of Portland Place, showing the new Radio Centre shining brightly in the failing light of an autumnal evening.

1982-1983   Autonomous House
for Buckminster Fuller

Until Buckminster Fuller's death at the age of 87, just 10 days after giving the oration at Norman Foster's RIBA Royal Gold Medal investiture in 1983, the close friendship and working relationship between 'Bucky' and Foster had been extremely fruitful. The theatre for St Peter's College, Oxford, and the Climatroffice project, both 1971, and the International Energy Expo pavilion of 1978, all remained unrealised; but many of the constituent ideas informed later projects, not least their last collaborative venture.

This was to have been a residence for Fuller and his wife in Los Angeles; an 'autonomous house' based on a five-eighths sphere, double-skin dome generated by a new structural geometry which Fuller had recently developed.

Writing in 1983 at the time the house was being designed, Fuller recalled, "when I invented

low-friction sealed hydraulic race which required very little fluid to support the structural load.

It was a principle that Fuller had tested in the early 1970s with his 'rowing needles' – tubular hulled, catamaran scullers – which, as a keen oarsman, he had designed for his own use. In these, the water played the part of the hydraulic fluid. Using the same hydraulic principles for the house, it became possible to move the domes with very little effort, opening up a whole range of new possibilities.

The external skin was to be a 50-foot diameter 'fly's eye' dome capable of rotating independently around a similar inner dome which would support the space-deck living floors. Each dome was to be half glazed and half solid-clad in polished aluminium panels so that the house could be closed up completely at night or track

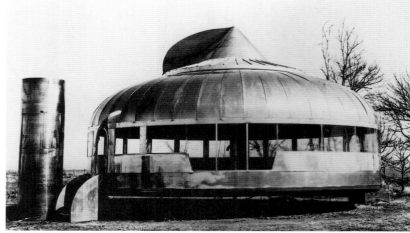

Buckminster Fuller's interest in the use of curved forms for domestic dwellings predates his early work on geodesic structures in the 1940s *(left)*, stretching back to even earlier designs for a 'Dymaxion House' *(right)*, first exhibited at Harvard University in 1929.

and developed my first clear-span, all-weather geodesic dome, the two largest domes in the world were both in Rome and were each 150 feet in diameter: St Peter's, built around AD 1500, and the Pantheon, built in AD 118. Each structure weighs approximately 30,000 tons. In contrast, my first 150-foot diameter all-weather geodesic dome weighed just 30 tons — one-thousandth of the weight of its masonry counterparts".

The refinement of lightweight, high-performance structures had occupied Fuller throughout his career, and here the concept reached its logical conclusion, the continuous bottom tubes of the inner and outer domes both 'floating' in a

the sun during the day; an idea that can be traced back to Foster Associates' rotating 'sun-scoop' rooflights, developed to trap the low winter sun in the Norwegian Vestby office project of 1974.

Between the two domes, the environment would be controllable, warm or cold air circulating between the two skins, depending upon the outside air temperature. The interior would be planted to create an internal micro-climate.

The design was advanced in a series of meetings in London attended by Buckminster Fuller, Norman and Wendy Foster and others in

Twelve years after work ceased on Buckminster Fuller's house, many of the ideas that had informed that project resurfaced, in simplified form, in the design for a new dome for the Reichstag in Berlin.

During his last visit to London, on the occasion of Norman Foster's RIBA Royal Gold Medal investiture, Buckminster Fuller and Wendy Foster discuss ideas for his new home in Foster Associates' model shop.

Fuller's sketch for a triangulated floor structure for the new house (left) sought to draw on the same geometric reasoning that had informed the structure of the external dome (right).

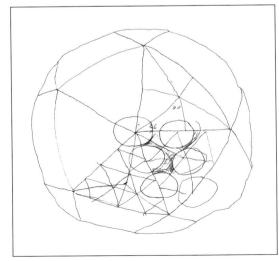

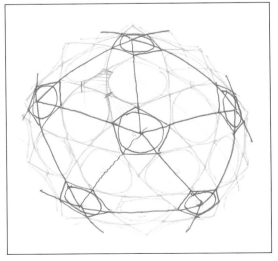

the Foster Associates team. A full set of design drawings was sent to Fuller's office in California where the final complex three-dimensional geometry was calculated.

Unlike Fuller's earlier geodesic domes, in which the surface is divided into a structural pattern of triangulated polygons, the Autonomous House domes rely on an interlocking series of parallel segmental lines to define the structure; an effect analogous to taking the equator and lines of latitude on the surface of the Earth, then tilting and repeating them at set intervals. These lines were joined by a pattern of regular framed hexagons and triangles. Irregular pentagons were formed by the intersecting segments.

A large-scale model was made in the design studio of a US aircraft manufacturer. This

Shortly after his death, the model of Bucky Fuller's final design was photographed against the evening sky on Dunstable Downs, complete with a selection of prototype cladding panels — both glazed and transparent.

was completely demountable into a portable kit which Fuller brought with him to London where it was assembled in Foster Associates' model shop near their Great Portland Street office.

Fuller was tremendously excited by the project and the success of his collaboration with the Foster team and felt that, "it was really going to happen". But after his death the project was inevitably shelved, although the model held pride of place in the Foster office until it was again dismantled when Foster Associates moved to their new premises in Battersea in the summer of 1990.

Martin Pawley

Carré d'Art
Nîmes
France

The historic heart of Nîmes, the grid of its Roman street plan still discernible, stands out in this aerial photograph as the area bounded by the approximate triangle of modern boulevards. The Roman Arena lies at the southern tip, while the Maison Carrée stands in the square straddling the western boulevard near the north-west corner.

Often used by Norman Foster in lectures, these are just two of the many posters he photographed while on his early visits to Nîmes that, for him, captured "the spirit that animates the city".

The Carré d'Art project began to take shape in 1983, soon after Jean Bousquet was first elected Mayor of Nîmes. As every French school-child knows, Nîmes is the administrative centre of the Gard *département* and is chiefly famous for Roman monuments, bullfighting and a textile industry that once cornered the market in denim (originally *de Nîmes*). But despite its illustrious past and picturesque *férias*, the Nîmes of the 1970s and early 1980s lacked the dynamism of its rapidly expanding neighbour, Montpellier.

Jean Bousquet entered local politics in 1983 because he believed his native town needed to change if it was to have a future. He admired the Georges Pompidou Centre in Paris, and was particularly impressed by the way it had brought new life to a run-down neighbourhood. (The Beaubourg site had served as a lorry park since pre-war part-clearance of the capital's most notorious slum, "*îlot insalubre numéro 1*".) Even before his election, it had occurred to him that a contemporary art centre might provide Nîmes with a much-needed fillip.

Grand architectural gestures were high on the political agenda in the France of the 1980s, in forms expressing a new modernity in tune both with the future and with the past, and conceived to symbolise the revitalisation of French culture deemed essential to national survival in a changing world.

In Paris, the spectacular conversion of the redundant Orsay railway terminus to house a new museum of nineteenth-century French art and civilisation, and the transformation of the vast but obsolete post-war meat market at La Villette to create a museum of science and industry four times bigger than the Pompidou Centre, were planned before President Giscard d'Estaing was voted out of office in May 1981.

Both projects were continued – with some modifications – by President Mitterrand, who soon launched six more *grands projets* in and around the capital: a new Opera House at La Bastille, an 'International Communications Crossroads' at La Défense, a new 35-hectare public park at La Villette, an Arab World Institute on the Left Bank, a new building to house the Ministry of Finance at Bercy, and the complete re-organisation and enlargement of the Louvre museum. (In the process, existing projects for Tête-Défense, Parc de La Villette & the Arab World Institute were scrapped.) In parallel, several major state-sponsored projects in the

Below: the Maison Carrée, photographed during Norman Foster's first visit to Nîmes, surrounded by iron railings and a sea of parked cars.

The Maison Carrée and the Arena are among the most complete Roman buildings still in existence and, together, they have shaped the development of Nîmes for nearly 2000 years. The new building could not ignore their presence.

provinces were announced by President Mitterrand in March 1982.

Prompted by the devolution of a series of executive powers to regional and local authorities from 1982 onwards, local mayors soon began to follow the presidential example. Before long, virtually every town in France seemed to be promoting at least one architectural project designed to rejuvenate its image, reinvigorate the community and create a favourable climate for the regeneration of the local economy.

If by no means all such local initiatives received state subsidy, a few were accorded the

status of 'associate' *grands projets*, among them the *Maison du Livre, de l'Image et du Son* at Villeurbanne, near Lyons. This multimedia library was agreed by the town council in March 1983, Mario Botta was appointed architect and 40 per cent central government funding was secured for a project deemed to be of "symbolic and monumental character, expressing the permanent mutation of a town that has led the field in urbanism for nearly half a century".

Soon after taking office in March 1983, Mayor Bousquet received a report stating a multimedia library, or *médiathèque*, was needed

in Nîmes, as the linchpin of the radical modernisation and reorganisation of the municipal library service envisaged by its newly-appointed director. A purpose-designed building was required, to encompass audio-visual material, a music library with loan collections, a newspaper and magazine section, an art loan service, exhibition areas and activity workshops, special provision for children and the blind, improved accommodation for reference, loan and rare book holdings, and a department specialising in material on bull-fighting.

The preferred location suggested for the new médiathèque was in the town centre, on the site of Nîmes' nineteenth-century theatre, which had been gutted by fire in 1952. Like the Place Beaubourg in Paris, the site had long been used as a car park. Little survived of the theatre, other than its imposing Neo-Classical entrance façade of 1827, overlooking one of Nîmes' best known historic monuments: the Roman temple known as the Maison Carrée, which is thought to date from the end of the first century BC or from the early years of the first century AD.

It struck Mayor Bousquet that the former theatre site would provide the ideal location for a 'Beaubourg of the South', combining the

The theatre in 1905. Following a fire in 1952, all that remained at the time of the competition was the colonnade. Its future was to play a major part during the project's early stages.

functions of a médiathèque and a contemporary art centre. The broad range of activities offered would attract a wide public to the town centre and its proximity to the 2000-year-old Maison Carrée would endow the town's past with new relevance, particularly if the new building was conceived as an architectural symbol of the renascent Nîmes.

A meeting was arranged in November 1983, to discuss the idea with the Minister of Culture, Jack Lang, who is said to have been highly enthusiastic. According to a report in the newspaper *Midi Libre*, on 29 November 1983, Lang shared Bousquet's opinion that an outstanding example of contemporary architecture was appropriate for the site, encouraged him to approach architects of international repute for the design, and requested more detailed information in order to decide whether the project might be eligible for central government subsidy. Mayor Bousquet's team then drew up a project specification, in consultation with three departments in the Ministry of Culture, and, in March 1984, Lang agreed in principle to the use of the former theatre site for a médiathèque and contemporary art centre, and to the inception of the design process.

A visit to the local curio shops turned up a fine selection of old postcards showing the Maison Carrée and the nearby theatre when they were still in their prime.

The Maison Carrée, as seen from the corner of the site. Divided by what is now a busy boulevard, Norman Foster realised that the traffic was just part of the site's dynamic character — though he was determined to remove the parked cars.

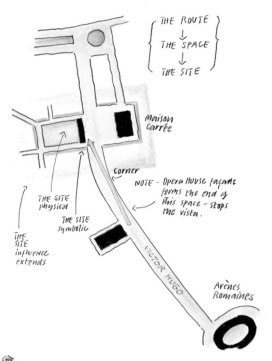

THE ROUTE
↓
THE SPACE
↓
THE SITE

Maison Carrée

corner

NOTE - Opera House façade forms the end of this space - stops the vista.

THE SITE physical

THE SITE symbolic

THE SITE influence extends

VICTOR HUGO

Arènes Romaines

Crammed full of drawings, notes and diagrams, Foster's sketchbook of his first visit to Nîmes is eloquent testimony to the excitement aroused by both the project and, perhaps more importantly, the site. Repeated frequently, it is the space created in front of the new building that is emphasised and the building itself is hardly mentioned.

NIMES IS A CROSS ROAD ↓ THE SITE IS A CROSS ROAD

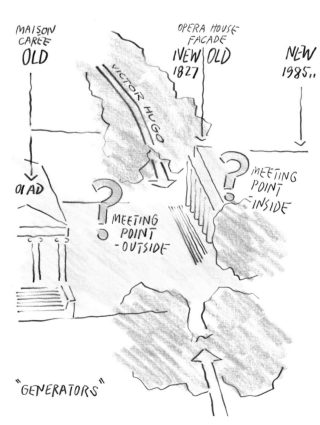

MAISON CAREE OLD

OPERA HOUSE FACADE

NEW 1827 | OLD

NEW 1985,.

VICTOR HUGO

OLD

MEETING POINT - OUTSIDE

MEETING POINT - INSIDE

"GENERATORS"

The Competition

The architectural competition was organised by the Nîmes town hall administration, in consultation with two government ministries. Patrick O'Byrne and Claude Pecquet, who had worked on the brief for Beaubourg, were appointed to draw up the competition brief. But an open international competition along the lines of that held in 1970/1971 for Beaubourg was ruled out, on the grounds that time and money would be wasted as the majority of candidates would not be of the required high calibre.

Mayor Bousquet opted instead for a limited competition between four or five candidates, selected by interviewing architects short-listed on the strength of visits to recent museums and cultural buildings around the world.

Twelve architects — nine from abroad (Norman Foster, Frank Gehry, Hans Hollein, Arata Isozaki, Richard Meier, Cesar Pelli, Aldo Rossi, Alvaro Siza and James Stirling) and three French (Paul Andreu, Christian de Portzamparc and Jean Nouvel) — were invited to spend 48 hours in Nîmes, to study the site and to discuss the project. Each was sent a dossier, describing Nîmes' history and climate, illustrating the site and its setting, outlining the scope of the project and detailing the competition conditions.

Attention was drawn to the key location of the site, the exemplary architectural quality sought for the new building and the role it was expected to play as the flagship of the renascent Nîmes.

The demolition of the 1827 theatre colonnade was presented as a question of fundamental importance to be resolved by competitors. Diagrams were supplied showing daylight angles governing the height of the future building, indicating existing basement levels, and drawing attention to the existence of two large sewers under the boulevard running parallel with the entrance façade of the former theatre.

The multi-functional character of the project was emphasised but, at this stage, the amount of floor area to be housed in the new building was not specified, nor was a schedule of accommodation supplied.

The deadline for individual interviews in Nîmes with those interested in competing was mid-July. The final choice of candidates was to be announced in August, and their competition sketch schemes were to be submitted by 1 October 1994. The winner would be expected to

Approaching the site along the Boulevard Victor Hugo, from the direction of the Arena. As Foster's photographs and sketches show, he was much taken both with the "dark tunnel" of trees lining the boulevard and with the angled view of the colonnade it created.

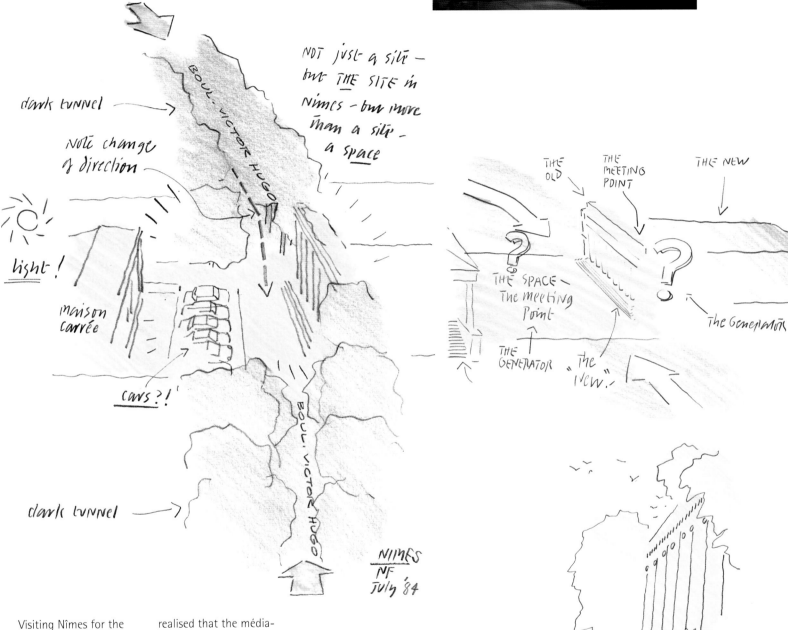

dark tunnel →

Note change of direction

light!

maison carrée

cars?!

dark tunnel →

BOUL. VICTOR HUGO

BOUL. VICTOR HUGO

NOT JUST a SITE — but THE SITE in Nimes — but more than a site — a space

NIMES NF July '84

THE OLD

THE MEETING POINT

THE NEW

THE SPACE — The meeting Point

THE GENERATOR

"THE VIEW"

THE GENERATOR

← VIEWS OVER TRAFFIC

STEPS - SYMBOLIC MEETING PLACE - ELEVATED PLATFORM VIEWING TERRACE

Visiting Nîmes for the first time in July, Foster was immediately impressed by the richness of street-life he encountered all over the city — seemingly at all times of the day and night. Whether a formal *vernissage*, spilling out of the local museum, or the informal gatherings at street-side cafés, Foster realised that the médiathèque project held the potential of becoming not just a building, but the catalyst for the regeneration of an entire neighbourhood — in particular, the Place de la Comédie, the square in front of the site in which stood the Maison Carrée.

81

"I was saddened to notice that most of the great architectural projects completed since the First World War had happened abroad. I am deeply convinced that there is a direct correlation between architectural greatness, with all its aesthetic qualities, and the greatness of a people. A weak period in architecture, it seems to me, corresponds to a period of national weakness."

François Mitterrand, *Le Nouvel Observateur*, 14 December 1984, explaining the philosophy behind the *grands projets*.

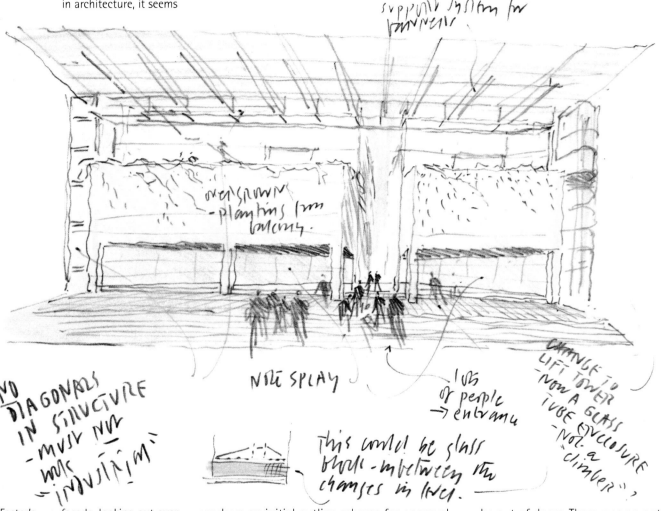

One of Norman Foster's earliest design sketches, drawn soon after his return from Nîmes, indicating his main concerns. Anything of an industrial flavour was to be rejected in favour of a welcoming simplicity that drew people into its embrace. Unsurprisingly, like many of the early representations of the project, the sketch concentrates on the main entrance façade, looking out over the Place de la Comédie and facing the Maison Carrée. Success here was essential if the rest of the scheme was to be accepted.

work up an initial outline scheme for approval by 1 December, and the scope of any subsequent stages of design work was to be determined after that.

Although the 12 architects were not contacted until 26 June, all but Meier and Stirling accepted the invitation. (Stirling was prevented from attending by pressure of work, but later agreed to sit on the competition jury.)

Shortly before his official interview, Norman Foster travelled to Nîmes and spent a few days there incognito, sketching, taking photographs and getting to know the town. He has since said the clues to the concept of the future building emerged from this initial research, "not all at once, but over time, as a delayed reaction".

Particularly memorable, he says, was the chance discovery of a street packed with people attending a *vernissage* at the Beaux-Arts museum: "It was a warm evening and they wanted to be out of doors. There was no outdoor space in the museum so, in characteristically Mediterranean fashion, they took over the road — it was completely blocked."

The creation of a generous semi-public space, where people could gather and meet at the threshold of the future médiathèque and contemporary art centre, became a design priority from then on.

The site of the future building was bounded on three sides by narrow streets, whereas the fourth side — the eastern frontage — was occupied by the surviving theatre entrance. It completed a town square created in the eighteenth and early nineteenth centuries, to provide a seemly setting for the Maison Carrée after the mediaeval fortifications had been demolished and replaced by the boulevard encircling Nîmes'

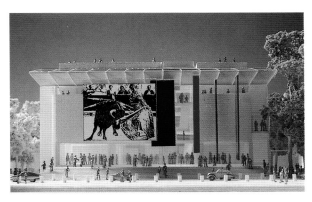

Enlivening an otherwise simple façade, Foster envisaged a display of colourful banners hung from a mobile support frame fixed beneath the building-high entrance canopy. Various options were shown on the competition model.

Below: people arriving, departing, waiting were a constant theme in all the early drawings of the building, which even at this stage were exploring the use of basements for storage and other facilities where daylight was not essential.

tight-knit core. The 1827 theatre colonnade was raised on a plinth approached by steps. It offered shade from the afternoon sun and provided a vantage point from which views were to be had, over the boulevard traffic, of the western flank of the Maison Carrée.

Analysis of such existing factors as the contrast between the explosion of light in the Place de la Maison Carrée and the tunnel-like effect created by trees bounding the boulevard leading into it, the way this route turned a corner on its way from the Roman Arena to reveal an oblique view of the 1827 theatre colonnade, the symbolic importance of the latter and its relationship with the Maison Carrée, led Foster to observe that what was at stake was "NOT just a site — but <u>THE</u> SITE in Nîmes — but more than a site — a *space*".

At his official interview in July 1984, Norman Foster spoke of his initial reactions to

Nîmes and of the key importance of the site and its surroundings. He suggested that simple improvements to the Place de la Maison Carrée, such as the removal of parked cars, would make this space more congenial to pedestrians. To revive its role as a forum and cultural focus at the very heart of Nîmes, he floated the idea that activities generated by the future médiathèque and contemporary art centre might spill out into the open and, perhaps, spread right across the boulevard into the square on special occasions when through traffic could be re-routed.

To make the point, he showed some of the sketches and photographs made during his incognito visit. To their great astonishment, Mayor Bousquet and his advisors found they were themselves featured in shots of the crowded street outside the Beaux-Arts museum on the evening of the *vernissage*. Mayor Bousquet has

since said it was clear Norman Foster understood the essentially Latin character of Nîmes from the start.

The Competition Brief

After the 10 architects had been interviewed, the final selection of candidates was announced: Foster, Gehry, Isozaki, Nouvel and Pelli. Only then was the competition brief issued.

A sober aesthetic, human proportions and an urban scale corresponding with that already existing in Nîmes were among the chief characteristics required by this 160-page document, which went on to specify that high quality finishes and directional clarity were also expected.

It demanded that the main public entrance should be easily accessible to everyone, and should lead directly into a general reception area. The médiathèque was to be related as closely as possible to the main entrance, whereas the contemporary art centre galleries were to be housed at the top of the building, to benefit from natural light. Unnecessary changes of level were to be avoided within the building, and public access between the different floors was to be provided by means of ramps and lifts.

Also included in the brief was a detailed schedule of accommodation, with a diagram indicating the relationship to be achieved between the various facilities to be provided. In all, a gross floor area of 13,435 square metres was required — *excluding* an independent 300-400 place underground car park — giving a plot ratio of 5.4:1 for the 2500 square-metre site.

Candidates were informed categorically that there was no question of burying the boulevard in an underground tunnel (the re-routing of existing underground services would be prohibitively expensive), nor of the permanent closure of the boulevard to through traffic.

Competition Submission

Norman Foster visited Nîmes twice more before finalising the competition submission, which took the form of "a diagram, to suggest priorites", intended "to serve as a basis for dialogue between client and architect". He proposed the new building should not only respect the height and mass of the former theatre, but should also occupy the same footprint. As he has since put it, "I saw no good reason to play around — the space was absolutely right as it was".

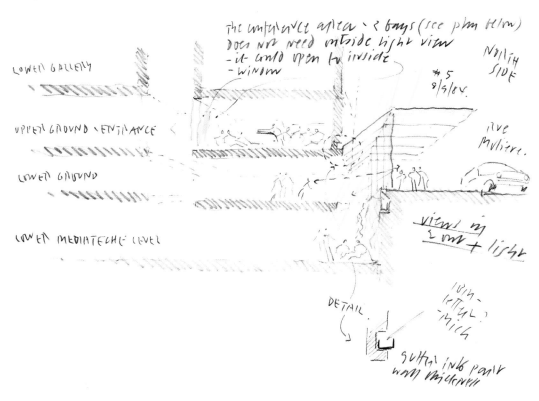

Very much in the spirit of the BBC competition entry, Foster's drawings for the Nîmes competition put forward *ideas* for a building, rather than a complete scheme. The basic diagram was simplicity itself and, with handwritten notes, quite self-explanatory.

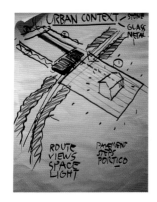

URBAN CONTEXT - STONE
GLASS
METAL

ROUTE
VIEWS
SPACE
LIGHT

PAVEMENT
STEPS
PORTICO

During his final presentation, Norman Foster surprised the competition jury by turning his back on them and talking through his ideas for the project with the help of a sequence of free-hand sketches which amplified many of the points already made in the official presentation document.

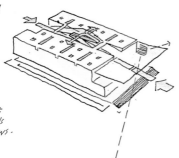

All levels are connected by gentle ramps at the lower levels - for everyone including the disabled.
The upper levels are connected by stepped ramps.

A glass "wall climber" lift connects all public levels - provides spectacular views.

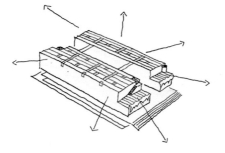

.The roof could become a viewing terrace - long views over the surrounding buildings - the countryside beyond - monuments - connected by steps and stairs to the lower balconies

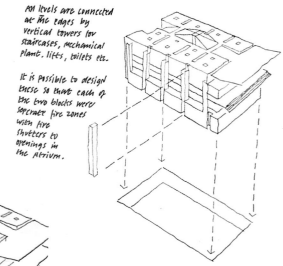

All levels are connected at the edges by vertical towers for staircases, mechanical plant, lifts, toilets etc.

It is possible to design these so that each of the two blocks were seperate fire zones with fire shutters to openings in the Atrium.

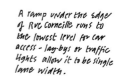

A ramp under the edge of Rue Corneille runs to the lowest level for car access - lay-bys or traffic lights allow it to be single lane width.

glass & metal - No painted steel. steel is either stainless or clad with bronze.
state of the art" optics & lighting design.

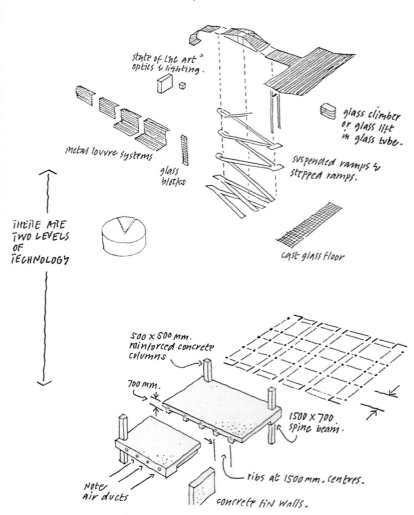

state of the art" optics & lighting.

metal louvre systems

glass blocks

glass climber or glass lift in glass tube.

suspended ramps & stepped ramps.

cast glass floor

THERE ARE TWO LEVELS OF TECHNOLOGY

500 x 500 mm. reinforced concrete columns

700 mm.

1500 x 700 spine beam.

ribs at 1500mm. centres.

Note air ducts

concrete fin walls.

concrete & stone facing

BUT NOTE that the structural & environmental engineering are integrated - a "massive" traditional shell is approproprinte for this low energy concept. see later section for more detail.

Reinforcing the basic presentation of ideas, tantalising glimpses of model photographs were included, but again in the spirit of showing possibilities, not a final solution.

In place of the 1827 theatre colonnade, a giant canopied proscenium raised on a plinth and approached by steps, signalled the presence of the médiathèque and contemporary art centre. The semi-public space so created was intended as a focus for open-air events such as concerts, laser or film shows, and as a venue for outdoor exhibitions and trade shows, as well as serving as a meeting point at the threshold of the new building where people could enjoy views over the boulevard traffic to the Maison Carrée.

The route into and through the new building was defined by a relatively narrow top-lit atrium. Placed slightly off-centre, this axial slot was presented as a space full of life and movement that would serve as a locational reference point for visitors, as well as a source of natural lighting. At entrance level, the atrium was conceived as a melting pot where visual and literary cultures would come together within a shared reception area. From there, ramps led down to the médiathèque (below entrance level), and stepped ramps led up to the contemporary art centre galleries (on the two uppermost floors). Large landscaped terraces offering views over Nîmes and the surrounding countryside were proposed on the roof, linked to smaller, gallery-level terraces beneath the main entrance canopy. Vertical services — lifts, emergency escape stairs, lavatories and so on — were to be housed in towers projecting from the flank walls at the perimeter of the building, while storage, services and car parking were to occupy basement levels.

At this stage, a concrete structure faced externally with natural stone was envisaged, with metal louvres to protect areas of glazing from the sun. Among other features of the design, the plinth under the entrance canopy was to have a cast glass floor, to let natural light into the areas below during the day. After dark, it would "glow, jewel-like, lit from below".

The proposals submitted by the three other short-listed competitors could scarcely have been more different.

Gehry proposed a sculptural composition designed to evoke the playful atmosphere of Beaubourg: a mountainous urban fragment, crowned with forms inspired by elements of the Nîmes roofscape which were intended to signal some of the facilities on offer, while the boulevard frontage sported a spiralling access point combining the imagery of a helter-skelter with that of Nîmes' Roman Magne tower.

A substantial amount of accommodation was to be housed in two main basement levels which not only occupied the former theatre site to its full extent but were continued beneath the boulevard, to a smaller secondary access point outside the Maison Carrée. As for the existing 1827 theatre colonnade, Gehry suggested it should be re-erected elsewhere in Nîmes, perhaps in a public park, as he felt it was out of scale with the Maison Carrée.

Nouvel proposed an entirely subterranean building, above which the boulevard was to be transformed into a minimalist bridge, traversing uninterrupted space west of the Maison Carrée. Set slightly below the level of existing pavements, the glazed roof of the new building was to resemble a lake, or the glass lid of a giant showcase over an archaeological dig revealing

Central to Foster Associates' proposal for the Nîmes competition was the idea that what took place around the building was just as important as what happened within. This theme was developed to include the revival of a public square at the heart of the city.

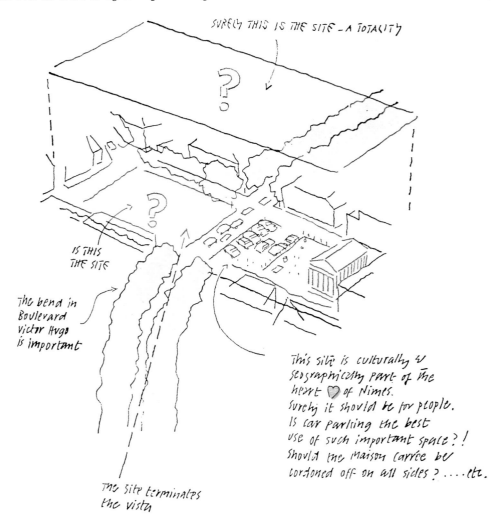

SURELY THIS IS THE SITE – A TOTALITY

?

?

IS THIS THE SITE

The bend in Boulevard Victor Hugo is important

This site is culturally & geographically part of the heart ♡ of Nîmes.
Surely it should be for people.
Is car parking the best use of such important space?!
Should the Maison Carrée be cordoned off on all sides? ....etc.

The site terminates the vista

85

Appropriately, the 19-strong jury met for their final two days of architectural presentations and deliberations in the Maison Carrée, surrounded by the entries of the four finalists: Cesar Pelli, Frank Gehry, Jean Nouvel and Foster Associates.

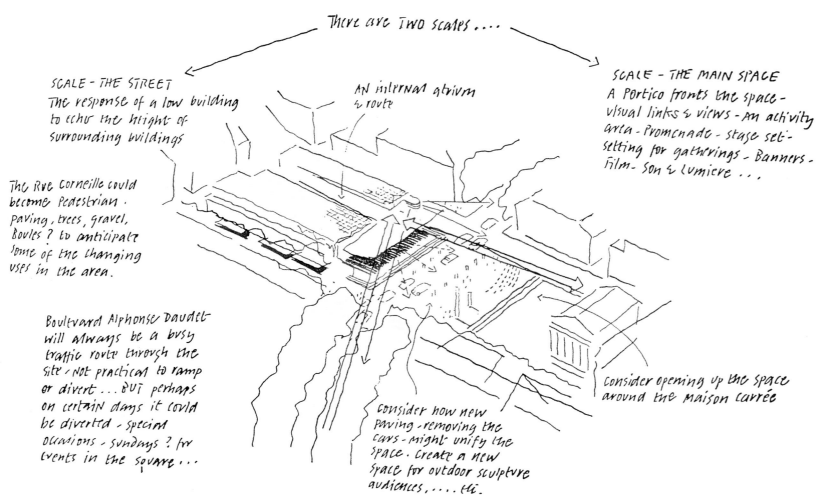

There are two scales....

SCALE - THE STREET
The response of a low building to echo the height of surrounding buildings

The Rve Corneille could become Pedestrian. Paving, trees, gravel, Boules ? to anticipate some of the changing uses in the area.

Boulevard Alphonse Daudet will always be a busy traffic route through the site - not practical to ramp or divert ... But perhaps on certain days it could be diverted - special occasions - sundays ? for events in the square ...

An internal atrium & route

Consider how new paving - removing the cars - might unify the space. Create a new space for outdoor sculpture audiences, ... Hi.

SCALE - THE MAIN SPACE
A Portico fronts the space - visual links & views - An activity area - Promenade - stage set - setting for gatherings - Banners - film - son & lumiere ...

Consider opening up the space around the maison carrée

Foster Associates' proposal sought to reconcile the conflicting demands of its location, respecting the almost domestic scale of the surrounding streets but with a main façade appropriate in grandeur to the square in front and the Maison Carrée opposite. The building's response to the town around it, and its connection to existing routes past and through it, were always

as carefully explained as the facilities within. In an interview after the competition, Bousquet recorded his approval: "With two pencil strokes I knew he understood the city — its heritage and its Mediterranean character".

accumulated layers of history. It was to offer spectacular plunging views into the média-thèque and contemporary art centre below, within which cascades and other water features, created by exploiting a culvert of Roman origin, would highlight the importance of the natural spring upon which Nîmes had been founded.

The 1827 colonnade was to be re-erected immediately underneath its original location, as a permanent feature of the new building, commemorating the town's nineteenth-century urban history.

Pelli proposed to bridge over the boulevard, by means of a link building designed to mark the importance of the site when seen from passing cars while also protecting the interior of the médiathèque and contemporary art centre

from traffic noise. Contained within this bridge were temporary exhibition galleries and a pedestrian route, connecting a gleaming box of a building on the former theatre site with a modern reinterpretation of the Mars Ultor temple colonnade, with which he proposed to surround three sides of the Maison Carrée. He suggested the 1827 theatre colonnade be re-erected, within the building, as a decorative feature.

Isozaki was unable to meet the October 1984 deadline and withdrew from the competition. In response to representations from local architects, Mayor Bousquet had agreed the competition brief should be made available to all those who wished to submit a sketch scheme for the jury's consideration. But only one local architect registered as a competitor and no sketch project was received.

Sidestepping what was becoming something of a controversial issue, Bousquet appointed Foster Associates winners of the competition, on condition that their design was amended to include the theatre colonnade. This model of the revised proposal was on show in Nîmes within weeks.

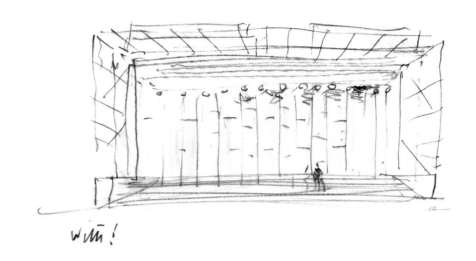

Having demonstrated their willingness to work around the existing colonnade, Foster Associates went on to prepare a decisive analysis that proved that keeping it would be both expensive and would limit the development potential of the site.

The 19-strong jury, presided over by Mayor Bousquet, met in the Maison Carrée on 17 and 18 October 1984. When called upon to explain his entry to the jury, Foster demonstrated his grasp of the scheme by turning his back on the material he had submitted and making a series of new free-hand sketches which illustrated his approach to the project in relation to the Maison Carrée and the urban fabric of Nîmes.

Gehry and Nouvel also presented their proposals to the jury in person, but Pelli was unable to travel to Nîmes and his entry seems to have been placed fourth fairly swiftly. By all accounts, the fortunes of the other three entries fluctuated wildly during the course of subsequent deliberations. Eventually, Gehry was placed third, Nouvel was awarded a special mention and Foster was voted the winner.

On 19 October, the result was officially announced by Mayor Bousquet: Foster Associates had won the competition, but had been asked to amend their design, to retain the 1827 colonnade as an integral part of the project.

By then, fierce controversy was raging in Nîmes on the subject of the colonnade. An opinion poll, "*Référendum pour ou contre le maintien sur place des colonnes de l'ancien théâtre*", had been launched in February 1984 by the newspaper *Midi Libre*. Initially, 54.9 per cent of respondents favoured the use of the site for a médiathèque and arts centre, while 41.1 per cent considered the colonnade should be retained as an integral part of the project. *Midi Libre* had pursued the matter and, by October, a petition demanding the colonnade be retained was supported by some 12,000 signatures.

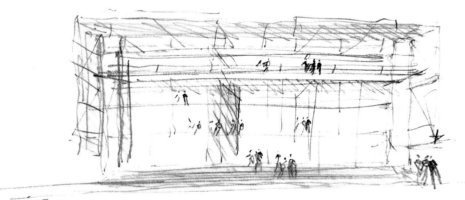

"Foster — Avec les Colonnes"

The French technical press was disappointed by the outcome of the competition. Several Parisian critics considered the sketch scheme submitted by the office to be somewhat dull; they would have preferred to see the project develop without the theatre colonnade — a point of view cogently expressed by Patrice Goulet in his analysis of the competition in the *Architecture d'Aujourd'hui* of December 1984.

Local architects interviewed by the magazine *Calades* in November 1984 felt the 1827 colonnade was a red herring that had distracted attention from the real issue: the presence of the Maison Carrée and an appropriate architec-

tural response to it. "*La gravité, l'enormité de l'affaire, c'est qu'on transfère le vrai débat — qui est la présence de la Maison Carrée — sur celle de ces colonnes*", said one. "*La réintégration des colonnes, c'est anecdotique, et surtout très révélateur de la manière dont on conçoit l'architecture en France; révélateur d'une fausse culture qui but sur des symboles*", said another, who regretted that Foster's potentially interesting concept of the new entrance façade, as a setting for events, should have been abandoned.

Only two weeks after the announcement of the competition result, Foster Associates submitted revised sketch proposals, showing how the retained theatre colonnade might be integrated in the design of the new building. The project was accompanied by detailed analyses of the cost of retaining the colonnade, of the effect it

would have on the design of basement storeys and their future expansion, and of the degree to which it would hamper the design of a free-flowing main entrance space.

The results of these investigations indicated that the costs and difficulties would be greatest if the whole colonnade was retained, but these would diminish as elements were discarded, to a point of near-insignificance if only one or two columns were kept.

In the meantime, an archaeological dig was begun on the site, and Mayor Bousquet held a meeting to discuss the future of the project with the Minister of Culture, Jack Lang.

Having demonstrated that the retention of the existing theatre colonnade would compromise the overall project, the design team were

Retention of the theatre colonnade was abandoned in November 1984, and almost immediately Foster Associates were investigating, in model form, far more dramatic proposals for the main entrance façade than had previously been indicated on the drawings.

The first plans and sections were based on the competition scheme, and show three floors for the médiathèque, partly sunk into the site, with two floors for the art galleries above and two floors of storage below.

instructed in November to proceed with alternative proposals. Three months later, Lang allocated five million francs of central government funds, to pay the architects' fees for design work on the médiathèque and contemporary art centre.

"Foster — Sans les Colonnes"

On 24 November 1984, Mayor Bousquet announced to the press that the project was to go ahead — with Foster Associates as architect, but without the theatre colonnade which would now be re-erected elsewhere. A new sketch scheme was released for publication.

In this version, the oversailing canopy was abandoned in favour of an entirely glazed entrance façade, angled to define a semi-public

As the sections of the competition scheme show, considerable ingenuity was employed to ensure daylight was drawn down into the heart of the building, using a series of deep 'funnels' and side shafts.

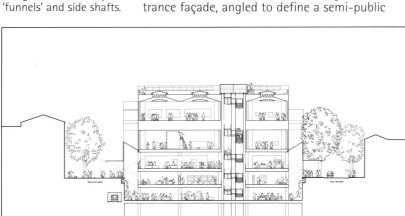

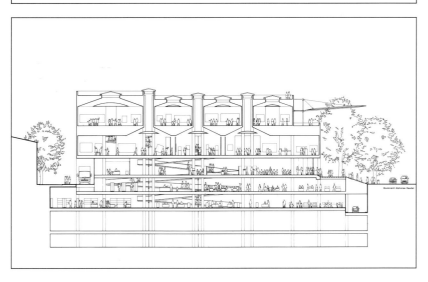

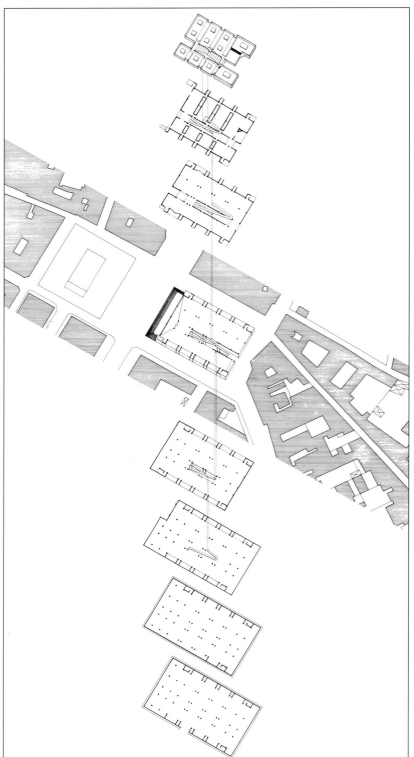

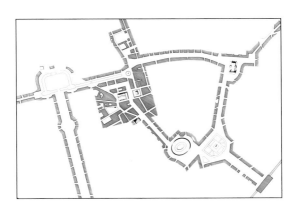

The site lay across a natural route between the Arena, to the south-east, and the Jardins de la Fontaine, to the north-west. By allowing access to the atrium from both ends, it was hoped passing pedestrians would be lured into the building's cool interior.

A central atrium to accommodate the main vertical circulation route was introduced at the competition stage and evolved through several variations before the design was finalised. In this early scheme, the planning grid, too, is just one of many variations, its irregular form responding to the demands of individual spaces. Later variations would seek a more regular rhythm.

area at the threshold of the new building and to channel the public into a wide, centrally-placed atrium. To integrate the project more closely with its surroundings, the retention of a very fine mature tree on the north-east corner of the site was proposed, as was the introduction of a diagonal route through the building at entrance level, to create a pedestrian short-cut between the Maison Carrée and the eighteenth-century Jardins de la Fontaine.

The office's appointment as architect for the next stage of the design was confirmed in December 1984. They were asked, among other things, to rework the design of the main entrance façade, for the client's approval.

The project then went through numerous mutations, to clarify priorities in dialogue with the client. Different ways of entering the build-

ing and the interplay between internal and external spaces were explored, in relation to a variety of plan configurations and elevational treatments. As may be appreciated from the many study models made at this stage, ideas were often tested initially in relatively extreme forms, to clear the air.

On the strength of this process of investigation, Norman Foster established the final form of the future building in a series of sketches drawn in May 1985. Thereafter, a calm, translucent external elevational treatment was researched, means were sought to tighten the relationship between the future building and its urban context, and the internal planning was developed around a monumental staircase — a major departure from the ramps specified in the competition brief.

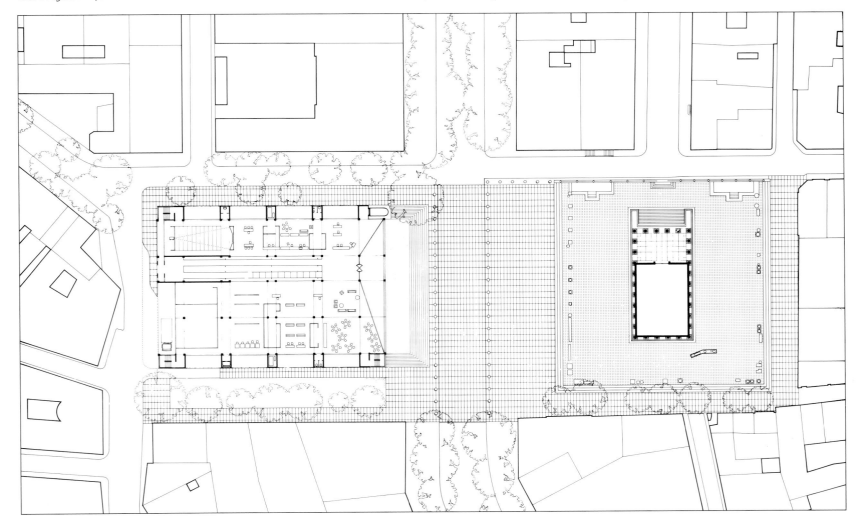

"The scheme evolved over time to reflect the traditional ingredients of steps and courtyards particular to that part of France. We didn't want to copy these traditions mindlessly, but to capture something of their spirit and let that inform the design. Today, the heart of the building is a courtyard filled with light and a cascading staircase — a glass staircase which lets the light through."

Norman Foster, lecture at the Joslyn Art Museum, Omaha, Nebraska, 6 July 1993

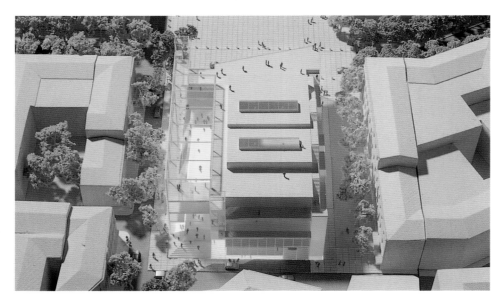

Between December 1984 and March 1985, the project went through an almost bewildering series of options as the brief was improved and various ideas were tested. Models were made of many of these, the different designs being dropped into a site model first prepared for the competition entry.

Foster's earliest sketches had illustrated the building's potential to act as a social focus in terms of the spaces around it. As the design developed, the architects realised this potential could be drawn into the heart of the building with a dramatic atrium. Options were explored, with the atrium offset to one side *(left)* or positioned centrally *(below)*.

The discrete entrance façade of the competition entry, with its banners and overhanging canopy, was dropped in favour of a far more dynamic and open solution where the whole façade, now entirely glazed, was cut back at an angle to sweep visitors into a bold, bright galleria — reminiscent, in many ways, of the office's final proposal for the BBC Radio Centre.

"In some ways the French critics have been proved right — Foster is an excellent tactician. Having won the competition with his respect for the Nîmes townscape, he then bowed to local wishes, retaining the colonnade, and once this obstacle (although Foster is adamant that had the colonnade had to stay, he would have worked around it) was out of the way, went on to generate more the kind of building that the French were expecting from England's 'sublime mechanic'."

Jonathan Glancey, *The Architectural Review*, May 1985

If the building's relationship to the Maison Carrée and its degree of accessibility were open to experimentation, its reinforcement of the ancient Roman street pattern and its deference to surrounding building heights most definitely were not. In one presentation, Foster had referred to this harmony with an older tradition as "almost sacred". It was this striving for a better sense of harmony that led the architects to reconsider the design's more radical elements.

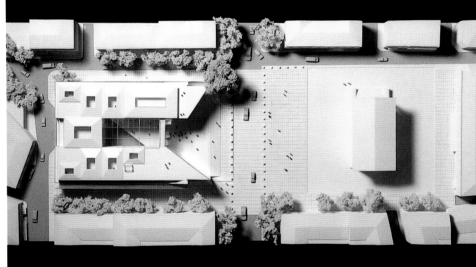

Hand in hand with the overall design, many of the more detailed issues were also refined, each in turn being added to the growing number of study models. Rooflight options, external terraces, different elevational treatments; all were tried out to provoke further discussion, in part within the team and in part with the client.

The radical reappraisal of the scheme, and the many bold proposals put forward, encouraged a better understanding of the building's true nature. The openness of the new design had certainly created new opportunities. Some of these would be retained in the final design, others discarded.

91

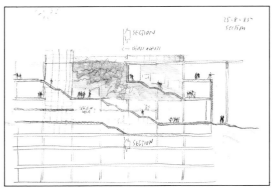

Stairs and lifts had been proposed as a replacement for the circulation ramps specified in the brief during the interim design stage. Foster now took the idea one stage further and proposed a grand ceremonial staircase, linking all the main floors, at the very heart of the building.

"The line of the roof relates to its domestic neighbours, and by expressing the individual galleries, each with its own roof, the building is discreetly tied into the historic fabric of the town."

Norman Foster, *SD Magazine*, September 1993

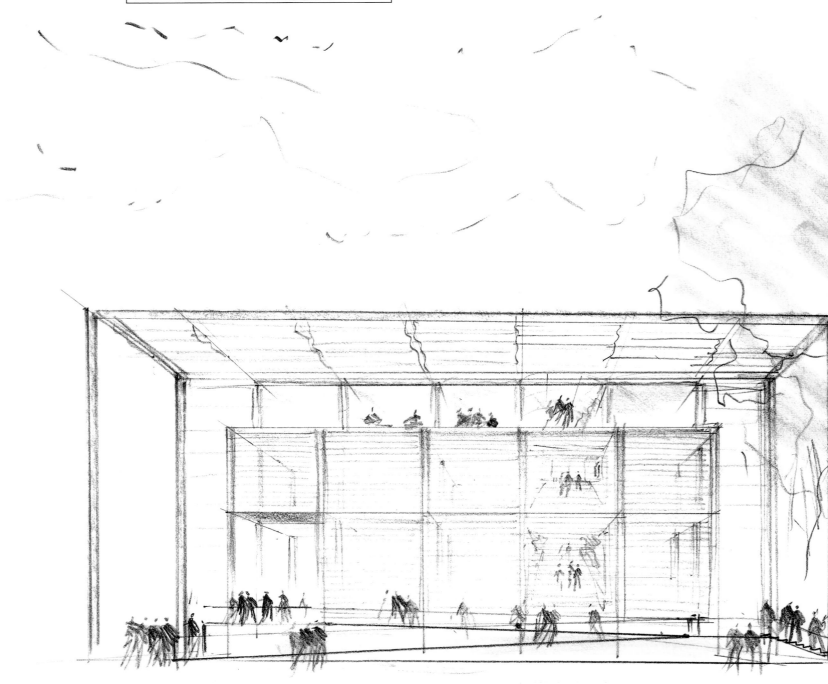

Over the course of three days at the end of May 1985, Norman Foster prepared a sequence of sketches that sought to identify and bring together the best parts of the previous proposals. The result was a scheme that encompassed nearly every element of the final design.

"In its final guise the building is lighter, more sophisticated and more self-referential than the competition winning scheme, and much more recognisably a Foster building."

Jonathan Glancey, *World Architecture*, April 1989

As with earlier designs, the top floor of the revised scheme was given over entirely to gallery space, though now with open-air terraces added to the front and back of the building. Reviving an idea first expressed at the competition stage, the front terrace overlooking the Maison Carrée incorporates an open-air cafeteria in a reinterpretation of the traditional street-side café.

The *Galerie Inférieure*, immediately below the top-floor galleries, is an open-plan space suitable for temporary exhibitions. The structural grid was now rationalised into bays of equal width, seven bays across and eight bays deep. The lifts and grand staircase occupy one whole bay, offset to one side, while the two side bays are given over to services and escape stairs.

Approached by a long ramp at the front, or by stairs from the rear, the building's entrance lobby was located on the upper-ground floor. In this sketch, the main entrance is aligned with the staircase, though a preferred option shows this closer to the corner, responding more directly to the diagonal route across the site.

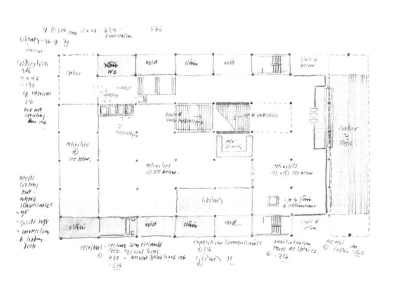

93

"In the heart of the building is a courtyard with generous terraces, which encourage the visitor to move from one culture to another, integrating two cultures which are normally held to be quite separate — the culture and world of fine art and the culture of information technology, the past and the future coming together in the present."

Norman Foster, lecture at the Architectural Institute of Japan, Tokyo, August 1988

Below: prepared for a major client presentation in August 1985, the latest design model showed a generous central atrium, two bays wide rather than the one bay initially proposed in May.

— now composed to respond to the proportions and massing of the Maison Carrée's western flank. The main entrance was contained in two recessed bays at the crucial south-east corner, closing the vista from the boulevard leading from the Roman Arena.

As previously, the entrance was raised half a level above the street and approached by steps. However, the remaining five bays of the front elevation were glazed almost to pavement level, to maximise daylight penetration into the médiathèque — via voids just inside the window-wall, which lit the area half a storey below ground level, and a glazed strip in the pavement, which funnelled light down a storey and a half below ground.

French expertise with concrete had led to the choice of an exposed concrete frame, within which the elevational treatment — inspired by traditional Japanese architecture and by Chareau and Bijvoët's 1928-1931 Maison de Verre in Paris — was composed of clear glazing, translucent double glazing, white glass and a variety of sun-shading systems.

Internally, a monumental staircase with broad stone treads linked all public levels. It rose through a top-lit space inspired by the central

As with all previous options, the new scheme was immediately reproduced in model form. A fully glazed roof protects the one-bay wide main staircase, set between barrel vaults — reminiscent of Louis Kahn's Kimbell Art Museum — which delineate the four bays of gallery space. At this stage, the service bays running along each side of the building are clearly expressed as separate elements, which expose the workings of the building behind fully glazed façades.

The ideas explored in Norman Foster's concept sketches of May were taken up by the design team and were soon being developed in detail. Ideas fell into place and a new scheme was worked up in time for a presentation in early August. It proved an immediate success and was accepted by the client as the basis for the definitive design. The following month, a formal application for a *permis de construire* (the French equivalent of planning consent) was made.

At this stage, eight floor levels were provided, four above and four below entrance level — the two lowest being reserved for services and storage. As in the competition proposal, the contemporary art centre galleries were located on the top two floors and the médiathèque remained closely related to entrance level, where the concept of a melting pot prevailed.

The pedestrian route through the building, which had been explored in diverse splayed configurations in study models, had been much simplified: principal and secondary public entrances were placed at diagonally opposite corners of a basically orthogonal overall volume.

A lightweight fabric canopy oversailed the full seven-bay width of the boulevard frontage

Jean Prouvé's Maison du Peuple in Clichy. The all-glass pitched roof over the central atrium was located on rails, allowing it to be rolled to one side during good weather — as shown here. A similar idea was proposed for the Carré d'Art.

courtyards of traditional Nîmois houses, to which surrounding interior spaces were linked visually, and above which was a glazed roof that could be opened in fine weather.

The opening roof had a heroic precedent — the 300 square-metre rolling roof of the Maison du Peuple at Clichy. Conceived and erected between 1935 and 1939 by Prouvé, Beaudouin, Lods and Bodiansky, this seminal building was remarkably innovative for its period. As Jean Prouvé pointed out shortly before his death, "long before Beaubourg, the Maison du Peuple sought to provide an everyday cultural and communication venue for local people, a free forum for our epoch".

In the course of developing the 5 August 1985 scheme to contract stage, further refinements were made. To improve daylight penetration down through the atrium, the stone treads envisaged for the monumental staircase were

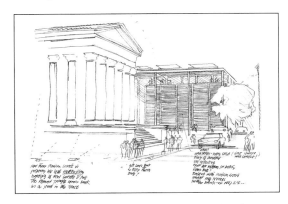

replaced with translucent glass; to make the lowest level of the atrium more congenial, a café was introduced in the area beneath the staircase (in addition to the café-restaurant at the top of the building); to accommodate the roots of the mature tree retained at the northeast corner of the building, basement walls were realigned; and, at the request of the client, an extra basement level was added, for the storage of town hall archives.

But although building work was eventually begun, a series of vicissitudes led to still more modifications.

Delays

Continuing objections to the relocation of the surviving theatre colonnade resulted in administrative delays and impeded funding negotiations

Models (above) and sketches (left) of the new entrance façade, immediately revealed many of the key features and the calm serenity that mark the final design. The transparency of the interim scheme was retained, though modified behind louvres.

A close-up view of the central atrium as proposed in August 1985. At this stage the space was encased within solid stairs and walls, similar to the traditional courtyards found throughout the region. The subsequent introduction of glass transformed the space — and the project.

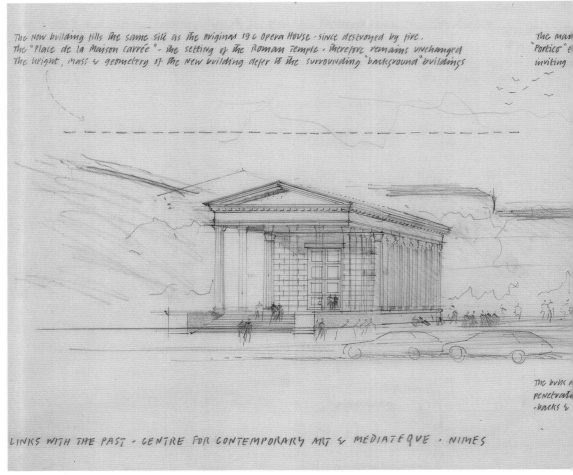

Approached by the Japanese magazine *A+U* for a sketch suitable for a calendar they were planning, Foster took the opportunity to prepare a new drawing of the Carré d'Art, delineating for the first time its relationship with the nearby Maison Carrée.

with central government. In addition to growing local pressure for a public referendum on the colonnade's removal, the matter had excited interest as far afield as Belgium. In 1985, the Brussels-based magazine *Archives d'Architecture Moderne* published a 20-page article, detailing the history of the Nîmes theatre and arguing that the merits of the colonnade had been sadly underrated, both as an admirable example of early nineteenth-century French urban design and as an enlightened architectural response to the Maison Carrée.

Moreover, the colonnade's removal required the equivalent of listed building consent on two counts: the theatre was itself a listed building, and the Maison Carrée's legal status as a Historic Monument meant any demolition or construction within a 500-metre radius required approval from the relevant authorities. Such consent was refused, first by the regional *Commission des Sites*, then by its national counterpart, and the dossier was referred to the Minister of Culture, Jack Lang.

Poised between his cultural policies, his political commitment to local decision-making, and his party loyalty to the Socialist candidate against whom Mayor Bousquet had decided to stand for election as *Député* (member of parliament) at the 1986 general election, Lang made a knife-edge decision. On 17 January 1986, he overturned the decision of the *Commission des Sites* and granted a *permis de construire* for Foster Associates' project. But he recommended that the opinion of the people of Nîmes be sought before any demolition or construction work was begun, and, to ensure local opinion was respected, he ruled that, apart from the five million francs already allocated by central government, all monies required for the project must be raised locally.

Two months later, the Socialist government lost its parliamentary majority at the general election and resigned. A period of 'cohabitation' ensued, during which President Mitterrand completed his first seven-year mandate with the Gaullist, Jacques Chirac, as Prime Minister.

Jean Bousquet — who had been elected *Député* for the Gard *département* and was to combine this role with his duties as Mayor of Nîmes — was appointed Secretary to the Assemblée Nationale's Finance Committee by the incoming government.

The political affiliations of the new Minister of Culture, François Léotard (also the Mayor of

The new building fills the same site as the original 196 Opera House - since destroyed by fire. The "Place de la Maison Carrée" - the setting of the Roman Temple - therefore remains unchanged. The height, mass & geometry of the new building defer to the surrounding "background" buildings

LINKS WITH THE PAST - CENTRE FOR CONTEMPORARY ART & MEDIATEQUE - NIMES

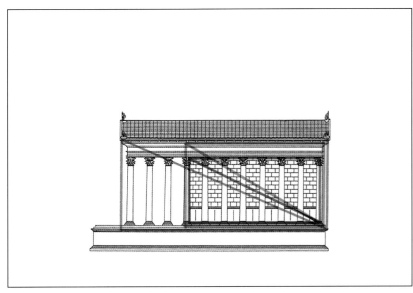

"Here then was a simple, rectangular building with a big portico facing a public square; just like a Roman temple.

The façade, however, was not symmetrical. The main entrance was placed to the left of a three-storey projection with a terrace on top, under the all embracing portico. But then, since the temple was side-ways on to the public square, its façade was not symmetrical either. A subtle game of imitation and reflection was being played. The idea was that the proportions of the portico, projection and open terrace would correspond exactly to those of the whole temple façade, its solid side wall and its entablature."

Peter Davey, *The Architectural Review*, July 1993

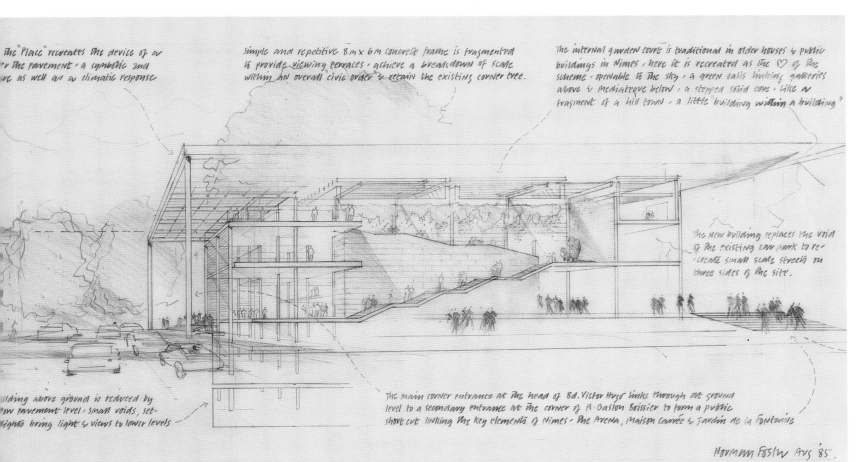

The "Place" recreates the device of over the pavement · a symbolic and ve as well as a climatic response

simple and repetitive 8m x 6m concrete frame is fragmented to provide viewing terraces · achieve a breakdown of scale within an overall civic order & retain the existing corner tree.

The internal garden court is traditional in older houses & public buildings in Nimes · here it is recreated as the ♡ of the scheme · openable to the sky · a green oasis linking galleries above & mediatheque below · a stepped solid core · like a fragment of a hill town · a little 'building within a building'

the new building replaces the void of the existing car park to re-create small scale streets on three sides of the site.

ilding above ground is reduced by ow pavement level · small voids, set-lights bring light & views to lower levels

The main corner entrance at the head of Bd. Victor Hugo links through at ground level to a secondary entrance at the corner of R. Gaston Boissier to form a public short cut linking the key elements of Nimes · the Arena, Maison Carrée & Jardin de la Fontaine

Norman Foster Aug '85.

It would be true to say that the overall design of the main façade was developed with little regard to its proportional relationship to the side elevation of the Maison Carrée. However, once the similarities had been identified, comparative drawings were prepared to help resolve issues of detail.

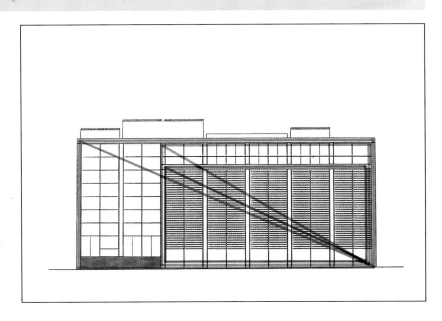

The *permis de construire* drawings, submitted in May 1987, 21 months after the design had been accepted in principle. Several refinements had been introduced in the intervening period, not least the change from a seven to an eight bay wide structural and planning grid.

On 3 October 1988, 10 months after construction of the building had begun, Nîmes was struck by a devastating flood that brought work on the project to an abrupt halt. Fears for the safety of the art treasures to be stored in the basements led to a major revision of the design before work recommenced.

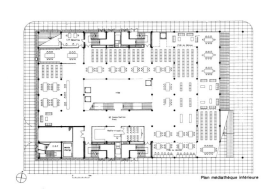

Plan médiathèque inférieure

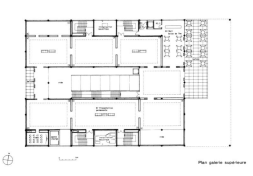

Plan galerie supérieure

Plan sous-sol un

Plan galerie inférieure

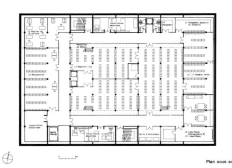

Plan sous-sol deux

Plan médiathèque supérieure

Plan sous-sol trois

Plan accueil

Fréjus), coincided closely with those of Mayor Bousquet. Despite the Chirac government's determination to cut public spending, Léotard decided the Nîmes médiathèque and contemporary art centre should be accorded status as a state-subsidised *grand projet* and, in November 1986, he committed 60 million francs of central government funding to the Foster Associates project – in addition to the five million francs allocated by his predecessor.

A further contribution of 32 million francs was received from the Languedoc-Roussillon regional council before the year was out. Nevertheless, Nîmes' municipal council still had to pay over 65 per cent of the total project costs.

The preparation of tender and contract documents was begun in January 1987 and excavation work started in January 1988. In March 1988, François Léotard visited the site and the project acquired a new name – the Carré d'Art.

François Léotard's ministerial role ended two months later, in the wake of the May 1988 presidential elections, when François Mitterrand was re-elected president of the Republic for a second seven-year term and the Chirac government resigned. A new Socialist government was formed, Jack Lang resumed his activities as Minister of Culture and acquired several additional ministerial responsibilities to boot.

Progress on the Carré d'Art site was unaffected by this change of political climate. However, work was brought to a halt on 3 October 1988, when a freak storm hit Nîmes. The town centre suffered severe flooding, a national disaster was declared and extensive improvements to Nîmes' surface and storm water outfall systems were put in train – with 670 million francs of central government aid.

Some say the Maison Carrée was saved only because so much flood water flowed into the huge hole on the Carré d'Art site, where excavations had just reached completion. Either way, building works had to be suspended while the site was pumped dry.

The Final Redesign

The flood prompted the design team to ponder what lessons might be learned from the 2000-year survival of the Maison Carrée, and it occurred to them that its remarkably high plinth

"Heavy rains, pouring down from the *garrigue* above the city, inundated the site. . . Facing up to the real danger of floods, Foster made a virtue out of necessity by elevating the entire building on a 'podium' 1.5 metres high, which encircled it completely. As a Classical feature, it might have seemed at odds with Foster's architecture, but the effect of the addition was to tie the building even more clearly to its setting."

Kenneth Powell, *Carré d'Art, Nîmes*, Blueprint Extra No.11, 1993

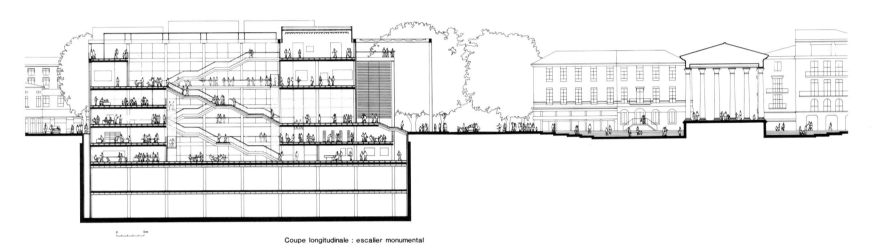

Coupe longitudinale : escalier monumental

A long section through the final 'pre-flood' design, dominated by the ceremonial staircase at the heart of the building that links the two basement levels of library and ancillary spaces with the two levels of the médiathèque and, above them, the two levels of art gallery. Only the two lower levels of secure storage in the basement are not immediately accessible to the public.

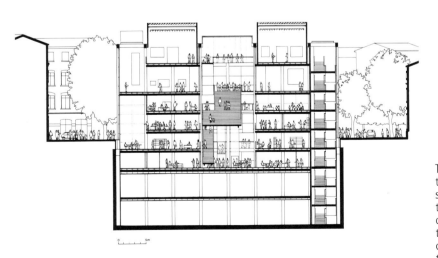

The switch from a seven- to an eight-bay wide structural grid necessitated a rethink of the overall planning, in particular the repositioning of the offset atrium of the early scheme to a new central location.

"When [Foster] received the commission to design a library and art gallery on the site facing the Maison Carrée, a powerful tension was set up. The temple was a kind of silent challenge. It couldn't be ignored or dismissed as a freak survival. It was not some piece of nineteenth-century pomposity, like the existing building on the médiathèque site, it was the real thing, 1700 years old. The process of the design of the média-thèque was not so much informed by the presence of the Maison Carrée as haunted by it."

Peter Davey, *The Architectural Review*, July 1993

In January 1988, to mark the start of work on site, a final presentation model was prepared, incorporating all the latest design developments. Further changes would be made, but here, for the first time, was an accurate representation of the final building.

might well have been designed to protect the building from the effects of flash storms.

The client, too, was concerned and together they decided that it would be prudent to re-design the basement areas of the Carré d'Art within a waterproof tank, protected by a perma-nent flood barrier in the form of a plinth rising to a height of 1.5 metres above pavement level, to ensure the contents of the building would be safe from future storms. Other modifications were also introduced — for example, the idea of an opening roof over the central atrium was abandoned, in case the closing mechanism should fail in an electric storm.

The far-reaching implications of these various revisions — particularly on floor levels, daylight penetration and the building's overall height — led to a thorough reappraisal of the brief. Following discussions with those who were to run the future building, other changes were introduced to reflect the division of administra-tive responsibilities between the médiathèque and the contemporary art centre. During the ensuing design stage, virtually every aspect of the building evolved: the plans and the plan-ning grid, the circulation routes and the central staircase, the elevations and the main entrance canopy.

In its final form, the Carré d'Art was de-signed to provide a total area of some 20,000 square metres — giving a plot ratio of 8:1 in relation to the 2500 square-metre theatre site — as against the 13,435 square metres envisaged

"Foster considered the entire plaza around the Maison Carrée as part of his brief, trading the cars that parked there for new outdoor cafés, and repaving the space in the local limestone of which the temple and much of the city is built."

David Cohn, *Architectural Record*, October 1993

The building in context. From the very beginning Foster had selected this as his favoured view: the Maison Carrée and the Carré d'Art seen as a single composition.

The long section and south elevation of the scheme as built. The flood of October 1988 led to a major design review that included not only the introduction of a raised podium around the entire building, but also the addition of an extra floor in the base-ment, following the division of administrative responsibilities between the library and média-thèque. The mature tree on the north-east corner of the site was retained, rounding off the base-ment wall at that point to minimise disturbance to the roots.

The January 1988 pre-sentation model, with the atrium roof remov-ed. Proposals for a re-tractable roof had to be shelved when it became apparent that it was impossible to guarantee that the closing mecha-nism would never fail.

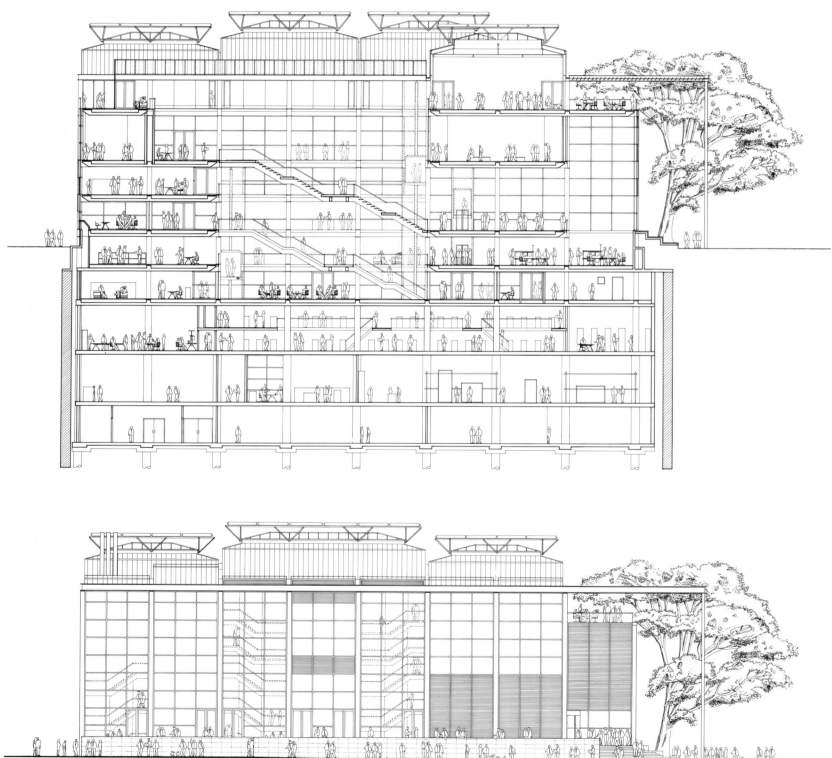

Below: with the side of the model removed, interior as well as exterior views were possible of and from all the main spaces in the building. This is a view from the main entrance lobby.

Made before the scheme was reviewed following the flood, the January 1988 model was not accurate in every detail. Future changes would include extra columns to support the canopy, and fixed louvres in place of the retractable canvas blinds.

by the original competition brief. Yet the basic thinking that informed the design from the outset remained unchanged. Indeed, in its final form, including the townscape improvements undertaken in the Place de la Maison Carrée to the architects' designs, the finished building more closely resembles the diagrams originally submitted in October 1984 than it does some of the alternative forms explored in the interim.

The Carré d'Art Inaugurated

In May 1993, 10 years after the creation of a Beaubourg of the South in Nîmes had first been mooted by Mayor Bousquet, the Carré d'Art opened to the public amid much media hype — the bound volume of cuttings collected by the Nîmes town hall press office weighs 2.25 kilos. Jean Bousquet has since said the finished building is the only example of modern architecture

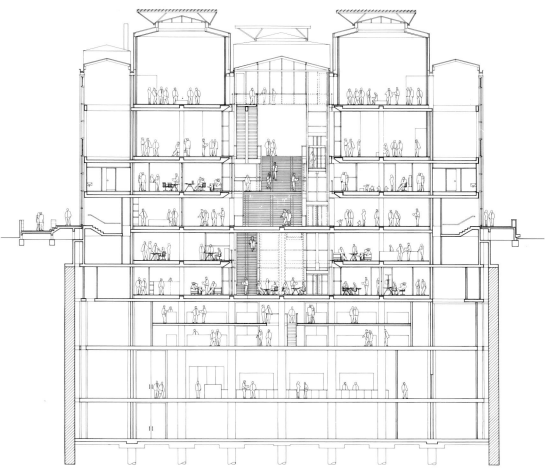

he can think of that confronts a historical gem without cowardice or compromise, while also according it due respect.

By the time the Carré d'Art was inaugurated, many other examples of Mayor Bousquet's far-reaching architectural and urban policies were in evidence in and around Nîmes, ranging from extensive restoration and rehabilitation in the town's historic core, to a multiplicity of new buildings and interventions.

Looking back, Norman Foster describes his former client as "an impressive individual. Many French towns have been ruined by over zealous mayors — but Jean Bousquet recognised the best in Nîmes and he didn't play around. He knew where to leave well alone, where to build on to what already existed, and where to place new buildings".

Charlotte Ellis

The introduction of the extra floor in the basement — in fact, a double-height space which included a substantial mezzanine floor — caused an increase in the overall height of the building. It proved possible, however, to retain the height of the service areas along each side of the building to their original level, and so matching the eaves' height of the surrounding buildings. Only the gallery roofs extended further, their mass disguised by expressing each gallery individually.

Mayor Jean Bousquet
an interview with Charlotte Ellis

Charlotte Ellis qualified as an architect in London. After working at Lambeth and in the GLC Historic Buildings Division, she was appointed news editor of *The Architects' Journal*. Working freelance in Paris since 1983, she has written numerous articles on architecture in France, notably for *The Architectural Review*. A member of the editorial team for the three-volume *Archi-* *tecture: Une Anthologie* (IFA-Mardaga 1992-93) and a contributor to the *Dictionnaire de l'Architecture du XXe Siècle* (IFA-Hazan 1996), she has recently co-authored the book *Dom Bellot: moine-architecte* (IFA-Norma 1996) on the work of the French monk and architect Dom Paul Bellot (1876-1944).

This interview took place on 22 February 1990.

* *Elected members of Nîmes town council:* M Ardrieu, Bernard Durand, Jean-Paul Fournier; *ministry representatives:* Claude Cousseau, Claude Joly, Pierre Lajus, Jean-Louis Pradel; *celebrities:* Robert Calle, Gabriel Clauffret, Jean-Pierre Dufoix, Martial Raysse, P. J. Tn. Snoots; *architects:* Stanislas Fiszer, Daniel Mazet, Jean-Rémy Negre, Alain Sarfati, Roland Simounet, James Stirling, Georges Wursteizen.

Mayor Bousquet has never doubted Nîmes could be run exactly like his own highly successful company, Cacharel. "The population wants the best product at the best price, just like clients. You have to sell it to them and, to do that, you must communicate. Of course, you can't sell a product unless it is good. To succeed, a city must have a more positive image than its competitors — it must have added value. Years of experience in the fashion industry teaches you what added value really means. To achieve it, you have to raise your sights and think globally."

Born in Nîmes in 1932, Jean Bousquet qualified as a tailor at the local technical school. He left for Paris, aged 20, with "nothing but a pair of scissors" in his pocket. Ten years later, he launched his first collection of women's blouses, using the name Jean Cacharel. He stuck to the name for business purposes — a *cacharel* is a type of small duck, indigenous to the Camargue — and created the Cacharel company in 1965. The first Cacharel factory was installed at Nîmes the very next year.

To Bousquet, Cacharel represented the "democratisation of a dream", by making available good quality ready-to-wear clothes at a time when home dressmaking was virtually the only alternative to expensive *haute couture* garments. More factories followed, mostly in the south of France, including Cacharel's first fully automated plant, complete with laser cutting equipment, which was set up at Nîmes in 1979.

By 1984, the Cacharel empire extended to textiles and perfume as well as ready-to-wear clothes for women, men, children and babies, with 2000 sales outlets in 42 countries and an annual turnover of 1500 million francs (800 million in the ready-to-wear sector). Only a year later, Cacharel-L'Oréal's 'Anaïs, Anaïs' topped the world perfume market, with sales of 15 million bottles. It has since proved the worldwide best-selling perfume of the 1980s.

Bousquet's political career has often been described as a triumph for the extreme centre. Nîmes city council had been controlled by various left-wing groupings since the turn of the century, with the Communist party predominating from the mid-1960s onwards, when Bousquet was first elected Mayor in March 1983. Disliking party dogma, he stood as an independent candidate — endorsed by the liberal Union Républicaine — and won 50.3 per cent of the vote. He was elected to the National Assembly as *Député* (member of parliament) for the Gard *département* in March 1986 and has since been re-elected twice — as *Député* in 1988 and Mayor in 1989.

"I have travelled a good deal in connection with my business and I am aware of what is going on elsewhere in the world. By comparison, Nîmes seemed permanently asleep. The city had long been renowned for its magnificent Roman remains and for its bullfighting traditions. Yet on average, tourists stayed in the city for only two hours or less. No effort was being made to realise Nîmes' full potential for cultural tourism, still less to attract new industries and businesses to the city. I love Nîmes. I want to see it surviving post-1992 Europe. To do that, it needs a present and a future as well as a past. That is why I put myself up for election in 1983."

Once in office, Mayor Bousquet reformed the city's administration radically. Various council services were privatised, including the school dinner service — thereby cutting the cost to the council of each meal by half, while maintaining quality — and the town hall staff was persuaded to work four extra hours per week for no extra pay. New cultural and sports policies were formulated — Bousquet has been president of the Nîmes Olympique football club since 1981, a role which he claims is far more difficult than Mayor of Nîmes or founder-director of Cacharel. And an urban study was initiated to establish how the city might be enhanced for the benefit of the existing population and visitors, while taking into account means to attract new industries and businesses, and their future personnel.

One result was the designation of the *secteur sauvegardé* (conservation area) in the city centre. Extensive restoration work has already been undertaken there, more is planned and in progress. Needless to say, the purpose of all this refurbishment is to show Nîmes' rich architectural heritage to best advantage. So far as Mayor Bousquet is concerned, that means complementing the best of the old with the best of the new, as is illustrated by the 1986-87 upgrading of the town hall, a late seventeenth-century building at the heart of the *secteur sauvegardé*.

While the exterior was painstakingly restored, the interior was extensively remodelled in an uncompromisingly modern idiom to designs by Jean-Michel Wilmotte — a leading French designer responsible, among other things, for much of the interior design beneath I. M. Pei's Louvre pyramid in Paris, and for standardising

Norman Foster and Jean Bousquet in the Carré d'Art, on the occasion of the building's official opening in 1993.

"Architecture is now part and parcel of the making of a city's image. It enhances urban regeneration. Some towns, in particular, excel in this: Nîmes chose Norman Foster to design a landmark building housing a médiathèque and a centre for contemporary art, sometimes known as the 'Beaubourg of the South'; it also called on Jean Nouvel for several buildings and on Vittorio Gregotti for its new stadium.

Montpellier commissioned Ricardo Bofill to create a new masterplan for the Antigone quarter, while Claude Vasconi designed the combined Congress Hall and Opera House. Though separated by only a few kilometres, there is a lively rivalry between the cities of Montpellier and Nîmes, all the more fascinating since the mayor of the first is [politically] of the left while the mayor of the second is on the right."

Jacques Lucan, *France: Architecture 1965-1988*, Electa Moniteur 1989

the image of some 100 Cacharel shirt shops. Norman Foster and Philippe Starck also made contributions to the town hall interior.

The same thinking has been applied to Nîmes' Roman Arena, which is said to be the best preserved in the world. Management of the Arena had been let to private contractors by the previous administration. Mayor Bousquet considered the use of so important a monument should be controlled directly by the city council and the contract was terminated. A wide-span inflatable roof is now erected over the lower tiers and central space during the winter months, so the Arena can be used throughout the year for major public spectacles, from pop concerts to opera, boxing matches and bull-fighting.

"Nîmes has been marked by many centuries; the built heritage is fundamental to the city's identity. But if it is to live, it must coexist with the present," says Mayor Bousquet. "I want to see the very best of the twentieth century represented here too." He has no qualms about bringing in leading architects and designers from elsewhere. "They have a very positive con-

tribution to make, both by raising the horizons of local people, and by projecting a dynamic image of the city nationally and internationally." He sees their role as exactly parallel to top fashion designers. "Fashion is a very important business. It is deeply serious and very difficult to do. A good fashion does not date. Look at Dior, or Saint-Laurent. To succeed in the fashion industry you need a global outlook. The same applies to architecture."

Well-known architects and designers have been commissioned to design a very wide range of projects in Nîmes since 1983, notably the Nemausus 1 housing development (completed in 1987, to designs by Jean Nouvel and Jean-Marc Ibos) and the 'Grand Stade', a football and rugby stadium with a total capacity of 25,000 (18,000 seated), completed in 1989 to competition-winning designs by Vittorio Gregotti and Marc Chausse. But the project Mayor Bousquet sees as the key to the revitalisation of the city centre is the médiathèque and contemporary art centre, now under construction to designs by Foster Associates on a highly sensitive site opposite the remarkable Roman temple known as the Maison Carrée, which was once the centrepiece of the Roman forum.

"The Centre Georges Pompidou in Paris has attracted thousands of people a day since it opened in 1977. I have long wanted to see such a facility in Nîmes, to bring young people back into the city centre. There is a splendid location for it, the site of the former theatre, which was built in 1827 but burned down in 1952, leaving only its great colonnade. The site remained empty for 30 years, because nobody knew what to do with it.

"The design of a major new building so close to the Maison Carrée demands a real master. I decided to hold an international architectural competition, for a combined médiathèque and contemporary art centre — we have called it the Carré d'Art. Twelve architects of international repute were invited to spend 24 hours in Nîmes. They were asked to look at the city and the site and I saw each of them afterwards, to see which I had most affinity with. Five were shortlisted and invited to compete.

"Norman Foster was selected the winner by the jury. It was a jury of some importance,* comprising local politicians, personalities, representatives of government ministries and several architects. Foster had presented a sketch, rather than a finished design — in other words, the jury

chose the architect, not the project. They asked him to see if the surviving nineteenth-century theatre colonnade could be incorporated in the design. They had no option. People here were not against the Carré d'Art as a project, but a virulent campaign was raging to save the colonnade.

"Foster's investigations showed the colonnade's retention would prevent the creation of a work of real architectural quality on this key site. Although obviously of sentimental value, expert opinion later deemed the colonnade to be of very little inherent architectural worth. It was taken down and put into store and will be re-erected as a feature of the Nîmes service station, on the new Nîmes-Arles motorway."

On 3 October 1988, a freak storm caused severe flooding in Nîmes. "We had to ask Foster Associates to reappraise the Carré d'Art project, to ensure it would be adequately protected from any future floods — an absolute necessity, considering what the building is to contain: the city's contemporary art collection and an outstanding collection of books and manuscripts, many of them irreplaceable, as well as reference works, audio-visual and computer facilities and a music library.

"The provision of so much under one roof will offer residents and visitors alike a unique cultural experience. Such variety could not be achieved by a smaller town, while a similar range in bigger cities would become too large and unwieldy. It can be done in a city of this size and, with our warm climate, the new urban square proposed by Norman Foster, between the Carré d'Art and the Maison Carrée, will certainly become a major public meeting place.

"Of course, the Carré d'Art project is of more than purely local interest. That is why we have asked the State and the Regional Authority to pay a proportion of the costs. Of the 270 million franc total estimated building costs, 65 million will be contributed by the State, 32 million by the Region and 173 million by the City.

"Some might think the contrast between Foster's architecture and the Maison Carrée too brutal. They would be wrong. The confrontation of the two buildings, and the tension created by their co-existence, is exactly what is needed in a Nîmes that is alive to the times. The Carré d'Art will give new life to Nîmes by providing a modern forum for the young."

As Norman Foster had hoped, the Carré d'Art has rejuvenated the area around it, in particular the square it overlooks which has now become the social heart of the city. It is at its most lively during the *férias (far right)* when dancing and performances last long into the night.

106

Light and Culture
by Norman Foster

The Carré d'Art and the Maison Carrée at night. Foster Associates were responsible for the re-planning and landscaping of the entire square.

I still have vivid memories of my first visit to Nîmes. I had flown in alone to the airport at Garrons with an overnight bag, sketchbook, camera and without any preconceptions of the place. After checking in at the hotel I walked for hours, late into the night, and was up again at first light to explore further.

Thinking back over the memories from that visit, two themes keep recurring: the culture of the place — the city and the surrounding landscape — and the impression of a particular light. The same key words, 'culture' and 'light', can best describe the experience of the Carré d'Art, which opened almost nine years

of light and by the unexpected prospect of a Roman temple, the Maison Carrée, the central focus of the space.

Architecture is both an interior and exterior experience. From the outside, the new building was shaped by the history of Nîmes, which surrounds it, and by the traditional architecture of the region. The spaces inside the building now play a part in shaping the lives of those who use them — the generations of today and those who will succeed them. The experience of viewing the contents of the new building, the works of art on display there, the books and periodicals in the library reading rooms, will be modified by

later. As both were powerful influences on the design, though, this is hardly surprising.

The site brings these two themes together. I can recall emerging out of the dark tunnel of trees which line Boulevard Victor Hugo into the Place de la Comédie — as it was then known — to be dazzled simultaneously by the explosion

the context of the new. In turn, the historical setting outside has been transformed by the impact of this latest intervention — even though it grew out of an urban grain bequeathed by the past.

Médiathèques are a relatively new concept, but can be found in most towns and cities in France. Typically, they embrace the world of information technology, books, magazines and

The main entrance, flooded with the bright light of a Mediterranean morning. Located at the south-east corner, in line with the route from the Arena, the entrance immediately establishes the diagonal route through the building to the smaller entrance on the north-west corner.

"The elevation to the square is calm, neither over-demonstrative nor obviously recessive or over-respectful. It has the simple dignity of finely judged proportion and fastidious detailing. Below the canopy, the façade is indented, expressing the entrance and the internal galleria beyond. Ascend the steps to the entrance and you get views down into the library reading room."

Kenneth Powell, *Carré d'Art: Nîmes*, Blueprint Extra 11, London 1993

newspapers, as well as music, video and cinema. Less common are new galleries for paintings and sculpture. But what is unusual, possibly unique, about the Nîmes project is the way that it integrates both museum *and* médiathèque, and blurs the edges between so many different worlds — young and old, residents and visitors, art and literature, sculpture and information, present and historical.

At the time of the building's creation, the appeal of that part of the building dedicated to the visual arts was never questioned. It was always assumed that the galleries, with their permanent collection and visiting exhibitions of paintings and sculpture, would attract visitors from afar. I remember summarising my first impressions with the Mayor, Jean Bousquet, by writing that the project should communicate at all levels — internationally as well as in the context of Europe, the region and the city.

Having followed the progress of the building in the years since it first opened to the public, there is no doubt that such predictions have proved well founded. Visiting the centre on a typical summer's day, it is apparent that the building has proved to be a magnet for many visitors to the city, possibly tipping the balance in favour of visiting Nîmes rather than other nearby tourist venues.

They linger in the newly-named Place de la Maison Carrée outside, ascend the steps and filter through the concourse level to view the galleries and finally arrive on the café terrace. From there they contemplate the surrounding roofscape and life in the square below. At every step and turn, the visitor is reminded of the visual and historical connection with the Maison

The Carré d'Art is basically an inward-looking building, with the service spaces set around the perimeter behind walls of white or translucent glass. Apart from the secondary access on the north-west corner and the heavily shuttered service bay, there is no direct contact with the streets to the side or rear. Only at the front, on the main east façade, does the building open up, with clear glazing rising the full height of the building, protected from the sun by fixed external louvres and by the louvred canopy.

"The Carré d'Art fits into Nîmes much better than Foster's critics anticipated. It is not an alien High Tech structure dropped as if from outer space into a delicate old city, but an arts centre and library that appears to have grown from the heart of the site, to have filled a hole that had always existed in the city's fabric. . . [It] is a model of how to bring a big modern building into an old city centre by employing the best architecture of today — in civic service — to raise the profile and fortune of a provincial centre."

Jonathan Glancey, *The Independent*, 24 March 1993

Below: the north-west entrance, seen from the street that connects the building to the nearby Jardins de la Fontaine.

The north facade, as seen from the secondary entrance at the rear of the building, on the north-west corner.

Carrée — a continuous dialogue which is sometimes only hinted at by a glimpse of its portico at the end of a long gallery vista.

Less apparent to the casual visitor is the fact that the public areas of the building occupy less than half of the total volume — the building has almost as much storage space below ground as it has galleries and libraries above. More significant, however, are the mixing spaces in between, which have transformed the life of the local community.

It was the city librarian who pointed out that more people now pass through the doors of the Carré d'Art in a typical month than the entire population of Nîmes. On my most recent visit, a local taxi-driver expressed this with even greater enthusiasm, commenting that, over the course of a year, more than 1000 people a day pass through the building.

The dominant pulse of the life this has introduced into the building is on the lower floors, around the various library reading rooms which cluster around and below the entrance level. They provide a continuity of activity which offsets the inevitable low ebb of visitors to the city in the depths of a hostile Nîmes winter.

At the competition stage, our project was the only one to propose that the square containing the Maison Carrée should be respected and developed as a social focus. It was also suggested that this should inform an equivalent space within the building which, in turn, could create a pedestrian short-cut across the site. Some years later it is fascinating to see how the main and secondary entrances — each with

Part of the south façade, glimpsed from one of the narrow streets laid out on the Roman grid that surround three sides of the building. As intended, the new building reinforces this ancient street pattern with calm but distinctly modern elevations that match the height of the surrounding buildings.

"The Carré d'Art dissembles its mass through extreme lightness in the major members. Framing 'columns' at the end of the principal façade are pared away to become almost lines, the Classical grid raised to a notional existence. Textures are shimmering and semi-transparent, and the roof has the mildest pedimental slope, three times repeated. It resembles Roman architecture in its reliance on carefully calculated proportions. Yet, as in the best Roman buildings, calculation is transcended and the viewer is left with sensations of magical rightness."

Alastair Best, from a previously unpublished essay

Clear glazing lines the sides as well as the front of the main entrance lobby, connecting the activities within to the city beyond.

The external louvres protecting the main façade stop at sufficient height above floor level to allow the entrance lobby unprecedented views of the square and Maison Carrée beyond. Unsurprisingly, the entrance lobby is now a popular meeting place, drawing people into the building throughout the day.

111

The reading desks in the main library, as seen from the entrance lobby above. Much of the furniture — including these tables and all the special seating — was made specially for the building to designs by Norman and Sabiha Foster.

Below: videos, as well as books, can be borrowed from the main library, with facilities on hand for immediate viewing.

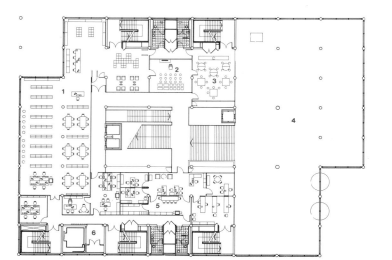

The First Floor — dedicated to the children's areas of the médiathèque and to offices.

1 children's library
2 words + picture room
3 children's workshop
4 void
5 administration
6 service lift

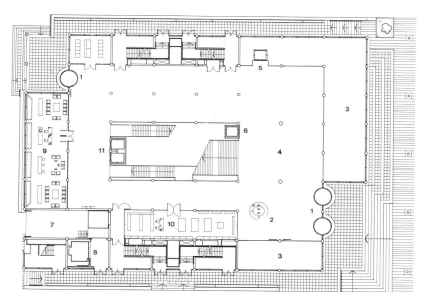

Upper Ground Floor

1 entrance
2 reception
3 void
4 main lobby
5 lift to rooftop café
6 lift to galleries
7 delivery bay
8 service lift
9 periodicals library
10 bookshop
11 lift to médiathèque

The periodicals library, seen here enjoying the late afternoon sun. Situated at the rear of the building on the main entrance level, it has become the most popular of the médiathèque's facilities.

their own porches, both protective and symbolic — lock the building into the circulation routes around it.

It was the Mayor's intention to create places for young people and it is gratifying to know that the main staircase and terraces have become one of the favourite meeting places for teenagers — quite apart from the facilities of the médiathèque which provide their own attractions. Perhaps less expected is the appeal of the building to the very young.

About a year after the opening, I met the family of a French architect with whom I had worked when he was part of the team at the local Agence d'Urbanisme. His young son, seven or eight years of age, was introduced to me and his father explained the connection between us. The little boy's immediate reaction was one of curiosity — what did I have to do with *his* building? He identified closely with the place; it had become a regular treat which he looked forward to after school on most days.

The social integration in the Nîmes project follows in the footsteps of earlier works, such as the Sainsbury Centre for Visual Arts, which blurred the edges between the public and academics, between the contemplation as well as the study and preservation of works of art. Here, too, the fusion of these normally separate worlds is realised by the creation of spaces which are inviting and friendly enough to help break down traditional barriers. In these endeavours, the handling of light — both natural and artificial — is a major ingredient.

The full-height glazing to the children's reading area on the north side of the building, where protection from the sun is unnecessary, has been left clear, affording animated views of the surrounding streets.

The reading area of the children's library. Like the furniture in the main library, the seating and storage units were designed specially by Foster Associates.

The reading room of the main library, on the lower ground floor, has been left open to the entrance lobby on the floor above – allowing daylight to flood the lower level and drawing attention to the many facilities to be found there.

An informal meeting area, also on the lower ground floor and open to the lobby above. Commissioned to prepare a mural for the space, Richard Long applied local clay direct to the fair-faced concrete wall.

"The main spatial event of the building, however, is down at the bottom of the atrium, two floors below ground. Here the whole point of those cascades of glass steps becomes clear. At some time in the development of the design there has been a trade-off. The exciting, canyon-like quality of the original atrium design has not been sacrificed in vain. It is like standing under a waterfall. The daylight filtering through and between the flights of steps transforms what could so easily have been a dingy cave into a magical grotto."

Peter Davey, *The Architectural Review*, July 1993

Beneath the waterfall — the main atrium stairs seen from the lower library floor, two levels below the entrance lobby. The stairs are based on the narrowest single flights required at each side. The cantilevered glass-infill treads — sandblasted three times for extra grip — spring from a central steel box-beam spine. The main double- and treble-width flights are essentially two or three of these single-width units joined together, maintaining the same edge cantilever and balustrade detail throughout.

At the Sainsbury Centre, the abundant green slopes of East Anglia encouraged what is essentially a single-level experience of low density. Nîmes could hardly be more different. The tight, multi-storey urban fabric of the historic city is replicated in the building itself, which is tightly layered above ground and buried deep into its site. It was a form that posed new challenges in the quest to permeate as many of the public spaces as possible with the special magic of natural light.

I can recall shading the competition drawings *(page 88)* with coloured pencil, to help explain the idea of the 'chimneys' that would funnel shafts of light down into the intermediate level galleries. In the end, the sheer density of development did not allow this luxury and the final arrangement is a combination of top-lit and side-lit gallery spaces.

What *has* prevailed is the development of other ways of enabling light to be pulled down into the lower depths, coupled with oblique views to the world outside. In the library spaces, for example, you are often aware of the ancient tree on the corner, even though you are well below pavement level. From other vantage points, the Maison Carrée is a constant point of reference.

The internal courtyard, with its cascade of glass terraces, bridges and stairs, could not have happened without the influence of earlier projects, such as the unbuilt glass plaza for the Hongkong Bank or the intricate glazed infill of

The children's workshop, overlooking the main atrium. As the principal point of reference, the atrium mixes rather than separates the building's diverse functions.

A small lecture theatre — fitted with a retractable screen and full projection facilities, has been installed at the lower basement level near the médiathèque lifts, where it is readily accessible for day or evening use.

Rising six storeys through the heart of the building, the atrium links all the main public areas to create a natural thoroughfare bustling with activity at all hours of the day. For the less active visitor, a clear-glazed lift provides direct access to the galleries above or to the library below.

115

"In a black and white photograph, the slender columns of the portico — as thin as flag poles — look like an uncomfortable attempt at a Festival of Britain revival. But Foster has played his strongest card: his mastery of the play of light, in this case the dappled light of Provence.

Foster has designed a glass box, which, if too assertive, would spark instant outrage. But though this building is large, it is extraordinarily gentle. The branches of the ancient plane tree spread round the corner column of the portico and even the *sous-sol* retreats to allow space for its roots."

Marcus Binney, *The Times*, 2 April 1993

"[The terrace's] chief delight, though, is that it affords a perfect framed view of the Maison Carrée — an appropriate homage to a building that has all along silently dictated the terms of this design."

Peter Davey, *The Architectural Review*, July 1993

The roofscape of Nîmes, as seen from the restaurant terrace *(right)* and from the Jardins de la Fontaine (above). With its array of horizontal louvres over the individual galleries, it is only from this distant vantage point that the technology that underpins the building is readily apparent.

lifts and staircases at the Royal Academy in London. But, at Nîmes, the scale and effect is of a different order. I am convinced that one of the keys to the social success of the building lies in this handling of light and views.

In the more specialised spaces, such as the galleries, the lighting is the outcome of painstaking exploration, both with our consultant, Claude Engle, and with the future curators of the museum. I can still remember unpacking large containers on the grass outside the offices of the local Development Agency.

These had been made in our model shop in London and air-freighted to Nîmes for a meeting. Although they looked like crude white boxes from the outside, when you peered in through carefully located peep-holes, the gallery interiors seen within were complete down to the detail of individual finishes, people and replica paintings on the walls.

The models provoked animated discussions, during which the angle of the louvres, both on the roofs and the ceilings would be endlessly adjusted. Although the location and function were different, it reminded me of similar studies we undertook when designing the lighting for

Overlooking the Place de la Maison Carrée (previously called Place de la Comédie), the terraces, steps and ramps that line the front of the building have become a natural vantage point for those with time to sit and watch the world go by.

The inner walls of the galleries, overlooking the atrium, are clear glazed and can be left open to the view or lined with simple fabric screens where extra protection from daylight is required. The bench was designed by Norman and Sabiha Foster.

All the galleries on the upper level of the building are top-lit, the central rooflight lined with internal louvres below and a fixed brise-soleil above to ensure direct sunlight is avoided.

The largest galleries of both upper and lower levels of the museum are linked by a double-height space, drawing attention to the continuing attractions above and below.

Below: the médiathèque and the art museum are considered important educational facilities and both are visited regularly by school parties.

Overleaf: the Maison Carrée and the Carré d'Art in the early morning. Changes of level and engravings within the new limestone paving of the square were employed to delineate the line of the Roman forum that once surrounded the temple.

Stansted Airport, where the model was so large that you could crawl underneath it and stand up inside.

Just as influential was a model we created to explore the urban landscaping of the square – the setting for the Maison Carrée and the Carré d'Art. This was a later commission, but it picked up some of the recommendations that I had made in sketch form during my first visit. Their implementation has provided benefits out of all proportion to the cost of the work.

Metal railings, parked cars and unsightly advertising have been removed and the line of the old Roman paving has been reinstated, with simple stone steps linking the changes of level. The traffic has been calmed and three of the streets given over entirely to pedestrians.

At night, the Roman temple is floodlit by specially designed fittings that have been recessed into the stone paving, and its present-day

counterpart, the Carré d'Art, basks in the reflected light from its elder architectural statesman.

The effect of these two projects – the new building and its related urban works in the Place de la Maison Carrée – has been to totally transform a whole quarter of Nîmes. The Place is now alive with people, a new outdoor café life has been born and there is a ripple effect which extends well beyond the site. The Carré d'Art is a powerful demonstration of the way in which an individual project, linked to an enlightened political initiative, can regenerate the wider fabric of a city.

Upper Gallery Level or Third Floor

1 upper reception area
2 galleries
3 void
4 video room
5 terrace
6 cafeteria
7 lift to entrance lobby
8 service lift

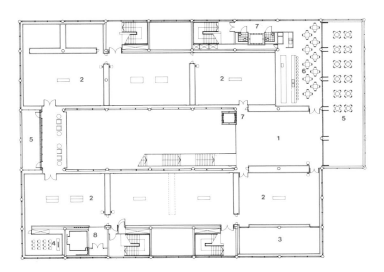

Lower Gallery Level or Second Floor

1 reception area
2 cloakroom
3 galleries
4 void
5 service lift
6 lift to entrance lobby

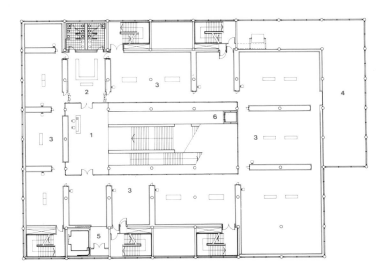

The galleries, like the rest of the building, are aligned on the simple 5 x 7-metre structural grid, allowing a variety of spaces two bays wide and one, two or three bays long.

1985 Pavilion Cafeteria
Jardins de la Fontaine
Nîmes

Below: based on the simplest of frames, the pavilion can be built in straight or curved forms. At the Jardins de la Fontaine, it followed the curve of the river bank.

Laid out in the 1760s, on either side of a small river diverted specially for the purpose, the Jardins de la Fontaine retain an impressive sense of military order, which the new pavilion was expected to match.

Major buildings and their architects may, on occasion, exert an influence that extends beyond the immediate task in hand. An example of this process was Foster Associates' proposal for reworking a small café in the Jardins de la Fontaine in Nîmes, commissioned while the practice was working on that city's médiathèque.

Laid out in the eighteenth century on both sides of a small river, by an army engineer called Mareschal, the Jardins de la Fontaine are decorated with marble vases and statues taken from Château de la Mosson near Montpellier and contain the imposing remains of the old Roman baths. The landscaping reflects an unequivocally military sense of order.

For the duration of the Nîmes project, the local Foster office was housed in one of a group of buildings that was mirrored on the opposite bank by a similar group, one of which had been converted into a riverside café called Le Pavillon. Over the years, the café had developed rather casually, with umbrellas and tables spilling out untidily on to the gravel path.

At the instigation of the Mayor of Nîmes, Foster Associates was invited to find a way of upgrading the café and converting its existing outdoor clutter into a scheme more in keeping with the design of the gardens. Their response combined the idea of a windbreak, achieved through vertical glass panels, with a form of overhead canopy to modulate the light.

Since the terrace on the médiathèque itself was being planned to incorporate an awning in the traditional style of the region — one capable of being rolled out and back again in response to changeable weather — this can be seen as an attempt to reprise that idea in miniature.

For the new outdoor section a curved central spine would be covered with split cane, a traditional shelter material much used in the south of France and resonant of the lattice shading over the Casbah in Marrakesh, a favourite Foster image. On either side a short tubular steel framework would support both the glass panels and overhead roller blinds.

The overall effect can be seen as a reworking of the French pavement café, where a zone

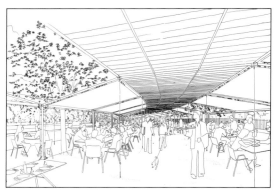

is created that blurs the boundary between indoors and outdoors. Here, though, the aim was to avoid the attendant sense of clutter that matters rather less on a city street than in the context of a formal garden landscape.

Though the proposal was well received and went on to feature in several exhibitions, sadly it was never implemented. However, in drawings and models, the riverside pavilion still represents an imaginative contemporary response to the legacy of an army engineer, dismissed by some eighteenth-century critics as "more qualified to build fortifications than decorative works".

Graham Vickers

122

Shading devices of split cane are very popular in the south of France, as Norman Foster's photograph of one of his favourite restaurants demonstrates. Like his photograph of the Casbah in Marrakesh, this image is frequently used in client presentations and general lectures.

Designed for use anywhere, the pavilion's structure is based on a series of simple, modular 'Y' frames, linked longitudinally by tubular cross-members that support the vertical panels of glass and overhead roller blinds, and laterally by lattices of split cane. Seen at ground level, in elevation or in section, the finished structure is all but invisible.

Salle de Spectacles
Nancy
France

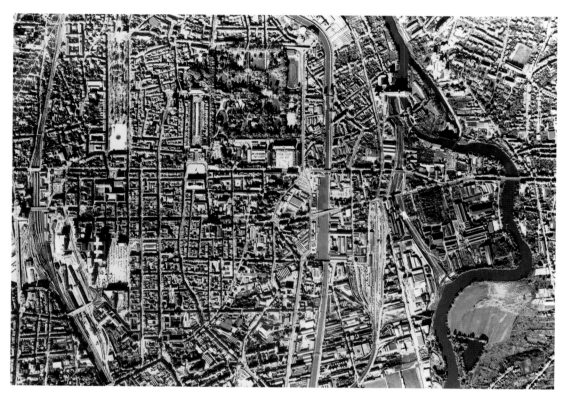

vigorous form of Art Nouveau (created at the turn of the century by a group of artists, architects, engineers and craftsmen known as the Ecole de Nancy), for having been the fulcrum of the French steel industry and for being the home town of Jean Prouvé.

Such prevailing perceptions scarcely suggest a city in crisis. Yet by 1986, heavy industries were fast being rendered redundant, a series of closures had left the area with only one operational steelworks and a couple of environmentally dubious chemical works, and rapid industrial decline had resulted in a net loss of 8000 jobs in Nancy since 1974. The most recent census recorded a 33,000 drop in the city's population (from 123,000 in 1968 to 90,000 in 1982). Migration away from Nancy seemed to be accelerating and even thriving businesses were beginning to think twice about staying.

Following the election of a new mayor in 1983, the City Council had decided to stimulate urban regeneration just east of Nancy's extensive conservation area, by building an auditorium large enough to stage pop concerts, jazz festivals, variety performances and other events likely to attract crowds of several thousands from all Lorraine.

The three most important phases of Nancy's growth are dramatically illustrated in this aerial photograph. At top left can be seen the warren of narrow streets that define the old medieval centre. To the south of this and stretching eastwards is the formal grid of the sixteenth-century 'new town'. The canal and the two basins that lie at the centre of the site run north-south to the centre-right of the picture, beyond which the nineteenth-century industrial sprawl spreads towards the river. The magnificent Ducal Palace *(right)* can be identified at the end of the long avenue of trees to the west of the park at the top-centre.

In July 1986, Nancy City Council invited Foster Associates to prepare a feasibility study for a large auditorium and multi-purpose hall, to be built on a site only some 600 metres from the celebrated Place Stanislas — a sumptuous eighteenth-century square rated 'world heritage' by UNESCO. The commission led to proposals Norman Foster has since described as "an attempt to solve the inner city problems of Nancy".

The city of Nancy, 306 kilometres due east of Paris, is nationally reputed to be staid, keenly patriotic and more than a touch conservative. No doubt such views are reinforced by images freeze-framed in countless French minds since their army days. National service is still compulsory in France, the army presence in the northeast remains massive, Nancy has its own military governor, the town plan is peppered with barracks and the main-line railway station seems permanently awash with bored teenage soldiers killing time.

Long famous internationally for its 'new town' which rivals counterparts at Edinburgh, Bath and Bordeaux, Nancy is now almost as well-known as the birthplace of a peculiarly

No such facility then existed anywhere in north-east France, but a low-cost lightweight structure with an audience capacity of 6700 was proving immensely popular in Paris. Called the Zénith, it had been erected in 1983 on disused land next to an elevated motorway at La Villette. Variants were being commissioned from the architects, Chaix and Morel, for several other towns and cities elsewhere in France and, initially, it was assumed a modified Zénith would fit the bill perfectly at Nancy — not least because J.-P. Morel was born in Lorraine and had trained at the Nancy school of architecture.

Below: the centre of Nancy has been beautifully preserved. Norman Foster photographed a number of the buildings there for his own files and was particularly taken with the many fine examples of Art Nouveau.

The centre of the French steel industry during the late nineteenth century, it is little surprise that Nancy was to spawn its own particular form of Art Nouveau, or that later it was to be the home town of Jean Prouvé.

Doubts that any type of tent structure could be adequately sound insulated to prevent events from causing serious noise nuisance in the neighbourhood of the chosen site put paid to plans for a Nancy Zénith. Instead, the City Council made the proposed auditorium the subject of a competition. Three entries were shortlisted: one by a Parisian, one by a local architect, and an eye-catching confection by an Italian. But none was deemed wholly satisfactory, especially so far as cost was concerned.

Having drawn a blank twice, the City Council then turned to Foster Associates for a fresh

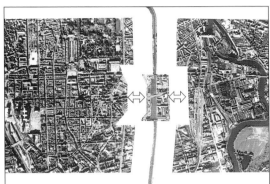

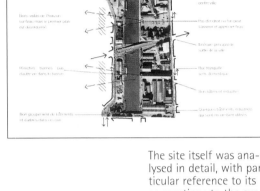

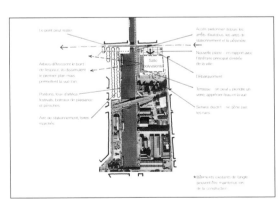

appraisal of the auditorium question. To assess how such a building might generate the desired neighbourhood revitalisation, the office examined the brief and site in the wider context of Nancy's urban structure.

Distinctly different textures have contributed to Nancy's urban fabric in three principal phases of development: the close weave of narrow streets surviving in an 'old town', founded in the eleventh century; the formal grid of the 'new town', developed from the sixteenth century; and a vast conglomerate fringe of heteromorphic parts, stitched together with diverse degrees of solidity as the city expanded with dramatic speed in the latter part of the nineteenth century.

Nancy had already been absorbed into the national rail and canal networks when Germany annexed Alsace and part of Lorraine in 1871, leaving the city closer to the frontier than any other major conurbation in France. An influx of French-speaking refugees arrived, including many wealthy businessmen from Metz. Exploitation of locally-mined iron ore, coal and chemicals intensified. Heavy, light and service industries proliferated. Suburbs and satellite towns

The office's first report used photomontages of the aerial photograph to place the site within the context of the city. The proposed solution sought to bind, not separate, the historical centre to its more recent suburbs, and to generate a new network of pedestrian routes uniting the city.

The site itself was analysed in detail, with particular reference to its connections to the surrounding neighbourhood, its best points of access and which areas should be opened up or required screening.

The report concluded that the site be laid out orthogonally in a continuation of the new town grid, to create a series of *îlots* that could be developed separately or as a whole. The first phase, the auditorium, would be at the north end of the site, nearest the major roads.

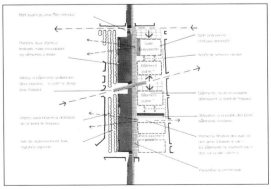

By the mid-1980s, the closure of obsolete industries and the migration of others to better served industrial estates had left the area around the canal as little more than an urban wasteland desperately in need of regeneration.

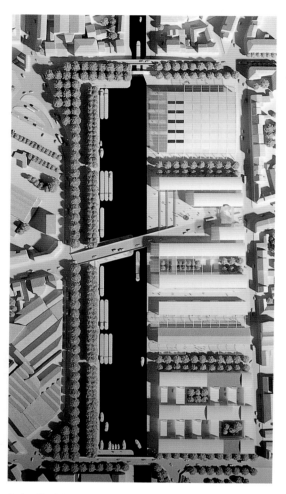

In its final form, the proposed masterplan established a simple grid of large *îlots*, 100 metres square, that could be developed wholesale (as shown on the presentation model above), or subdivided into any number of smaller plots suitable for local initiatives.

Where the site was bisected by a major road, the design team turned adversity to advantage by proposing a landmark development that would embrace and bridge the thoroughfare to create a new gateway to the city.

developed. By the turn of the century, the city had more than doubled in size and the population nearly trebled, to reach 103,000 by 1901.

Members of the Ecole de Nancy developed their ideas on the integration of art with industry in numerous commissions for new, modern business premises and residential accommodation, and many outstanding examples of Art Nouveau were executed to their designs, both in the city centre and the suburbs, in the early 1900s. But the imperative of national survival soon took priority over artistic preoccupations: after the German advance of September 1914, the enemy line remained perilously close to Nancy until the Armistice.

All annexed territories subsequently reverted to France and Nancy's steel industry retooled for peacetime purposes, notably Jean Prouvé's pioneering experiments in the use of pressed and folded steel for prefabricated building components, undertaken in his own workshops during the 1920s and '30s. The German Occupation (1940-44) put a stop to these activities and, although Prouvé made heroic attempts to alleviate the chronic housing shortage in Lorraine immediately after the Liberation (in 1944 alone, over 800 prefabricated emergency homes were produced in his workshops), his ideas for far more widespread application of lightweight prefabrication techniques in the post-war reconstruction of France were largely ignored.

Large-scale, government-subsidised developments were added to Nancy's extensive urban fringe (among them the Haut-du-Lièvre housing

estate, built 1956-62 and since claimed to include France's longest inhabited slab block); the city's historic core was designated a conservation area and painstakingly restored; Art Nouveau was re-evaluated and a museum devoted to the Ecole de Nancy was created. But by the early 1980s, the effects of economic recession were becoming very apparent in the city's industrial interstices.

The area earmarked for regeneration by the City Council was just such a case: an increasingly run-down strip of industrial development bounding the eastern banks of two basins, or ports, on the Marne-Rhine canal, just beyond the limits of the historic 'new town'. Light industries had been attracted to the area from the mid-nineteenth century onwards, after land drainage had been improved by cutting the canal through this part of the River Meurthe flood-plain and reclaiming large areas of previously unhealthy marshland. Initially, the continued risk of seasonal flooding was far outweighed by the cheapness of the land, and its proximity to the city centre and to transport by road, rail and canal.

These advantages diminished as the area became increasingly hemmed in by local road traffic, then virtually severed from the city centre by an inner ring-road. Distinctive industrial buildings and warehouses still survived, but access to the eastern canal bank was limited to three raised road bridges — each equally unattractive to pedestrians — and one narrow and flimsy footbridge. Waning commercial activity,

Where possible, it was proposed that the best of the existing buildings be retained and refurbished to accommodate new uses.

dilapidation, migration to modern industrial estates elsewhere and severe flooding in the early 1980s had all contributed to the decline of an area fast becoming a kind of urban no-man's-land at the interface between city and suburb.

On the strength of their urban study, Foster Associates suggested this process of marginalisation and decay might be reversed, by making the whole neighbourhood the linchpin in a long-term regeneration strategy designed to close the gap between Nancy's historic core and the eastern suburbs.

To this end, the design team recommended the discipline of the sixteenth-century 'new town' planning grid be extended east, as far as the River Meurthe but adjusted as necessary to allow for the retention of such existing roads, buildings and other features as might be deemed desirable, to provide a framework for future redevelopment. Within the resulting matrix of routes and streets, îlots of about 100 x 100 metres might be subdivided into a number of building plots or redeveloped wholesale. And they suggested means of realising the full public amenity potential of the canal and the river be investigated, as a matter of general policy, in tandem with a programme of environmental improvements centred on landscaping.

The office illustrated how this strategy might be applied in more detailed proposals for the land on either side of the two canal basins. To screen the whole neighbourhood from the inner ring-road, extensive planting was recommended, mainly in the form of avenues of trees

On the narrower western side of the canal basin, the office proposed a single linear car park, screened by an avenue of trees, which could serve as a venue for markets, fairs or other, more informal events at weekends or on bank holidays.

Barges and other craft would be encouraged to moor within the basin, bringing extra life to a new canalside walk, part of a proposed network of pedestrian routes that would help tie the site back into the city's urban fabric.

Antecedents for the office's final proposal for the auditorium were to be found all over Nancy, establishing the building as a fitting tribute to Lorraine steel and an earlier generation of craftsmen.

traditional to French towns and cities, defining and shading a long, linear car-parking area bounding the quayside to the west. They suggested this car-parking area might double as a location for markets and fairs, and that the public amenity value of the quayside would be considerably enhanced if the two canal basins were more fully exploited, both for use by pleasure boats, barges and other craft, and for outdoor events — festivals, firework displays and so on.

A canalside walk was envisaged along the eastern quayside on the opposite bank, to extend an existing pedestrian route from the Parc de la Pépinière — a magnificent 23-hectare park laid out from the 1760s onwards on land adjoining the Ducal Palace. The office saw this proposed pedestrian link as a means of threading the neighbourhood back into Nancy's urban fabric, as well as a public amenity in its own right — a place where people would come to enjoy the animation of the canal basins.

To anchor the area still more firmly to Nancy's urban structure, the discipline of the 'new town' grid was to be applied to future re-development of the industrial land abutting the canalside walk, to create a series of *îlots* separated laterally by tree-lined service roads. These cul-de-sacs were intended to ensure visual links with the canal from the east, as well as providing for off-street deliveries and car parking.

The design team highlighted a number of existing buildings that might be refurbished within this framework, particularly at the southern end of the strip where private sector development was anticipated in the long term, once the revival of the area had been established.

Towards the centre of the strip, an *îlot* was bisected on the diagonal by one of Nancy's busiest traffic arteries. The architects suggested that this thoroughfare could become a positive feature in an office complex designed to straddle part of the road, like a modern gateway to the city. They recommended that this challenging and prominent site should be used to provide new premises for the Conseil Général — the regional council, whose role and staff

In its final form, the roof of the proposed auditorium building was to be formed in three steel vaults, of different sizes but united by an economic system of standardised I-section beams and tubular tie rods.

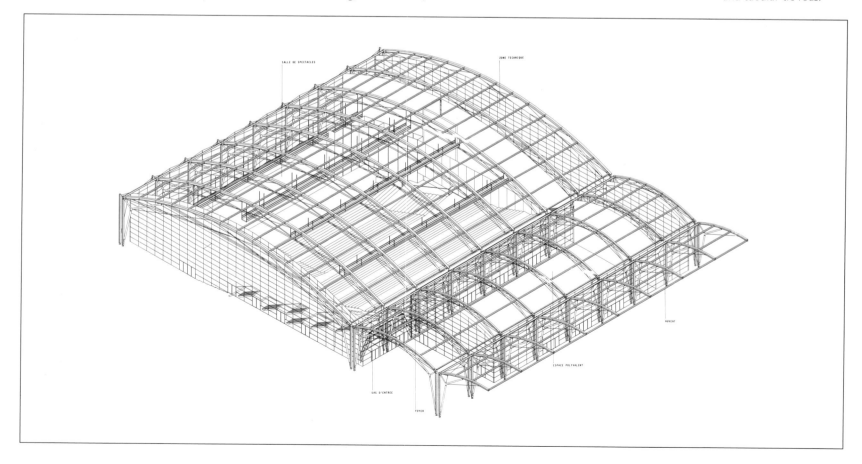

"We applied our research to the area in question, to create a sequence of traditional building blocks, blocks which other architects could work on, could respond to and, hopefully, would act as a catalyst for even greater regeneration."

Norman Foster, lecture at the UIA Congress, Brighton, 17 July 1987

Detail design of the auditorium building was already under way when the project was brought to a halt. Political uncertainty prevented the scheme from being realised, though some of the urban planning suggestions have since been implemented.

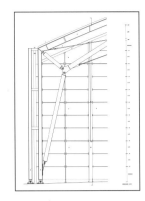

The triple vault solution evolved as a direct response to the three main spaces that were to be included within the building. The main vault was to house the auditorium itself, the *salles des spectacles*, with seating for up to 3000 people. The second vault contained a separate multi-purpose hall, an *espace polyvalent*, suitable for exhibitions or banquets with up to 1000 guests. The third and smallest half-vault was little more than a grand portico, though space was also set aside for a foyer and ticket office serving the whole building.

had been substantially increased following the devolution of a series of administrative functions from central government.

The adjacent and most northerly *îlot* corresponded closely to the site originally selected by the city council for the future auditorium. The architects recommended it be retained for that purpose, as it was well served by public transport and by road, could easily incorporate drop-off points for coaches, and was potentially the most conspicuous and easily found by strangers to the city.

After detailed discussion with their client, the architects established that the new building was to consist of three principal elements: an auditorium capable of housing a wide range of events, with an audience capacity of 3000-3500 (3000 seated, or 2500 seated and 1000 standing); a separate multi-purpose hall large enough to seat banquets of up to 1000 people (with contract catering, hence minimal kitchen facilities); and a foyer and ticket office serving both auditorium and hall.

In their usual manner, the design team embarked on a process of trial and experiment, honing possible solutions to the demands of brief, site and urban context. Some councillors were dismayed by the first version presented to them because they thought it looked too much like a hangar. Subsequent reworkings extended from radical revision of the internal planning to an entirely new structural concept. A fitting tribute to Lorraine steel, the Ecole de Nancy and Jean Prouvé might have emerged had these investigations not been cut short.

In the absence of any announcement by the city council of a clear-cut result following the earlier competition for the auditorium design, the project was never realised. However, some of the most important urban planning suggestions put forward by the office, particularly on tree planting, were subsequently implemented in response to local initiatives.

Charlotte Ellis

Urban furniture, as Foster partner David Nelson has noted, can address some interesting issues of scale since it occupies "an interim space, somewhere between architecture and product design". Neither a building, nor a commercial industrial design product, a piece of urban furniture must not only satisfy all of the aesthetic and practical demands made upon it, but also be capable of retaining its own identity when dropped into a wide variety of locations. In addition, as the office's successful association with the French company of JCDecaux demonstrates, the best urban furniture is usually created, installed and successfully maintained in very particular economic circumstances.

Foster Associates' involvement with office furniture in the late 1980s — their 'architecture in miniature' — has been fully explored by Penny Sparke in volume 3 of this series. However, any assumptions that designing urban furniture might represent a seamless extension of the Nomos and related office furniture projects are soon challenged by the public nature and high maintenance cost of the exercise.

An initial meeting between a representative of JCDecaux and the office took place during the building of Stansted Airport. Three years before completion of the project, the architects had begun to focus attention upon a variety of external elements including paving, shelters and some small-scale urban furniture. In part, this was a reaction to the British Airport Authority's approach to such elements, which was to use exposed aggregate as a matter of course. The office thought this an inappropriate solution and set about looking for an alternative method. By coincidence, JCDecaux were looking for international design partners at the same time, to create street furniture tailored to the tastes and needs of individual countries.

JCDecaux targeted Great Britain and approached the office with a view to enlisting them as urban furniture designers; JCDecaux was, in turn, asked if it would like to co-operate on urban furniture for Stansted. In fact, neither proposal proved practical at that time, mainly because JCDecaux's agenda involved creating products tied to advertising displays.

The office, therefore, proceeded at Stansted on its own, seeking a simple and attractive form for items such as light bollards and litter bins. A cylindrical shape predominated in these designs. The litter bin, for example, was a cylinder with an articulated top that returned to the closed

Foster Associates' first foray into the world of urban furniture was a series of cylindrical litter bins and light bollards for Stansted Airport *(top)*. Two years later they were developing study models of bus shelters for JCDecaux.

The urban furniture at Stansted Airport went beyond the standard litter bins and street lamps to include an extensive arrivals canopy in the lower car park (below left) and these 'totem' signposts.

position after something had been deposited. There was also a series of illuminated bollards designed in the shape of miniature beacons.

These elements were all eventually realised and used at Stansted, notably on the lower level of the short-stay car park where a long footpath was lined with both bollards and litter bins. The litter bins continued in production well beyond the completion of Stansted, as did the office's alternative to the standard issue concrete paving slab. A superior, ground granite slab proved sufficiently popular at Stansted to justify subsequent successful mass production.

The architects, then, had already demonstrated an interest in extending the aesthetic of a building to its perimeter and beyond wherever possible. Following Stansted, they became interested in resuming discussions with JCDecaux.

"Urban street furniture is a real minefield," recalls David Nelson. "The best intentions of city authorities often go wrong, usually because the economics of paying for urban furniture are quite daunting, not least because of the subsequent maintenance costs. What was attractive to us was that Decaux had found a really intelligent way of solving the problem."

JCDecaux's understanding of the advertising potential of urban furniture lies in its own post-war beginnings in administering poster sites. Over the years, the company has built up a reputation for providing cities and local

Selected by Jacques Chirac for use in the Champs Elysées, the Foster bus shelter can now be found throughout Europe. Its structure could hardly be simpler. Two tubular posts, connected at the middle by a crosspiece to which is attached bench seating, support the advertising display panel and the welded roof unit, itself fabricated from a tubular cross member and steel sections. The 10mm thick safety glass is mounted on cast aluminium brackets to protect against impact.

Based on the rear unit of the column, a free-standing civic marker was also developed, to stand at the roadside or on motorway junctions indicating town boundaries and any nearby attractions.

Foster Associates' final presentation model included a variety of optional extras, nearly all of which have since gone into production in forms almost identical to the original design. This mast variant is one of the few options that was not taken up.

Based on JCDecaux's standard advertising 'cylinder', usually designed to accept three separate posters, the Foster team proposed replacing one poster with an integrated tower unit, capable of housing a variety of public facilities from telephones to automatic public conveniences.

authorities with amenities that can be properly maintained through the revenue generated by advertising. In addition, it has usually sought well-designed original products that combine aesthetic quality with easy maintenance.

A contract was drawn up between Foster Associates and JCDecaux for two initial products, a bus shelter and an advertising column based upon the iconic French type known as the Colonne Maurice.

Edward Hutchison, who worked with David Nelson on these projects, identifies some of the issues surrounding the design of the deceptively simple-looking bus shelter. "JCDecaux had enjoyed considerable success in the UK and elsewhere with its public lavatory cubicles. That was the basis on which they were exploring the UK market with regard to bus shelters. David Nelson and myself set about going back to the basic principles of the shelter. That may sound odd, but in fact there were all sorts of requirements to be met."

Among those criteria the design team found that bus shelters needed to be as transparent as possible, in order to make the least possible impact upon prestigious sites. To enable easy cleaning and to avoid interfering with services beneath the pavement, they also had to make minimum penetration into the ground.

A further requirement was for the shelter to be strong enough to support anyone foolish or inebriated enough to clamber on top of it — up to a maximum, apparently, of three. In response to these demands for high strength

plus low visual and physical impact, the design team developed — with the help of Ove Arup & Partners — a prototype that was manufactured by JCDecaux in Paris.

The result was minimal in all respects except that of the element which paid the rent: the conventional 20cm-thick illuminated display panel could not be modified. In all other ways the shelter proved to be an elegantly understated piece of urban furniture and when the final version was displayed in JCDecaux's showroom it proved an instant success. Jacques Chirac, then the Mayor of Paris, liked it so much that it was installed the length of the Champs Elysées. Some 2000 shelters have been erected in Paris alone, and the London borough of Croydon and the cities of Hamburg and Brussels have since followed with significant orders of their own.

Reinventing the Colonne Maurice for various European countries offered a wider range of design opportunities. JCDecaux's long-term guiding principle had been to try and adapt its various street furniture elements to the tastes of individual countries. As Edward Hutchison recalls, the design team attempted to confer distinctiveness by promoting the columns almost as working statues, large city markers that could incorporate a range of amenities. "We set out to make them bigger and give them cultural overtones," he notes. "There were opportunities to add information technology, weather forecasts, shelters and seats. Some of these ideas were dropped, some survived."

Among the survivors were a distinctive canopy and seating. In some columns the process of incorporating practical amenities was

In its final form, the column is supported on a heavy cast-iron base — itself fixed to a precast-concrete anchor block — to the top of which is fixed a metal-slat bench and the advertising display 'cylinder'.

extended to incorporate telephones or automatic public conveniences. The office presented JCDecaux with a model, then a full-scale prototype in wood. In its final form, the column is a simple casting on to which different elements of standard sizes and details can be attached.

Again the result has found favour in France where a number of variations, very much in keeping with the office's vision of translating a passive display icon into a multi-purpose civic amenity, have been widely accepted.

The alliance with JCDecaux has also produced a civic marker in the form of a vertical panel, intended as a kind of graphic signature, to be installed on motorways, identifying exits to individual towns. These have been adopted in France and elsewhere in Europe, notably at the city limits of historic centres.

The office has continued to work with JCDecaux in areas like street lighting, and if the architects' contributions to JCDecaux's products have been significant, David Nelson is frank about what the office has learned in return. "What we now realise, and what Decaux have recognised for some time, is that it is not just a question of designing good furniture and depositing it in the street. You have to establish a whole process, where both designer and manufacturer have a vested interest in the continuing existence of a product that most city authorities just cannot afford to provide without the benefits of advertising revenue."

Graham Vickers

The column is based on a standard unit incorporating only the poster display panels and a low-level tower unit. To this can be attached a range of optional extras: from the bench seat and cantilevered roof to tower extension units, which can themselves be adapted to include information panels, clocks and so on. It has proved extremely popular, and examples can now be found in many cities around the world, including New York (left) and Dresden (above).

Authenticity in Old and New
by Martin Pawley

Martin Pawley is an architectural writer and critic with regular columns in *The Architects' Journal* and *World Architecture*, which he edited from 1992 to 1996. He studied architecture at the Ecole Nationale Supérieure des Beaux-Arts, in Paris, and the Architectural Association in London. From 1984 to 1991 he was architecture critic of *The Guardian,* and from 1992 to 1995 of *The Observer.* He has been a regular contributor to the BBC programme, *The Late Show.* Recent books include *Theory and Design in the Second Machine Age*; *Buckminster Fuller*; and *Future Systems: the Story of Tomorrow.* Forthcoming books include *Project 180* and *Terminal Architecture*, both of which are scheduled for publication in 1997.

Although it is not widely recognised, Europe has more architects working on old buildings than designing new ones. A moment's thought makes it clear why this should be the case. All over the Continent there is a legacy of historic buildings greater than all the additions made to it in the past century. In England and Wales, out of nearly 25 million dwellings, more than 12 million were built before 1914. Among them are 600,000 public buildings listed by the Department of the Environment, the vast majority of which were built more than 150 years ago.

Because of this formidable presence of the old, virtually all new urban building in the European Community, and much new non-urban building besides, invades history. Despite half a century of out-of-town building next to motorways, airports, distribution centres and retail parks, our old towns and cities remain the building blocks of the built environment.

As such, they have become a battleground between the forces of development and the forces of conservation. Over the last hundred years, the act of altering old buildings has ceased to be a technical event. Increasingly it has become a clash of cultures that can generate fear, anger and dissatisfaction.

The source of conflict over old buildings is the need for national economies to optimise efficiency. Just as no nineteenth-century brick-and-iron warehouse could ever be adapted to hold shipping containers, nor can any tiny grocer's shop in a narrow street compete with a modern superstore. This is why most historic buildings face a future of enlargement and adaptation. One way or another the elements of modern serviced floorspace must be shoehorned into every historic building. The art of the architect lies in the way this is done — as the aftermath of the fire at Windsor Castle demonstrated.

On Friday 20 November 1992, a fire, started accidentally in the course of renovation work, raged uncontrollably through the Royal state rooms and living quarters at Windsor Castle, near London. The fire destroyed the Queen's private chapel, the great St George's banqueting hall, several state rooms and two towers. It took fire-fighters more than 12 hours to save the castle and, by the time the battle was won, it was clear that at least £30 million would be needed to make good the resultant damage.

At first there was little debate about the proper architectural approach to the repair of this damage. Most commentators shared the

The destruction by fire, in November 1992, of several of the most important state rooms at Windsor Castle, started an intense debate between traditionalists — who believed the building should be restored to its former glory — and those who believed that, as this was itself little more than a nineteenth-century addition, there was no true historic identity to restore.

view of Her Majesty the Queen who, from an early stage, made it known that she wished the ruined parts of the castle to be returned to their condition before the blaze. But when the prospect arose of public funds being made available to repair the damage, an alternative school of thought emerged. The president of the Royal Institute of British Architects and others argued that the fire had created a golden opportunity for an architectural competition to design new state rooms at the castle using modern materials in a modern way.

There were arguments for and against this plan. The conservationist case depended upon the fact that the damaged parts of the castle had been part of a sequence of chambers, most of which had survived undamaged. For this reason, conservationists thought, the rest should be restored to their pre-fire identity, with the addition of concealed electronics and better fire precautions. The case for the modern solution was sharply contradictory. Its proponents argued that, because the architecture and interior design of Windsor Castle was nineteenth-century Gothic Revival in style, it had no authentic identity to restore.

In the event the progressive case did not win at Windsor. A year after the fire, the addition of a modern wing was officially ruled out and a £40 million reconstruction programme began. In a straight shoot-out between traditionalism and modernism, the latter had lost. Nor was such an outcome surprising. Like many projects before it, the legacy of the past had once again proved too powerful.

In general, the spectrum of public attitudes to historic buildings ranges from a fundamentalist belief in their importance as talismans of civilisation, to an equally fundamental conviction that they are no more than obstacles to the creation of newer and better ones. Between these two extremes lies a continuum of compromise that encompasses anything from the retention of façades to the preservation of heritage features, even when these end up in different locations and serve different purposes to those for which they were originally conceived.

The headquarters of Nomura International in the City of London is a good example of what is meant by façade retention. Designed by the Fitzroy Robinson Partnership and completed in 1991, this state-of-the-art financial services building started life as a six-storey Victorian post office headquarters. In its new guise it

Considerable energy has been expended in recent years in finding ways of adapting historic buildings to new uses. Several smaller buildings — such as François Espinasse's Michelin Building *(above)* — have been fully retained, though as little more than extensions to new, much larger developments behind. With larger buildings, only the original façades might be kept, as was the case at Nomura House *(right)* by Fitzroy Robinson, the longest façade retention scheme so far attempted.

has 10 floors, all tucked in behind the original post office façades with the aid of a tall mansard roof and a deep basement.

As for the preservation of historic relics, perhaps the best recent example is afforded by the planned rebuilding of the 1836 Euston Arch — demolished in 1961 — which followed close upon the discovery of some of its abandoned stones by a conservationist.

Compromise projects like Nomura House and the Euston Arch co-exist with surviving historic structures in the conservation areas of all major European cities. But in the 1980s, under increasing pressure of demand for more floorspace in conservation areas, they were joined by more extreme measures. Several relatively small historic buildings were converted into little more than mascots for large floor-plate commercial developments erected behind them. In London this happened to the 1911 Michelin building in

South Kensington, designed by François Espinasse, and to the former *Daily Telegraph* building in Fleet Street designed by John Burnet.

As these examples show, an agreed formula for the successful adaptation of historic buildings has yet to be discovered. However the case is not hopeless. Culture clashes of the Windsor Castle kind are the outcome of major stylistic and technical changes in the process of building that have made old and new seem incompatible for most of our century. These changes began with the engineering advances of the nineteenth century and led directly to the first generation of modern buildings that benefited from the shift from short-span, load-bearing construction using clay, stone and timber, to long-span frame construction using iron and steel, curtain walling and glass.

Foster's startlingly radical competition-winning proposal for the Reichstag has been tempered as the project developed, and now includes a modern reinterpretation of the original dome.

Layers of history. The competition-winning design for the reconstruction of the Reichstag, in Berlin, sought to bring together the building's past and future in a unified composition, but in such a manner that the different layers of history would retain their own identity and integrity.

Inevitably shifts of this magnitude created problems of compatibility. But now they are beginning to be resolved thanks to a new cultural insight based upon the concept of authenticity as the common ground of all historical periods.

As a result of this enlightened synthesis it now seems possible that the nineteenth-century solution of historical pastiche will finally lose its long-standing popularity, particularly among those observers who have seen that, exercised in projects of modern size, such as large city office buildings and out-of-town superstores, it threatens the end of all historical differences of style and period by homogenising them into a 'historicist', rather than a historical lexicon. By contrast, the new alternative, a much more honest accommodation of the differences between old and new, actually enhances the awareness of history by design.

The contribution of Foster and Partners to the success of this new approach has been no small one, even though it is true to say that its first manifestation was the modest extension to the galleries of the Royal Academy in London

that is described in detail elsewhere in this volume. In this small project, Foster Associates — as the firm was then called — contrived for the first time to set up a dialectic between existing and new work in a pair of connected buildings that was so perfect that it generated its own synthesis with an authenticity that satisfies all shades of opinion.

Working in association with a conservation architect and English Heritage, Norman Foster, the most modern of Modern architects, rediscovered and emphasised elements of the old in the context of an addition of undisguisedly modern design. The result was a limpid articulation of past and present that has been admired by Modernists and conservationists ever since. Today, it is not too much to say that the Sackler Galleries, with their modest demonstration of the value of authenticity across all periods, have become one of the most influential works of architecture in the last half century.

"The only constant in architecture is change," says Norman Foster, and he sees the proof of this statement in much larger projects, as well as in its modest beginnings at the Royal Academy. Today, wherever historic structures are concerned, Foster applies this law of continuous evolution.

"We have learned to peel away the layers of history to expose a dialogue between old and new," he explains. "The idea that the past has become so sacred and precious that you have to imitate it must be questionable but, by the same token, that does not mean that we ignore it. Research into the history of site and building is critical to our method. Authenticity is what gives history its depth, and the juxtaposition of historic elements with modern ones is what heightens our awareness of history. In architecture every age makes its mark, and in all projects that involve historic settings, whether disused nineteenth-century industrial infrastructure or eighteenth-century domestic architecture, we deal with past, present and future."

The results of Norman Foster's search for layers of authenticity and history can be seen at different scales, in projects as varied as the London shop for Katharine Hamnett and the enormous — but sadly aborted — King's Cross redevelopment. In the same way, where the triumph of the Sackler Galleries at the Royal Academy was created out of no more than a gap between two buildings, his competition-winning project for the reconstruction of the

Foster and Partners' proposals for the British Museum clear away the excrescences that have accumulated around Smirke's great Reading Room and return the great courtyard to its original splendour — though now protected by a soaring glass roof.

Reichstag in Berlin explored the gap between two eras of history. Taking the hulk of the Reichstag, the Imperial German parliament building that, through the grim vicissitudes of German history, had only housed a democratic parliament for 10 of its 100 years, the Foster team encased its battered stone shell inside a glass superstructure, thus symbolically encapsulating its first century and preparing it for a better second century in a united Europe.

More recently still, in what will be the largest construction project to be carried out there since 1914, Foster and Partners has undertaken to apply the same rigorous articulation of old and new to the reconstruction and enclosure of the courtyard around the circular Reading Room of the British Museum. There, in the shadow of the 150-year-old dome that epitomises the dawn of the modern age, the Foster team will install a glass enclosure rivalling I. M. Pei's pyramids at the Louvre.

The transformation of great buildings such as these, according to the principle of authenticity, heralds the advent of a wider acceptance of an architecture that will accept reconstruction as well as construction. Its success points the way towards a synthesis that will reconcile

land-based architecture with naval architecture and aircraft design, where the refitting of ships and the 'stretching' and re-engineering of aircraft is normal practice. It is a direction that promises to see conservation and modern design, at loggerheads for almost the whole of the twentieth century, fuse into a new millennial architecture just as a new century is born.

Martin Pawley

The Sackler Galleries
Royal Academy of Arts
London

Rising into the lobby of the Sackler Galleries at the Royal Academy is an elevating experience. The daylight that pours in through the glass cladding of the rooftop 'sculpture promenade' lifts the spirits, while the top-lit galleries themselves, with their clean, white shadowless outline, subtly concealed environmental controls, and simple picture fixings, stress the value of art as something more than a commodity traded in salerooms. Every detail, from the glass-edged floor of the entrance lobby precisely skirting a stone cornice on one side, to the translucent glass-cladding of the sculpture promenade lightly coming to rest upon an ancient parapet on the other, confirms this impression. The architecture of the Sackler Galleries is what Mies van der Rohe would have described as "nearly nothing", but in its very minimalism it pays

more genuine respect to the ancient brick and stone buildings to which it is attached, than it ever could by being more assertive.

The Sackler Galleries were completed in 1991, a year set on the knife-edge that separated the 1980s' building boom from the 1990s' recession. In retrospect, it is clear that, because of this, it encompassed the presentation of more long-awaited buildings, and projects, than any since. The completions of 1991 might now seem to be merely the aftershock of a vigorous decade, but even so, it is already inconceivable that there will be another year like it before the turn of the century. In the span of 12 weeks alone, from April to June, London saw not only the opening of Robert Venturi's Sainsbury Wing at

A place that "should not really exist". The assured calm of the new sculpture promenade and lobby *(left)*, floating in the 4.2-metre gap between the Royal Academy's two main buildings, comes as a complete contrast to the bustle of the building's approach from Piccadilly *(above)*.

Commissioned by Sir John Denham in 1665, the original house was sold on his death to the first Earl of Burlington, shortly before it was completed in 1667.

The original Diploma Galleries were themselves additions, commissioned by the Academy shortly after it moved into the original building in the 1860s. By the 1980s, the lack of adequate light and environmental controls had made them totally unsuitable for exhibitions.

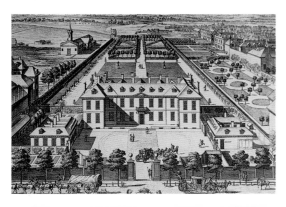

Burlington House was significantly remodelled into the form it takes today, when the third Lord Burlington commissioned Colen Campbell, in 1715, to add the Palladian façade to the main elevation, and William Kent, in 1719, to refurbish the main rooms of the *piano nobile*.

The work begun by Campbell was not completed until 1815, when Lord Cavendish bought the house and commissioned Samuel Ware to reorganise the building's interior and add the new garden façade.

the National Gallery, and the presentation of the ill-fated 'alternative' Paternoster scheme for the environs of St Paul's Cathedral — a project conceived with the help of the Prince of Wales — but also the opening of no less than three new buildings by Foster Associates: the epic Terminal building at Stansted, the magnificent ITN building in Gray's Inn Road, and the Sackler Galleries at the Royal Academy.

In terms of magnitude of architectural achievement there was little doubt at the time that Stansted towered above the rest. A vast and truly millennial structure with a roof as glorious as the cathedral structures of the Middle Ages, this building rightly attracted enormous critical acclaim. So much so that, compared to Stansted's 10-year gestation and £97.5 million cost, the reconstruction of three small galleries at the Royal Academy, in Piccadilly, seemed hardly to count. But size and cost are not the ultimate guarantors of influence. While the reputation of Stansted rightly stands undimmed, the judgment of recent history on the Sackler Galleries has been deservedly enhanced.

The consensus now is that in this one small project, on a virtually non-existent site, Foster Associates turned a page in the history of the popular acceptance of Modern architecture that had never been turned before. In short, through their unique approach to this task, the architects worked a sea-change in establishment attitudes to advanced technology architecture.

Best known for precisely the kind of High-Tech, green field building epitomised by their Stansted Terminal, the office had somehow achieved a design miracle in an utterly different context. However experienced in the use of deep

plans, big spans and suspended walls, the Foster team had never before built within a delicate Heritage framework.

Their contextual experience started and ended with the drastic but brilliantly successful 'zero lot line' masterpiece of the Willis Faber & Dumas building in Ipswich. Yet, as the first visitors to the new galleries at the Royal Academy in 1991 delightedly saw, in a dark and narrow gap between a much-altered stately home and a Victorian art gallery, the office had created something not only perfectly of its time, but also perfectly in place. As an icebreaker for the use of advanced technology architecture in a Heritage environment, the Sackler Galleries have proved invincible.

Of the press reviews of the rebuilt galleries only those in the *Spectator* and the *Catholic Herald* refused to share general critical approval. The former compared the sculpture promenade to "Fellini's bathroom", while the latter likened the refurbished galleries to "operating theatres in a hospital".

Today, such criticisms are no longer heard and it is the approbation of the majority verdict that has become universal for, at the last count, the Sackler Galleries had received no less than 15 national and international awards, and are universally accepted as a turning point in the relationship between the old and the new in architecture. Because of this they have become a convenient place of pilgrimage for the assessors of international competitions that involve additions to historic buildings, so that as well as exercising a powerful influence upon other architects, it is believed that the office has won at least two major competitions — the new wing

Sydney Smirke's masterly extension of Ware's original main staircase, leading to the main galleries beyond, leaves visitors quite unaware that they are passing between two buildings set 4.2 metres apart.

Burlington House as it is today. As well as Smirke's addition of the main galleries in the original garden, and of the Diploma Galleries to the building's third floor (behind a new façade of blind niches), refurbishment work was to continue within the house throughout the nineteenth century. In 1876 E. M. Barry added a new staircase to the Diploma Galleries and, some years later, Norman Shaw installed yet another, linking the ground and first floors. It was this confusing pattern of circulation that the office sought to rationalise.

for the Joslyn Arts Museum in Omaha, Nebraska, and the ongoing interior reconstruction of the Reichstag in Berlin — because of the powerful impression the Royal Academy galleries make.

As an architectural commission, the Sackler Galleries began life in 1985 as an instruction to improve the environmental conditions in three worn-out Victorian display rooms on the top floor of the Royal Academy. Called the Diploma Galleries, these small rooms dated from 1867 when the Royal Academy first took out a lease from the Government on its present home, Burlington House. Since then modern research has revealed that, prior to the arrival of the Royal Academy, Burlington House had already undergone 300 years of enlargement and alteration at the hands of architects.

As many as 14 distinguished practitioners are believed to have worked on the building over the years, including Hugh May, James Gibbs, William Kent, Colen Campbell and Samuel Ware, but few had as much impact as Sydney Smirke, architect of the great dome of the Reading Room at the British Museum and a Royal Academician himself. Smirke not only added the Diploma Galleries as a top-lit third storey to Burlington House, with blind niches instead of windows to the front, but also built the large Main Gallery that occupies what was once the garden at the rear of the house.

Part of Smirke's expansion of the Academy involved running the main staircase of Burlington House right through its rear wall to the first floor of the Main Gallery beyond. This new building immediately hid from view the north elevation of the original house, as well as the south elevation of his own gallery building.

Smirke's handsome elevation of polychrome brickwork was lost behind 100 years of *ad hoc* additions before Foster Associates proposed its reinstatement. Julian Harrap Architects were appointed to survey the surviving details of both this and Ware's garden elevation, and supervise their renovation.

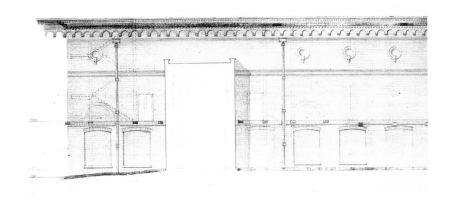

The gap between Burlington House and Smirke's new galleries as it was in 1985, crammed full with 100 years' uncontrolled growth of unwanted plumbing, lavatories and ancillary accommodation.

Thus was created the essential problem of the Royal Academy for future architects, which was – as the Foster team was to discover – that the institution occupied not one building but two.

Although the office had worked within the confines of a medieval street pattern at Willis Faber & Dumas in the 1970s, and later encountered other conservation issues when designing the unbuilt BBC Radio Centre at Langham Place in London, it had never worked on a historic building, let alone two of them so closely connected. In part, this explains the unorthodox approach the architects took to the problem of restoring the Diploma Galleries. But in equal part their laterally thought-out solution may have come from a long experience of work with adventurous commercial clients, who appreciated conceptual daring in organisational matters.

enhance quality of the existing spaces · respect mouldings · consider frameless glass infill only where essential · dialogue – old / new.

Unique opportunity to evolve magic combination of natural & artificial lighting · best balance of insulation · uv filtering · but quality of light vital !

tracks for hanging · discreet.

New floor finishes throughout

New environmental control systems · discreet floor grilles · use existing underfloor voids.

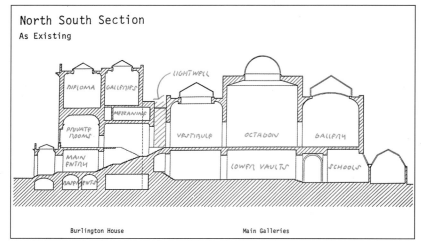

North South Section
As Existing

Burlington House   Main Galleries

With little funding available, the Academy's initial commission covered only the refurbishment of the Diploma Galleries. Norman Foster's early sketches explored ways of introducing improved lighting and environmental conditions suitable for modern travelling exhibitions. As this early research proceeded, however, it became increasingly clear that

the galleries themselves were only part of the problem and until the problems of access were resolved – for the art as well as the visiting public – the galleries would remain under-utilised.

Never content merely to follow a client's brief, the Foster office always studies the whole of its client's organisation and methods before advancing a proposal. Once, in the 1970s, they had even gone so far as to turn down the opportunity to design a building, by demonstrating that a clever reorganisation of the client's existing premises would make it unnecessary. Oddly enough, at the Royal Academy, a similar conclusion was to be reached but with different results.

In 1985, soon after they had begun their survey of the condition of the Diploma Galleries and discovered the problem posed by the two buildings, Norman Foster and his partner Spencer de Grey reached the conclusion that there would be little benefit in restoring the

The design team stumbled on the gap between the two buildings almost by chance, during an early meeting in one of the offices that overlooked the light well. Further investigation convinced them this was the undiscovered space that could solve the Academy's problems.

142

The architects prepared an early presentation model to explain the scheme to the Academy and potential benefactors. Made in sections, this included a proposal for a rooftop sculpture gallery that extended over the main galleries.

Though there was no funding to implement the scheme at this stage, the Academy commissioned Foster Associates to prepare a report explaining how the new circulation might work.

galleries to use without in some way improving access to them, both for visitors and for the movement of works of art. In their search for a better line of approach to this problem they began to consider using the slot Sydney Smirke had left between Burlington House and his own building as a possible site for a new vertical circulation system.

Over the years since it was created, the 4.2-metre slot between the north elevation of Burlington House and the south elevation of Smirke's Main Gallery had been progressively blocked up by the construction of lavatories and other ancillary accommodation. By the 1980s this process had culminated in a series of gloomy light wells filled with plumbing and bricked-up windows, alternating with stretches of outhouse roof. Embarking, as Spencer de

Grey has since remarked, on an "archaeological voyage of discovery" through this decrepit area the architects — with the support of English Heritage, and, in particular, Ashley Barker and Philip Whitbourne — were able to verify that the idea of reclaiming what the Academy called 'the gap' for a new staircase to the Diploma Galleries was indeed possible.

Possible perhaps, but more easily said than done. Opening up the gap meant exposing most of the much damaged garden façade of Burlington House designed by Samuel Ware, which had not seen the light of day for more than 100 years. It also meant exposing the south wall of Smirke's Main Gallery extension, which the architect had never meant to be seen. The architects, with their conservation adviser, Julian

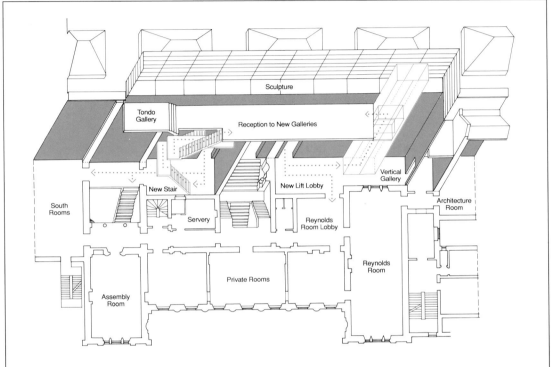

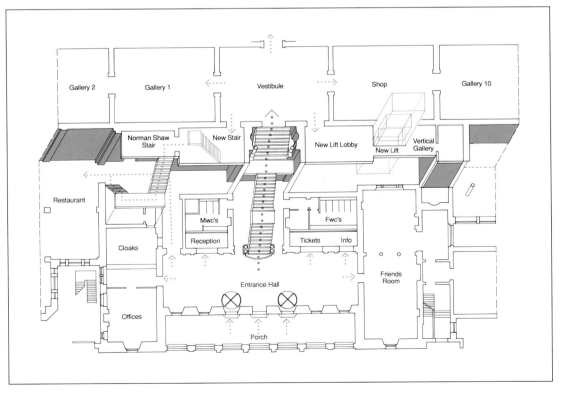

The working prototype of the glazed floor panels intended for the Hong-kong Bank's ground-floor plaza. Though the project was never realised, it convinced the office of the potential for drawing daylight down into previously unlit spaces.

Harrap, argued that not only should the façades be cleaned, but also that the original rendering, the lost mouldings, and the obliterated windows in Ware's façade should all be reinstated.

Such careful restoration work, combined with the insertion of a new staircase and the provision of a lift to provide disabled access and transport art works to and from the Academy's basement store, might well have transformed the utility of the Diploma Galleries, but it would also have vastly exceeded the budget originally allocated to the task.

Fortunately, at this point two wealthy philanthropists, Jill and Arthur Sackler, benefactors to a number of universities in the United States and long-term supporters of the Royal Academy, agreed to cover all the necessary costs. Both were enthusiasts for the new plan and with their

A large-scale presentation model was prepared that allowed the final design to be explored and refined in considerable detail. In its final form the model bears an uncanny resemblance to the finished scheme.

aid as principal donors — until his untimely death in 1987 Arthur Sackler became what Foster calls a 'working patron' — the budget was so enlarged that not only could the Diploma Galleries be transformed, the façades restored, and new stairs and a lift installed, but it also became possible to extend the brief to include a new display area for Michelangelo's tondo — one of the Academy's greatest treasures — and a new sculpture promenade, running the full width of the Academy on the additional floor-space that could now be created above the gap at second floor level.

Because Burlington House is Listed Grade 2* it was impossible to raise this promenade higher than the existing second floor parapet, but the architects believed there was sufficient

The 'before' and 'after' sections through the gap perhaps illustrate best quite how much space — and clarity — the office was able to create from the most meagre of resources. The improved circulation allowed the facilities to be relocated in the main building with the minimum of inconvenience.

Taken on completion of the demolition work, this photograph gives some indication of how badly damaged the original elevations were. Julian Harrap Architects initiated a detailed study of Ware and Campbell's original drawings to ensure the restoration work was completed with absolute integrity.

A shared philosophy that sought a clear separation between the new and the old allowed the restoration and the construction of new works to be carried out with the minimum of interference. Samuel Ware's original façade has been restored as accurately as research allowed, matching details and materials exactly though allowing the new work to stand out from the original. A new doorway was cut through from the new first-floor lift lobby, where previously only a window would have been possible: a period door was discounted in favour of one in glass to help identify it as a new intervention.

As no extra weight could be added to the existing structure, a lightweight barrel-vault design was chosen for the new gallery roofs. Gently curving beams, with tubular bracing, were installed at two-metre centres to form an effective portal structure.

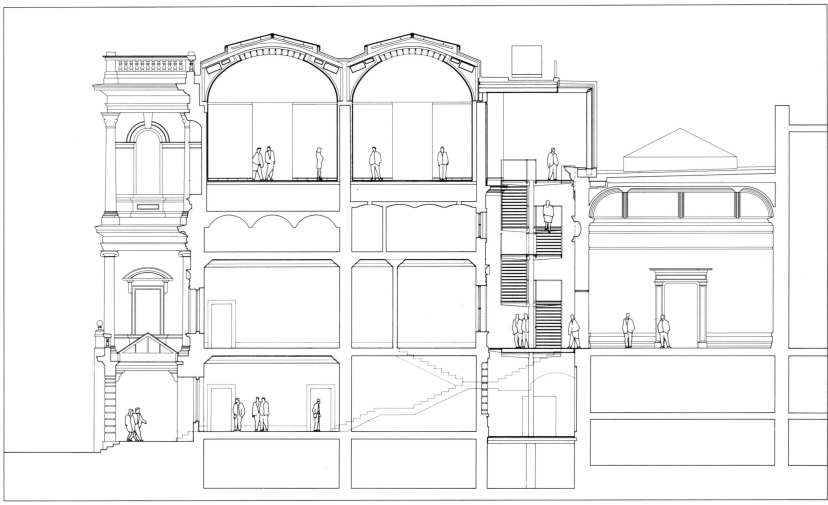

The floor for the new sculpture promenade was positioned just below the cornice line of the main galleries, allowing the cornice to act as a natural plinth for the sculptures and raising the height of the gallery floors to allow the installation of underfloor services.

room provided it nestled at cornice level, somewhat above the original, split-level Diploma Gallery floors. This, in turn, would make it possible to insert raised floors into the galleries, which would make it easier to provide them with the lighting and environmental control technology they required.

With a larger budget assured, the construction task at the Royal Academy thus divided itself into three parts. There was the conservation task of recreating the north façade of Burlington House; the work involved in designing and building a free-standing lobby and sculpture promenade on top of a minimal structure of three-storey steel legs, with a lift and staircase reaching down through the gap between the two existing buildings; and, finally, the interior

Every detail was carefully modelled to ensure the best possible solution. The positioning of the glass staircase and its landings was carefully analysed to ensure the existing windows were not obstructed.

Below: the extension of the sculpture promenade to the full width of the gap allowed the creation of a special 'gallery' for the Michelangelo tondo of *The Virgin and Child with the Infant St John.*

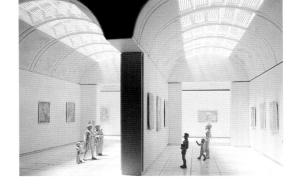

A considerable amount of research, including the making of this detailed study model, was undertaken to ensure the galleries would operate under the best possible lighting conditions.

work of stripping the former Diploma Galleries back to their brickwork, raising their floor levels to insert new services, and replacing the old roof with a new structure with barrel-vaulted ceilings and skylights with controllable louvres to monitor light levels at all times.

It was in the execution of these tasks that the office's legendary precision and attention to detail came to the fore. After painstaking research by Julian Harrap and his researcher, Wendy Hitchmough, which included studying the original drawings, the geometry of the 'lost' Burlington House façade by Samuel Ware was restored to as close an approximation to its pre-Smirke appearance as was possible, and Smirke's own robust brick façade was cleaned and repaired. Access to the rebuilt Diploma Galleries — now renamed the Sackler Galleries — was

Second Floor: the Sackler Galleries

1 lobby and sculpture promenade
2 tondo gallery
3 glass staircase
4 glass bridge
5 lift
6 north gallery
7 south gallery
8 west gallery
9 escape stairs
10 print store
11 library

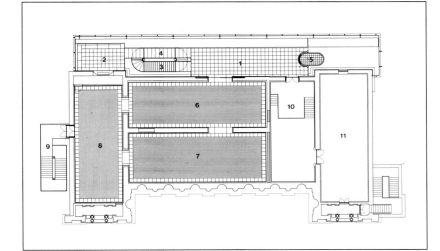

achieved by a new daylight-admitting steel and glass staircase and a glass-enclosed hydraulic lift, both located in the gap itself.

The top of the gap was closed by the floor of the sculpture promenade, a floor partly glazed to let daylight wash the restored historic façades beneath it, and also to stress its structural separateness from the two older buildings on either side. Finally, the roof and north wall of the sculpture promenade were enclosed with special daylight-balanced low iron oxide translucent glass from Czechoslovakia, supported on pin-jointed brackets that respond to any differential movement between the two buildings.

Finally the three galleries themselves were completely rebuilt— within the existing walls but

First Floor

1 entrance to main galleries
2 shop
3 glass staircase
4 main staircase
5 lift lobby
6 servery
7 ante-room
8 Reynolds Room
9 office
10 Norman Shaw staircase

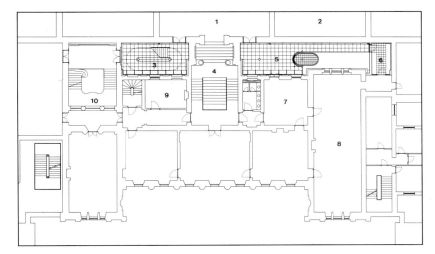

Ground Floor

1 entrance lobby
2 cloakroom
3 ticket desk
4 members' room
5 main staircase
6 lavatories
7 lift lobby
8 passage
9 Norman Shaw staircase
10 cafeteria

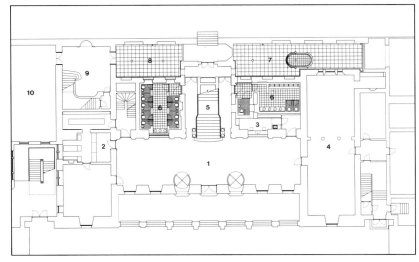

"At the Royal Academy, the past is encountered at such close quarters that discreteness, of itself, is not enough. It is not only a question, as in Nîmes or Ipswich, of placing new alongside old, but of creating a 'historic' space that has never previously existed. The original meaning of the garden façade is irrecoverable, since it is no longer a single composition, but is viewed obliquely and in fragments. This confers on Foster the role of an editor, or an interpreter of the past."

Kenneth Powell, *Sackler Galleries*, Blueprint Extra 04, London 1991

with an entirely new roof — as air-conditioned, light-controlled, barrel-vaulted, white-painted rooms, their complex servicing hidden beneath the new raised floor.

The minimalism of the modern parts of this project — the glass roof and glass cladding, the glass and steel staircase, and the noiseless hydraulic lift — is what throws the greater historic parts into such dramatic prominence. A visitor to the sculpture promenade, in effect, floats in space, on a level with the cornice of the Smirke building. A place that, as one critic wrote in *The Independent*, "should not really exist". The whole experience is, indeed, as the *Church of England Newspaper* remarked in wonderment, "as though new spaces have been plucked from the air".

Great care has been taken to ensure minimum disturbance of the existing fabric. The new work has been installed as a free-standing structure, supported off just three slender columns along the centreline of the gap, with outstretched tapered arms holding up the staircase and the two floors. The bracket is connected to the wall on one side only, to provide lateral support, but elsewhere the floors barely touch the walls, the separateness accentuated by glass margins along their edges. The stairs too are glazed — with open treads of sandblasted glass — allowing light to flood through from above.

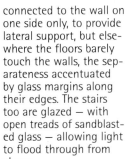

What was done by Foster Associates at the Royal Academy has a directness and honesty that has been evident to every visitor since the galleries opened. The relationship of old and new that was created does not require explanation, nor is there any question that the effect achieved was intentional. When the art magazine *Modern Painters* asked Norman Foster if, given an unlimited budget, he would not have preferred to design something that would have made 'the gap' entirely his own, he rightly replied, "It *is* entirely my own. It is a deliberate interpretation of how you relate the old to the new and get something richer and more dynamic out of both".

Martin Pawley

Fabricated specially for this project, the all-glass hydraulic lift rises along two tubular guide-rails that also support the glass doors at each floor. There is no shaft as such, the lift rising in free space and the floors cut back to allow a clear view up, or down, the full height of the gap.

The glass staircase employs no flamboyance whatsoever, other than to ensure the least possible structure to do the job. Thin steel stringers — each in two halves between which the glass balustrade is clamped — support narrow steel frames into which are set the sand-blasted glass treads.

"The whole experience has an otherworldly, almost sensual, quality. Far from fighting the older wings, the Modernist intrusion Sir Norman has designed seems to caress them. Architectural ornament that was once seen at a distance is now encountered up close, and it takes an altogether different cast. Indeed, in one of his most striking gestures, Sir Norman has turned the cornice of the main galleries into a long shelf for sculpture, a kind of podium running the length of the reception area."

Paul Goldberger, *The New York Times*, 31 May 1992

The south gallery during the Anthony Caro exhibition. Air quality is carefully controlled to provide constant levels of humidity and temperature, using packaged air-handling units which sit on the roof over the sculpture promenade. Trunking is installed behind the curve of the ceiling and supplies diffusers which run around the junction between wall and ceiling. By distributing the air upwards and downwards in equal proportions it has proved possible to mix the room air rapidly without producing high air velocities at the picture plane. The air is extracted at low level, through narrow slots just above the limestone skirting.

The south gallery in 1996, during an exhibition of the works of Roger de Grey, President of the Royal Academy 1984-1993. Natural top-lighting is controlled by two sets of louvres set at 90 degrees to each other. The outer set is electronically controlled while inside are larger fixed fins which also carry the spotlights. Lighting levels between 50 lux and full daylight are possible.

"Like all the best conjurors, [Foster] has extracted the maximum effect from a very shallow hat. It is particularly rewarding to produce a late-twentieth-century gem that dignifies the work of Ware and Smirke without artifice or compromise."

Extract from the report for the RIBA Architecture Award of 1992

The sculpture promenade at dusk. The height of the promenade was determined by the largest available sheets of laminated glass. Measuring 2 x 4 metres, the double-glazed panels have an outer sheet of clear laminated glass and an inner sheet of white low-oxide glass from Czechoslovakia.

A Client's View
by Piers Rogers

Piers Rogers trained as a Classicist at Oxford, though his first job was as a merchant banker in the City of London. In 1973 he moved to Paris, where he was Director of the International Council on Monuments and Sites, and a UNESCO consultant on the implementation of the World Heritage Convention. An interest in Islamic architecture led to his being an assessor for the Aga Khan Awards for Architecture in 1980 and 1983. In 1981 he returned to England and was appointed Secretary of the Royal Academy, a position which he held until 1996. As Secretary, with the then President, Sir Roger de Grey, he acted as client for the Sackler Galleries. He is now Director of the Royal Academy's Burlington Gardens project.

The choice, in early 1985, of Norman Foster as architect for the renovation of the Royal Academy's old Diploma Galleries was, in one way, a natural one. The Academy has always turned to its architect members when building work needed to be done, and though Foster, elected in 1983, had won himself a brilliant reputation abroad, he had never had the opportunity to work on a public building in London.

In other ways, however, the decision was paradoxical: the project was modest in scale when compared with the Hongkong Bank, then nearing completion, or Stansted Airport, his most recent commission which was just about to start on site. Moreover, Foster had never previously worked in the context of an existing building, let alone a building so redolent of history as Burlington House.

Interestingly, it was a straightforward appointment, without any of the competitive process which has now become standard. The Academy's Council was easily enough won over by Roger de Grey's insistence on creating something new, and when, some months later, he and I began talking to Arthur and Jill Sackler about our hopes and plans, this attitude certainly commended itself to them.

So the Academy appointed an architect, but did not commit itself to a design. In fact, the terms of the appointment were simply to "design the new Diploma Galleries, together with the approaches to them". Foster himself suggested the latter should begin in the entrance hall, and the brief was something which we worked on together.

In retrospect, it would have been folly to do otherwise, as this apparently simple project had extraordinarily complex implications for the fabric of the building and the operation of the Academy. These ranged from the underpinning of the foundations and the renewal of the drains, through the reorganisation of the kitchens and the displacement of public lavatories and a large proportion of the Academy's staff, to the restoration of the old garden front of Burlington House and the implementation of a fire strategy for the whole building.

Not least of these complications was the number of architects involved in this complex web of transactions. The Academy's Surveyor, advised by Trevor Dannatt RA, was responsible for all the works up to and including the ground floor slab, which was set out in such a way as to accommodate the Foster-designed structure above. John Partridge RA designed new kitchens, porters' rooms and circulation route in the basement area; Leonard Manasseh RA, a new escape stairs for the library. H. T. Cadbury-Brown RA was asked to fit out the new anteroom to the library — as created in the Foster plan — and Julian Harrap oversaw the restoration work. All were informed by a strategic survey undertaken by Arup Associates and Sir Philip Dowson RA. This arrangement was certainly unconventional and its success must be attributed to the finesse and skill of all involved.

It was, perhaps, unsurprising that design work continued for nearly three years, from the summer of 1985 to the summer of 1988, before the client committee — which involved yet more Academicians — was ready to recommend to the Council that the scheme be accepted "as proposed". And another year was needed before the start on site.

This lengthy process had a number of strands running through it. First, the Academy had very definite requirements for the showing of works of art, which necessitated a detailed study of lighting — both natural and artificial — air movement patterns, security measures and so on. The form of the gallery ceiling was largely dictated by the desire to have the light spill down the walls with a subtle gradation of intensity, and without the strong shadows of the original coffered ceiling.

Then there were the implications of working within the envelope of a historic building: after a brief flirtation with columnar and open-plan solutions, it was decided that the galleries should reflect the basic layout of the original seventeenth-century house, with a spine wall and two wings, the east wing being the library. The height of the roof was dictated by the sight-lines from Piccadilly, to ensure it could not be seen above the original parapet.

The terms of the commission did not specify how access was to be improved, and Foster's analysis concluded that there was no future in the dark, winding Victorian staircase. He proposed, instead, that the gap between the old Burlington House and the nineteenth-century Main Gallery must be used to establish new links between the public parts of the building, by enclosing an area previously open to the sky. In the end, this space was given an ambiguous, indoor/outdoor character.

The façades of the two buildings were restored as external walls — even to the extent of keeping the down-pipes which carry water off the Main Gallery's roof — and generous natural light was allowed to flood down from above, unimpeded by the steel-and-glass structures of the lift and staircase; the glass margins of the intermediate floors were designed to allow the passage of light and to enable the façades to be 'read' correctly.

The complexity of the project was equalled by the logistical problems of getting the work done in a very restricted space, with very limited access, in the heart of a building full of priceless works of art; and with an uninterrupted exhibition programme that would attract more than two million visitors during the construction period. Fortunately, the Academy recognised early on that it had none of the skills necessary to co-ordinate the project — let alone to schedule the work of 14 different trades in a space barely 14 feet wide — and appointed Bovis as management contractor.

At this point, the larger-than-life figure of Arthur Sackler must be mentioned. He and Foster hit it off from the start. Arthur was always pushing for more. He saw the lift-well as a 'vertical museum' — at one stage there were plans to 'hang' sculpture in it — and he imagined a 'sculpture court' cantilevered out over the Main Gallery roof: a problematical suggestion which Foster most adroitly resolved by extending the reception area over the Main Gallery cornice and placing statues along it, almost in the Baroque manner.

Roger de Grey's enthusiasm and Arthur Sackler's ebullience — until his untimely death in 1987 — carried all before them. I had the less glamorous task of ensuring that the Academy's practical needs were met, within the budget. But I gained enormous satisfaction from being involved with a bold attempt to integrate new architecture with old.

Years before, when I worked on architectural heritage at UNESCO, I had argued that conservation meant continuity, and that the qualities of an old building could be better served by sensitive additions in a contemporary style, than by feeble pastiche, but there were all too few examples of success to point to in support of this argument. To be involved in creating one was a privilege.

1986-1989 The Sackler Gallery
The Museum of Israel
Jerusalem

The involvement of Foster Associates with the Arthur M. Sackler Foundation for the Arts, Sciences and Humanities went beyond the Royal Academy project in London. For some time, Dr Sackler had wished to create, in Jerusalem, what he considered his most important project: a gallery to house part of his considerable art collection. It is a mark of the close relationship that had developed between Dr Sackler and Norman Foster during the Academy project — "speaking the same language", in the words of Dr Sackler — that he invited Foster to undertake the design. After the philanthropist's death, in 1987, this plan was actively encouraged by Dr Sackler's widow Jill, who continued as president of the Sackler Foundation.

Norman and Wendy Foster made their first visit to Jerusalem in 1986 and, after a series of meetings with the Sacklers, drew up an outline brief. Following Dr Sackler's untimely death a second visit was deferred until February 1988, when Norman and Wendy Foster, accompanied this time by Ken Shuttleworth and Rodney Uren, flew out to examine two possible locations for the new building that had been identified by the city authorities, and to gain a better understanding of the city as a whole.

The first location was a sloping site within the western curtilage of the Museum of Israel near the Shrine of the Book, a large building with a prominent golden dome that houses the Dead Sea Scrolls. Close by was the Billy Rose sculpture garden, designed in the early 1960s by the Japanese-American sculptor Isamu Noguchi.

Though enjoying excellent views out to the north-west, this site seemed impossibly compromised by the sloping terrain and its proximity to the sacred symbol of the shrine. The second site, on the other hand, about half a mile away to the north and near a large stadium, had no established architectural context. Here it would be possible to express a major new building with greater freedom, giving the collection — and its donor — a clearer identity.

Just as important as the site visits was the opportunity for the team to wander through the old quarters of the city, with their rich stone architecture suffused with the warm glow of the local limestone that had so impressed Isamu Noguchi a generation earlier. The experience was to have a strong influence on the project.

Before the team returned to London there was a review of the project, attended by the Mayor Teddy Kollick — who had been personally

During the early site visits, the design team took time to walk through the old quarters of Jerusalem and absorb the 'spirit' of the city, "that tangible but unquantifiable flavour" described by Norman Foster as the "vital ingredient in the design process of any building".

The use of stone in walls and floors was documented in examples which ranged from historic structures to the most recent buildings. The challenge of incorporating this strong tradition in the new project was to be an active stimulus throughout the early stages of the design.

"That same concern arises in a recent project for the Sackler Foundation in Jerusalem. Here, we were presented with the challenge of designing a building next to the Shrine of the Book, the home of the Dead Sea Scrolls and symbolically a very important building. Our new gallery needed to establish its own identity and had to respect the landscape, yet at the same time defer to the Shrine."

Norman Foster, lecture at the Architectural Institute of Japan, Tokyo, August 1988

The design team was highly critical of recent attempts to incorporate local stone in buildings in the form of thin veneers, preferring instead the solidity of traditional building methods. It was this quality that Norman Foster would seek to express in his early design sketches.

involved since the beginning — and other interested parties. The museum's representative and the city engineer understood the appeal of the remote location but felt compelled to express their preference for the museum site, not least on the grounds of the readily available access for services and visitors. Unexpectedly, the Foster team agreed. Not only were they sympathetic to the practical arguments, but they were also becoming increasingly excited by the challenge of deferring to the historic context and creating a subterranean, cave-like gallery.

Once back in London, the Foster team considered a number of outline design studies, resulting in their clear preference for the Museum of Israel site. Then, in conformity with an agreement made with the Sackler Foundation and the museum vice-chairman, their first proposal was forwarded to Jerusalem. This was not a fully worked out design, but various sketches by Norman Foster — supported by photographs of the old city, concept drawings and a study model — which proposed adapting the indigenous stone crescents built for centuries in the region to prevent soil erosion on hill slopes, crescents which had already served as an inspiration for the mounds in the Billy Rose sculpture garden.

Immediately adjacent to the preferred site for the new gallery were two stone crescents of the kind used traditionally in the region to terrace the available arable land and prevent soil erosion. Their structural form was to inform the first design proposals.

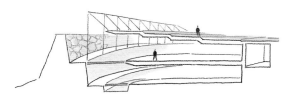

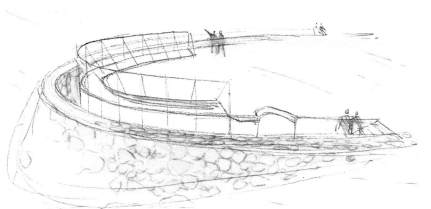

The possibility of building underground, yet creating a space flooded with natural light, captured Norman Foster's imagination and led to a sequence of sketches that sought to convey the spirit of the new building. Better than any orthogonal drawing, these formed the first submission to the Museum of Israel.

Norman Foster's sketches invest the building with a complex layering of space — with floating floor-plates set back at different distances from the external wall; sweeping ramps that encircle an indeterminate boundary between inside and out; and viewing platforms for the visiting public at every level.

The new gallery tied into the existing circulation patterns on the museum site in such a way that it was possible to maintain the strict separation of public and private areas throughout.

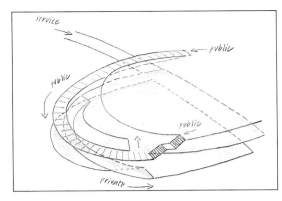

As Foster developed his ideas through the sketches, the absolute solidity of the external crescent wall he envisaged became ever more apparent, with the wall sculpted on its internal face to create a series of wide access ramps and viewing platforms reminiscent of ancient fortifications.

walking down the ramp even when the gallery is closed could be an exciting public event.

A small pool was proposed for the lowest gallery level, positioned beneath the soaring rooflight. Animated with fountains, a traditional cooling device in hot climates, this would help reflect the daylight back into the gallery floors, the action of the fountains dappling the light and filling the gallery with the sound of running water.

157

Though all but invisible at ground level, in plan view it is immediately apparent just how large the new gallery would be, far larger than the two existing crescents alongside it and larger, too, than the Shrine of the Book.

The initial proposal was intended to house only part of Dr Sackler's collection. The concept was so well received, however, that questions of how the building might be expanded were soon raised. Ken Shuttleworth explored possible options in a series of sketches.

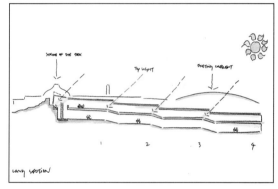

A model was made to accompany the initial sketch presentation, which unfortunately showed the new gallery rising somewhat higher than the Shrine of the Book. Later revisions placed the gallery further down the slope.

Two of the crescent structures that so intrigued the Foster team already marked the western boundary of the museum site. Foster proposed to excavate the space required by the new Sackler Gallery on a series of descending levels behind a third, much larger stone crescent of the same kind.

As Foster's sketches illustrate, access to the underground gallery space, both for visitors and service vehicles, was to have been by a curving ramp that led to floor levels set well below the top of the proposed sweeping crescent wall. The wall itself would have no projections, windows or openings to the outside. Only on the inside would a spiral ramp and steps lead to and from a viewing gallery located above and behind the parapet, sheltered from the wind and rain by a steeply pitched glass roof. Outside the building, visitors would be able to enjoy the view from a grassed roof, with the projecting glass serving as a partial wind and safety barrier.

The two existing crescents were to be landscaped to the same level as the gallery roof and integrated into the overall design. Once completed, grassed and planted with trees, the gallery itself would have been, to all intents and

Shuttleworth's revised design proposed that the original gallery would be only the first of four phases stretching along the hillside, below the existing crescents.

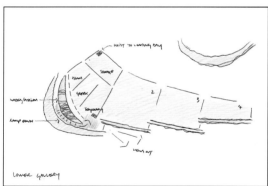

As before, the new design was to be fully integrated into the existing landscape of the museum campus, with only a raised rooflight to indicate the building's presence.

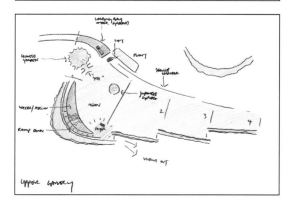

158

With its undulating grass roof, the original gallery integrated itself into the site almost as a continuation of the natural landscape. This was more difficult to achieve with the revised design but, positioned further down the slope, it would remain equally invisible from the rest of the museum.

purposes, invisible against the slope of the hill, with only the glass prisms signalling its presence from afar.

Originally the proposed gallery space was to have been relatively small, consisting of two subterranean floor levels opening on to a large, curving double-height space, set behind the parapet of the crescent retaining wall. The bottom level was marked by a small pool, positioned to cast dappled reflections upwards. This space was to have been articulated by means of giant steps formed in the wall itself, like fire steps in a nineteenth-century fortress. These steps, in turn, would have acted as a system of intersecting ramps, providing access to the gallery from outside via a descending path orbiting the curve of the crescent, and internally providing access to the lower level for the staff.

The proposal received enthusiastic approval, but raised the question of future expansion. The outcome was a more ambitious project in which four stepped galleries of increasing size would have skirted the slope of the site behind straight, battered stone walls before finally opening on to the original double-height space. In this final variant of the scheme, the culminating gallery was to have been only the first

of a four-phase excavation destined, when completed, to yield between 4800 and 7100 square metres of underground gallery space, with each gallery overlooking its downhill neighbour as it stepped back up the slope. Designed as an important extension to the Museum of Israel, the enlarged version of the Sackler Gallery would have contained Egyptian, Greek, Roman, Islamic, Iranian, Anatolian and Syrian exhibits, as well as temporary exhibitions and items from China, Korea and Japan.

The project remains in limbo through lack of funding, in part complicated by the legal circumstances which followed the death of Dr Sackler. However, it remains of interest as one of a sequence of designs stretching from the Retreat, overlooking the Fal estuary in Cornwall, to the Museum of Prehistory, close to the Gorge du Verdon in France; from the Son Recreation Centre, in Norway, to the Crescent Wing at the University of East Anglia and, more recently, to proposals for the extension of the Prado in Madrid — all designs that are partially buried in the landscape, but all of which maintain access to natural light, views and orientation.

Martin Pawley/Norman Foster

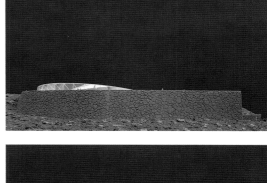

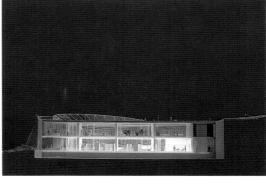

The hillside elevation and a cross-section through phase one of the revised design. Support spaces for the main galleries, including the plant rooms and a significant area of secure storage, were placed on the inside of the slope, away from the available daylight.

In the final presentation model, made shortly before the project was put indefinitely on hold, the rooflight marking the entrance atrium was supplemented with further rooflights marking the steps between the different phases and a new circular opening over the centre of the original gallery.

The Crescent Wing
University of East Anglia
Norwich

The Sainsbury Centre for the Visual Arts, set on the edge of the University of East Anglia's campus outside Norwich, is one of Foster Associates' most completely satisfying achievements. Its impact is as immediate and, indeed, as sensational now as it was on the opening day in 1978.

Like many of the office's most significant buildings, the Sainsbury Centre reflects something more than just a clear and decisive response to a client brief — the vital ingredient in any good building. Norman Foster had never built a museum or gallery before, but this was to his advantage, perhaps, in the eyes of Sir Robert and Lady Sainsbury, whose much-loved and very personal art collection the building was to house.

The Sainsburys disliked the idea of a conventional museum. They had warmed to Foster's view that "the experience was all-important", that the new building should be "a nice place to be", more like a living room than a museum gallery, and an enjoyable place for students — including, in particular, those in the School of Fine Arts — and the public. There was from the beginning a close sympathy, a fellow feeling, between architect and client and an implicit understanding as to the nature of the project.

The serenity of the gallery — or 'living area' — containing Robert and Lisa Sainsbury's extraordinary collection, remains total. The building itself, defined by the great extrusion that forms its walls and roof — conventional terms that hardly seem relevant — is totally uncompromised by the smaller structures and objects that sit beneath it.

The building is, however, underpinned — literally — by a domain that public and students never see, a narrow undercroft of storerooms, conservation laboratories and workshops running its full length and connected to the gallery level by lifts and inconspicuous spiral stairs: one emerges in the middle of the gallery's information and sales desk. At the west end of the building, a ramp dives down to provide vehicular access to a loading area. From the restaurant, looking westward through the glazed end wall, this great slit in the land is not seen but it is vital to the functioning of the centre.

The Crescent Wing, opened in 1991, can be seen in the context of the original Sainsbury Centre as a radical change in mood and direction. Yet the vital clues to its eventual form and character are clearly present in the 1970s building. In response to critics who suggest that the

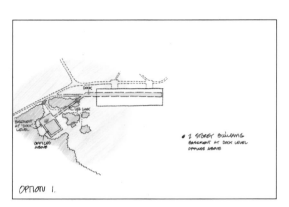

OPTION 1.

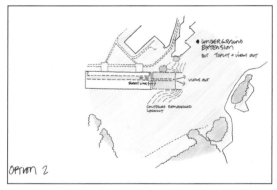

OPTION 2

Although the new building could not work independently of the Sainsbury Centre, it could work at one remove. A variety of options was explored, including building in the nearby woods, but the idea of an underground extension seemed to offer better possibilities.

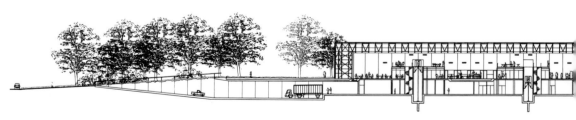

Both had a clear, and shared, vision of what they were trying to achieve.

The fine arts students and their teachers were to share the building, using seminar rooms and a library contained within the great space of the building, so that the objects in the collection would be part of their everyday working lives. Separate buildings were considered, but the "vast and sleek shed", to use Reyner Banham's phrase, the last word in a long line of such structures designed by Foster and his team, happily embraced every activity, including a heavily-used restaurant.

Wing is not the 'obvious' solution to the problem of extending a structure that had already attained near-canonic status, Norman Foster responds: "we don't do the obvious — we're always open-minded, ready to discard our preconceptions."

Foster had always envisaged the possibility of an extension of the Centre to the east, taking advantage of the natural fall in the landscape to the artificial lake — created as part of Denys Lasdun's UEA masterplan. When the idea of extending the building was first seriously discussed,

As this sketch demonstrates, Norman Foster's first reaction to the proposed new extension to the Sainsbury Centre was to look at ways of expanding the original building. It soon became clear, however, that the brief made this approach inappropriate.

By 1986, the original collection had more than doubled in size. Rather than hide most of it away in storage, the Sainsburys proposed adding a new 'reserve gallery', based on the Metropolitan Museum's highly successful Study Centre in New York *(right)*, where art in storage remains accessible at all times.

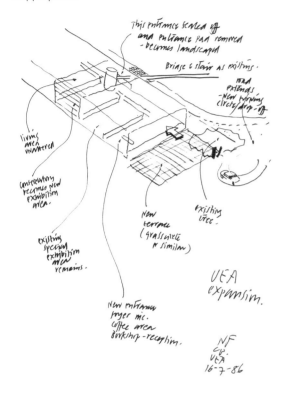

however, in 1986, the scale of what was envisaged seemed to imply that the original envelope of the building would grow. Possible options for extending the shed, a natural enough solution, were sketched. "If that approach had been right, we would have fought for it", Foster insists. But it soon became clear that there were very sound reasons, quite apart from the Sainsburys' great affection for the building as it stood and reluctance to see it changed, for adopting a very different approach.

The brief for what became the Crescent Wing was well defined and quite distinct from that of the original building. Although the Sainsburys had donated a number of works of art to the Centre since its opening, there was no great pressure of space in the main gallery. That said, there were very good arguments for rotating the items on display so as to avoid any impression that the Centre was a static entity.

However, there was a growing belief that it should also be possible for works in reserve to be made available to the public and scholars who came to study them, rather than locked away unseen for years. (The Sainsburys had seen, and admired, the study centre at the Metropolitan Museum in New York, where pictures were kept

secure but accessible in a system of sliding glass cases.) They should be displayed in an attractive, but quite distinct, space: the first element in the brief for the extension.

The Centre's laboratories and workshops had proved inadequate in scale: more and better facilities were badly needed. Neither was there anything more than token office space. Visiting exhibitions, too, had become an important part of the Centre's activities. Such was the nature of the building, however, that light levels — perfectly acceptable for most art works — could not be dimmed to the level demanded for delicate watercolours and drawings, and the latter could not be shown in the Centre. None of these facilities, it seemed, could be very readily supplied merely by extending the building. But the fact remained that the Centre was becoming too small for all the activities it housed.

The empathy between architect and client which had characterised the original project was rekindled as a solution to the problem was developed. Implicit to the scheme which did emerge was the realisation that the new space would be ancillary and subsidiary to the rest of the Centre. That being the case, one approach was to locate the addition away from the main building in a nearby wood, thus responding to the founders' preference that the latter should be left uncompromised. An underground passage could link the two. In terms of security, convenience, economy and architectural logic that solution was quickly ruled out. In any case, the idea of deliberately hiding the new building away, as if it were something to be ashamed of, seemed quite perverse.

The inevitable way forward, it was eventually concluded, was to extend the existing basement. By taking advantage of the fall in the land towards the lake, the extension could be allowed to 'emerge' into daylight. In that way,

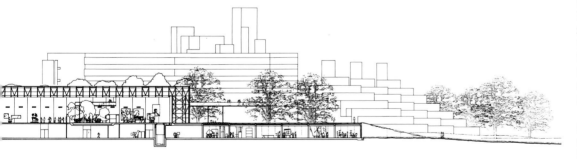

Hidden from view, many of the Sainsbury Centre's existing service areas are already located in an extensive undercroft. The underground extension formed a logical expansion of this area, while also creating a secure link for the movement of art between the two buildings.

Placed at the east end of the Sainsbury Centre, where it was closest to the rest of the campus, the new building was also able to take advantage of the fall of the land and emerge 'naturally' into the daylight.

It was no secret that Sir Robert and Lady Sainsbury considered the existing building as one of the highlights of their collection, and they soon made it clear that they were reluctant to see it — or its relationship to the site — changed to any great extent.

It is interesting to note that an extension of the undercroft had been considered during the design of the original building *(see volume 2, page 97)*. Norman Foster's sketches for the new building picked up where that long-forgotten proposal had left off.

both dark and daylit spaces could be provided: an office without natural light was clearly unacceptable. The attractions of a basement level extension were manifold, not least in terms of economy. The new facilities would be yards away from the gallery.

With ecological issues increasingly to the fore — though the original Centre had never been an energy-extravagant building — an earth roof made sense. Moreover, the grass would extend right up to the eastern elevation as it had always done and the view out would remain uncompromised. The geometry of the extension, it was assumed, would reflect that of the original Centre: the new wing would terminate in a straight edge to the landscape. In July 1988, however, the brief was extended to include provision for a new lecture hall. In due course, this space was to be critical to the plan of the Crescent Wing.

As the concept design developed, the particular needs of the various spaces were more closely defined. Photographic darkrooms — one requirement — obviously needed to be capable of total black-out. Other rooms needed carefully controlled daylight. In the offices good natural light was vital. One problem was that the end

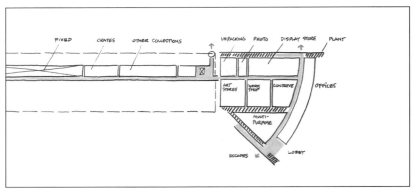

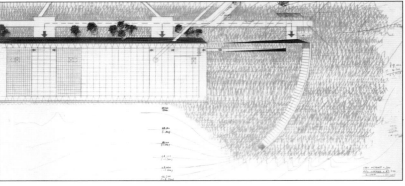

elevation of the extension would be relatively narrow — matching the dimensions of the original building — limiting the number of office spaces which could benefit from daylight and views, even though the client had steadily increased the office element in the brief.

The revised brief demanded an extension of around 2300 square metres, which implied a relatively deep building with limited exposure to natural light. In one of those adroit moves which underscores its claim to operate without preconceptions, the Foster office thought again — and came up with the idea of the curve, the sickle, the crescent. Norman Foster describes this move as "more radical than extending the original building — that was obvious. This was a response to real needs, not a mere gesture".

It also offered a counterpoint to the shed — a 'cave', if you like, to the original 'tent'. (Were there echoes here of the little seaside 'retreat' Foster designed, in his Team 4 days with Richard Rogers, for the Brumwell family?) In retrospect, the move away from a strictly rectilinear geometry seems forward-looking, a step towards a more organic and freer architecture — and to themes which have become apparent in the

Reconciling the needs of the brief with the natural slope of the land was *the* major challenge during the early stages of the design, and it was only resolved when the design team realised the multi-purpose gallery would work equally well as a triangular space or as one that was rectangular. The 'crescent' was born.

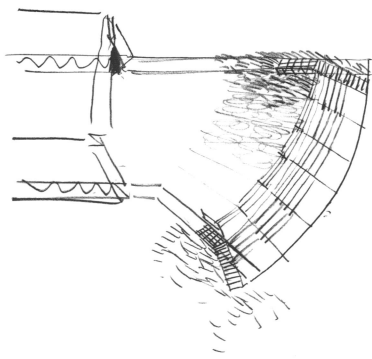

The definitive view from the Sainsbury Centre, looking out from the east wall towards the lake, over an unsullied landscape. It was decided at a very early stage that this view should not be compromised in any way.

office's architecture of the mid-1990s. Foster insists, however, that it was simply a response to a specific functional requirement, a 'natural' solution.

At one stroke, the problem of how to incorporate an adequate area of daylit offices was solved: the offices were strung along the sweep of the crescent, looking out to the park. Individually small in size, they could be all-but square, with only a slight canting of walls to take in the curve.

The planning of the other spaces remained difficult. "We struggled with the plan", admits partner Graham Phillips. It was illogical to have workshops and storerooms that were anything but rectangular. The architects, however, were coming up with some odd and awkward spaces that seemed to bring into question the whole 'crescent' strategy.

The lecture room, which was required to double-up as an occasional gallery, became the crux, the pivot, on which the difficulties of the plan were resolved. By making the lecture room triangular, the design team was able to reconcile the two geometries — the rectangular, a continuation of the 1970s building, and the curvilinear of the new extension.

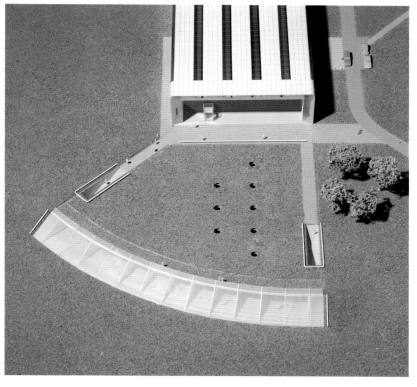

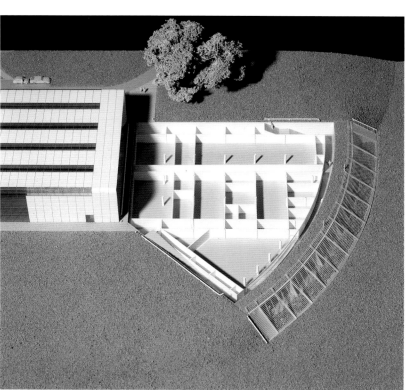

Once the idea of the triangular gallery had been accepted, the planning of the other major internal spaces — and their relationship with the daylit offices that form the crescent — fell into place with relative ease. This is not to say that options were not explored, however, including this early proposal that extended the basement corridor of the original building right through the new wing.

With only a seemingly arbitrary pattern of rooflights, ramps and glazing visible above ground, it is not immediately apparent that the 3000 square metres of floorspace provided in the new wing is actually two-thirds the footprint of the original building. With so large an area, the early plans assumed two access ramps would be necessary to satisfy means of escape. In the final design, however, escape doors were incorporated in the crescent of glazing, allowing the secondary ramp from the multi-purpose space to be omitted.

163

In the final design, the conservation laboratories form the core of the plan, around which are arrayed service areas, the reserve gallery and offices, and the multi-purpose space. Circulation is generous to ensure large works of art can be moved between the various areas with the maximum of ease.

1 entrance ramp
2 reception
3 glazed corridor
4 offices
5 multi-purpose gallery
6 internal corridor
7 reserve gallery
8 lavatories
9 conservation laboratories
10 projection room
11 workshops
12 original service area

Below: though useful in detail planning terms, the presentation model proved less successful in conveying the spirit of the building in the landscape — though this view of the model internally lit captures something of the drama of the building at night.

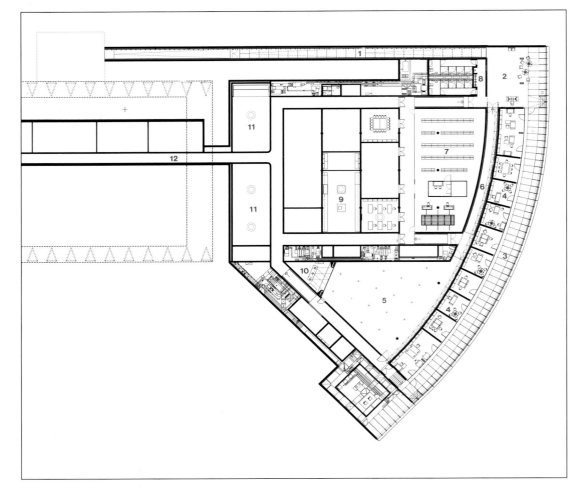

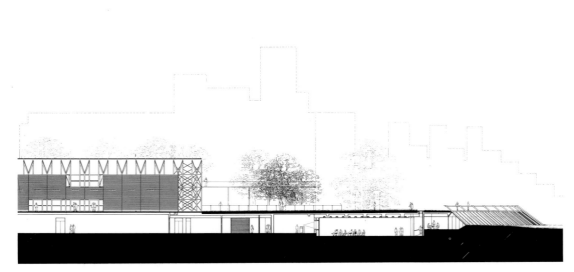

An architect working in the Classical tradition would have used a circle to the same effect. The office's rationalism ruled out such an obvious device. In effect, the lecture room is a left-over wedge of space. It is, at first sight, a curious space, though it works very well for its purpose.

In its final form, the plan combines an area of rectangular spaces connected by corridors, a projection of the footprint of the 1970s basement, counterpoised by the curve of the office wing. The space housing the reserve collection is curved to the east, where it abuts a ramp down to the lecture room. By setting the offices back from the external edge and providing access to them along a generous curved gallery on the perimeter, the need for an artificially-lit internal corridor is removed, though the offices remain generously daylit.

Since the Crescent Wing — as it became known — was conceived as ancillary to and an

extension of the original Sainsbury Centre, the need for a separate entrance might not seem obvious. However, there is no interconnection for the public between the Wing and the original Centre. Instead, the visitor proceeds down a long ramp, which begins exactly opposite the Centre's main door, and arrives in a separate reception area, from which he or she chooses to go into the offices, the lecture room or the reserve collection.

The stores and workshops, of course, are also accessible from this route but can equally be seen as a continuation of the private world of the undercroft, restricted to staff and to the storage or conservation of objects. The Sainsburys had always reacted against the idea of extensive basements, and to the notion of activities being hidden away — but, in the end, practical requirements prevailed.

Being self-contained, it proved possible to build the new wing without disrupting the day-to-day operations of the older building above in any way. The final link to the existing service areas was made only at the last possible moment, when the new wing was nearly complete.

The client insisted on separate access to the Crescent Wing, with the result that it offers a quite distinct experience from that of the main building. To enter it, visitors must leave the latter and go outside. Architecturally, the decision allowed for a dramatic device: the long ramp leading to a reception area which, far from being the dark underground space one might expect, instead opens on to a panorama of the lake beyond. Initially, the ramp was floored in non-slip rubber, but there were problems with this finish and granite was substituted.

The fact that the Sainsbury Centre had not been air-conditioned was questioned at the time of its completion in 1978, even though the cost of running an air-conditioned gallery could never have been sustained. The decision was soon justified, however, when climatic control by more 'natural' means proved just as effective, and with substantial savings in running costs.

In the Crescent Wing, extensive mechanical ventilation and cooling was inevitable, particularly in workshops and laboratories — where sophisticated extraction and filtration systems were needed to cope with the effects of chemical fumes and dust, and to comply with health and safety regulations. However, with the building being below ground, a high degree of insulation was secured. Consequently, the offices are not air-conditioned, but have mechanically adjustable blinds to give occupants a degree of control over their micro-climate.

The Sainsbury Centre had been built for flexibility. In the Crescent Wing, the spaces are largely fixed — with solid blockwork walls, plastered where appropriate. Close attention was given to the quality of the plasterwork to achieve an impressively exact 'sculptural' look.

The external face of the Crescent Wing is the curved, glazed wall looking out over the

The final position, radius and length of the crescent of glazing was carefully calculated to match the existing contours of the landscape as closely as possible. In the final design, the glazed corridor at the 'front' of the building has been supplemented by individual rooflights over the workshops and a strip of glass set flush with the grass roof that illuminates an internal corridor.

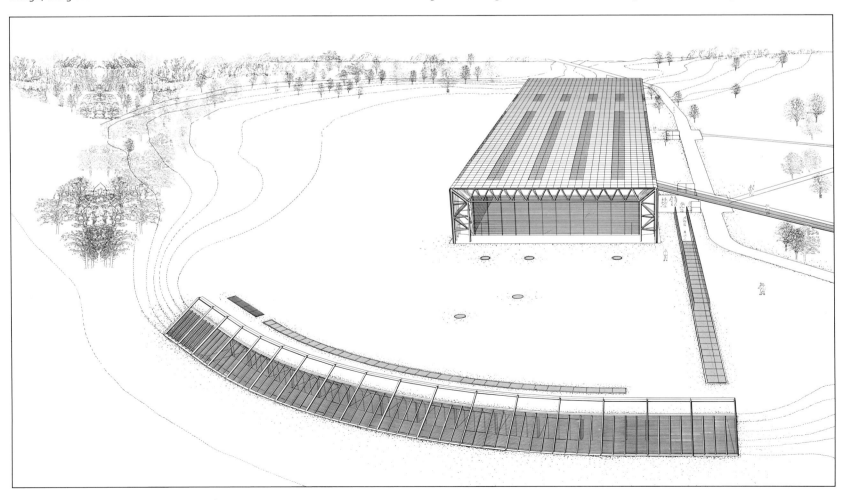

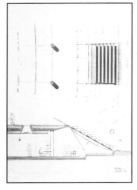

A variety of options was explored for the crescent of glazing, including this early proposal which set the actual glass wall behind a screen of external louvres.

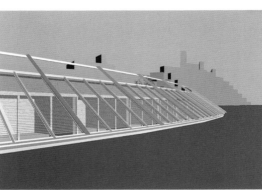

Though the glazed corridor faced east, away from the heat of the afternoon sun, solar gain was a major concern, and the effectiveness of various blinds, louvres and glass treatments was carefully studied. Most promising was a system whereby white ceramic stripes or dots are baked on to the surface of the glass.

Below: the offices lining the glazed corridor are fitted with internal blinds, to give their occupants control over levels of brightness and privacy.

green parkland. Initially, this was designed to consist of vertical glass panels. The addition of a sloping bank of louvres was a device that not only helped to mould the elevation to the contours of the land, but was, in fact, also functionally necessary to act as a sun screen. By using fritted glass, a material pioneered by the practice to combat solar gain, the office was subsequently able to dispense with the louvres and substitute inclined panes of glass — a much more elegant solution.

The engineering of this wall was far from straightforward and was explored in drawings, models and in the form of a full-size mock-up. The double-glazed elevation also had to accommodate a fire escape door, but this has been successfully inserted in a way that does not disturb the serenity of the great sweep of glazing.

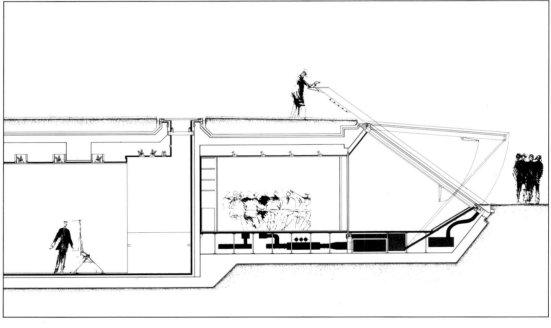

While the glazed corridor presented one set of problems to be solved — not least a safe mechanism for the escape doors — the desire to set the rooflights flush with the surface of the grass roof created quite another. The solution required concrete work of the highest precision.

In the final design, the glass wall of the external corridor is coated with a regular grid of white ceramic dots — or frits — the dots progressively increasing in width to create a sheet of glass virtually transparent at the bottom and opaque at the top.

Achieving a balance between natural and artificial lighting was a key element in the success of the final scheme. The Wing's flat, grass-covered roof is pierced by five circular rooflights which bring daylight into internal workshop spaces by means of reflecting lenses. Daylight floods into the depths of the building down the long ramps.

In contrast, the lecture room/gallery is entirely artificially-lit. Indeed, it contains a highly sophisticated lighting system — devised by George Sexton — which is adaptable to a wide variety of uses and occasions, thus providing a valuable learning resource for students of museum design. Lighting elsewhere ranges from recessed floor uplighters, on the entrance ramp, to low-voltage spots in the office corridor. All is carefully thought through to ensure the Crescent Wing makes highly effective but unshowy use of advanced building technology, taking its cue from the ecologically-friendly Sainsbury Centre.

Manufactured by MBM, the external glass wall required a level of technical virtuosity rarely seen on a construction site. The escape door, in particular, demanded meticulous attention to ensure it could be opened at all times with the minimum of effort.

It would be easy to see the Crescent Wing as a symbol of changing attitudes to architecture in Britain between the 1970s and 1990s. By 1991, when the building was completed, Foster Associates' Willis Faber building in Ipswich had been listed Grade I – ranking it alongside Hampton Court and Westminster Abbey. The Crescent Wing chose to go – largely – underground, a 'safe' solution it might be argued, but at odds with the radical spirit of the original.

This is an interpretation which Foster, not surprisingly, rejects: extending the original building would, he insists, have been a less radical way of achieving the desired ends. More importantly, it would have failed to meet the brief.

None the less, the completed Crescent Wing has a character quite distinct from that of the Sainsbury Centre proper. It reflects a growing concern for context which is present in a number of the office's projects of the period and which is paralleled in the work of Foster's contemporaries around the world. The fact that the immediate context – more important than that

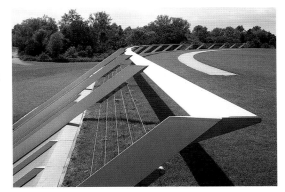

Accentuating the streamlined form of the glass crescent, the protective handrail was formed by simply extending the existing mullions up to meet a generously wide ledge, perfect for leaning on and enjoying the view.

A full-size mock-up of a section of glazed corridor was erected in a quiet corner of the Great Portland Street office to ensure that the junctions between what were otherwise standard elements were fully resolved before construction began on site.

The 70-metre ramp linking the Sainsbury Centre to the new wing sinks gently into the surrounding landscape, protected only by a minimal glass enclosure. Underfloor heating ensures it can never ice up during cold weather.

of the landscape or the earlier, much respected work of Lasdun – was an earlier building by the office was immaterial, if ironic.

Norman Foster's description of the relationship between the new and the old – the 'cave' and the 'tent' – is telling. The original Centre is notable for its clarity, immediacy and single-mindedness. The overriding idea behind the building is expressed with a strength and a conviction that overrides the conflicting demands of a multiplicity of uses, subordinating all to a calm serenity.

The Classical, even 'Platonic', qualities of the building have been the subject of extended critical comment. It sits in the landscape with all the assurance of a Georgian country house. The

"Inside, the new wing is coldly impressive. The study collection is housed in jewel-like cases — beautifully made and lit. The conservation workshops, photographic studios and storage spaces are all so lavish and state-of-the-art as to make most museum curators salivate in envy. Otherwise spatial excitement is muted. The only big gesture, ironically, is something the public will not see: the corridor that sweeps round in a curve beneath the glass windscreen. Tiger-striped with shadow, this is a marvellous piece of pure abstraction. "

Alastair Best, *The Independent*, 8 May 1991

Crescent Wing is, in comparison, secretive, subtle, complex, linked to its parent building yet with a life of its own.

From the south-east, the Sainsbury Centre now rises not from the grass, as it once did, but from a sweeping man-made ridge of glass, catching the sunlight by day and brilliantly lit after dark. The Crescent Wing is almost entirely underground, yet the 'ground' above it is mostly a relatively thin, 300mm layer of soil, sitting on a concrete slab, used as an energy-efficient roofing material. Only the rooflights which protrude through the turf give the game away. (Precautions were taken to prevent heavy vehicles from driving across this area — there is a defined route for emergency services.)

Seen in this light, the Wing can be read not so much as the solid podium on which the Centre sits but as a narthex in the tradition of that which fronts the Romanesque cathedral

During the day *(right)*, the glazed corridor is an ethereal space dominated by its silent, sweeping view over the Norfolk countryside. At night *(above)*, the view moves inward on to an animated scene of offices and sharp splashes of colour.

at Durham. The visitor walking across the grass roof is unaware of the building below until he reaches the crest of the ridge and peers over the balustrade — a feature of aerodynamic elegance — on to the inclined planes of glass below.

The eventual form of the entrance ramp takes the visitor down a deep slit — initially open to the air but largely covered in translucent sheets of toughened glass set into the grass — into a spacious reception area with fine views out to the park and lake. Its character is semi-public. Visitors pass through it to access

"The interior of the building, finished almost exclusively in non-reflective white, exudes an air of space-age hygiene. Low light levels, simple lines and hushed corridors prevail."

Matthew Coomber,
Building, 24 May 1991

In recent lectures Norman Foster has sought to convey the spirit of the building in two simple images that demonstrate how a minimal intervention in the landscape can create elegant, light-filled spaces where none should really exist.

"Close by is a spacious conservation room, quite unlike the cramped holes to which conservators are so often relegated, and a de-infestation room where exhibits can be deep frozen in order to rid them of their un-welcome visitors. Apart from all that, the study reserve is breathtaking. Glazed cabinets house the three-dimensional pieces, whilst rows of mechanically moveable frames, equalled only by the Metropolitan Museum in New York, house the larger two-dimensional work."

Tony Warner, *Arts Review*, 12 July 1991

Under the best environmental conditions, the reserve collection *(above and right)* is housed in glass cases of various sizes, suitable for two- and three-dimensional works, whether large or small. To maximise space, many of the cases were modified from the Bruynzeel moveable storage system more usually used for books or files, allowing them to be stacked in groups and rolled out only when required.

the reserve collection and the special exhibitions in the lecture room/gallery or, indeed, on their way to lectures held in that area.

The entrance foyer is equally the frontispiece to the building's administrative offices. The typical visitor is not normally given access to the office corridor and has to be content with a tantalising glimpse along its curved length. Though there was a case for making this a public space and, perhaps, relocating the Centre's public café there from its existing location a floor above, the determination to stress the ancillary nature of the new building remained firm. All the principal visitor facilities remain in the Sainsbury Centre proper. It is the administrative – and some academic – staff who benefit from the daylight and the views.

The transition from 'above' to 'below' is total when the foyer is left behind and the visitor enters the enclosed world of the lecture room or reserve collection. This is as far as most people will go. Beyond is a secure zone of stores, workshops and laboratories, tailored to the specific needs of curators, conservators and technicians, and merging seamlessly with the 1970s undercroft. Yet there is nothing mean or second-rate about these spaces: indeed, they are generous in scale, well finished and well lit without being extravagant in detail or finish.

The Crescent Wing may be a considerable remove from the building above, but there is an essential continuity of materials and finishes. The grey pinstripe carpet designed by the office for the original Centre could not be extended to the Crescent Wing – straight lines do not adapt well to a curve – but the flecked carpeting used gives a similar effect. Signage, too, is rigorously controlled, matching that applied in the 1970s.

Perhaps the greatest surprise of the Crescent Wing is the degree to which it is permeated by natural light. The architects went to great pains to maximise its impact – the rooflights, for example, are equipped with large, spun metal reflectors which have proved highly effective. Norman Foster's 'cave' turns out to be a very singular place, where his customary concern for light is brought to bear with surprising results.

Far from being a retreat from the radicalism of the 1970s, the Crescent Wing holds a special place in the Foster canon as a marker in the practice's increasingly fertile exploration of contextualism and ecology.

Kenneth Powell

The 1.5-metre diameter rooflights incorporate parabolic reflectors that focus the daylight into bright pools. Purpose-designed on the 'dark-light' principle, they appear dark when seen from anywhere outside the circle of focus.

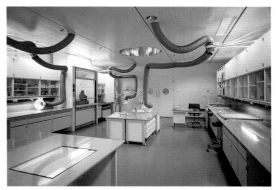

A specially-designed lighting system, where the lamps are incorporated in easily demountable ceiling panels, has been installed throughout the wing. Offering considerable flexibility, almost any lighting effect can be created, allowing each space to be lit to the highest standard.

The view from the far side of the lake on a cold winter's evening, the Crescent Wing's only true elevation glowing mysteriously in the mist.

"Standing on this lawn, looking towards the lake, or from inside the original [building], the new wing is virtually undetectable. Only the slender guard-rail, designed to prevent boisterous students or the careless visitor from tobogganing down the taut glass wall, calls attention to its presence. However, from the lakeside the effect is dramatically reversed. The Sainsbury Centre now stands at the top of a shining cliff of glazing, which apparently lifts it above its drab neighbours. It seems that Foster's Parthenon has at last found its Acropolis."

David Jenkins, *The Architects' Journal*, 8 May 1991

The cave below, the tent above. Designed on seemingly opposing principles, the Sainsbury Centre and its new neighbour, the Crescent Wing, have combined to create a unified composition that appears almost inevitable.

Katharine Hamnett
Brompton Cross
London

From the very beginning, Norman Foster sought to create at Katharine Hamnett a quite different space than that normally associated with the fashion boutique. Expensive details and compact planning were renounced in favour of honest finishes and a cool elegance.

Although "a two-storey rabbit-warren in an appalling state" when first seen, Norman Foster was aware that hidden within were elements of a more graceful past that might shine if given the setting they deserved. His early sketches attempted to express how the space might look once the detritus and surplus structure had been removed.

"Most shops seem to spend a fortune on expensive fit-outs and lavish materials, as though quality can be purchased by somehow spending more. It also assumes that quality resides in some materials to a greater extent than others. The attempt here will be to use more basic materials — not just because budget will be a major issue at some point, but also as a philosophical viewpoint, which I believe mirrors the thinking behind the clothes that generate the project. But these materials should be used well — quality as an attitude of mind — design as a tool to transform."

Norman Foster, hand-written letter to Katharine Hamnett, 19 March 1986

Katharine Hamnett first came to know of Foster Associates through her familiarity with the Joseph shop, whose proprietor, Joseph Ettedgui, had helped her earlier in her career by stocking some of her clothes. By early 1986 she had become one of Britain's leading fashion designers, famed, among other things, for raising the printed T-shirt to an art form. She also pioneered the use of parachute silk as a dress fabric.

Hamnett had, at one time, considered taking over the Joseph shop, but the timing had not been right. However, when the opportunity arose to open a new flagship outlet in London, she turned to Norman Foster for advice, when discussing the relative merits of alternative locations with her managing director Jerry Beeby and business associate Peter Bertelsen.

Foster's response was that, although most of the premises seemed fine as far as they went, they all lacked any kind of memorable quality of space. There was one location, however, which struck a chord — a former car repair shop and coachworks in South Kensington, hard by a District Line cutting, and just across the road from the Michelin building. It had not been seriously considered up till then as it had no entrance frontage and there was absolutely no possibility

KATHARINE HAMNETT

Lit from below, meandering on plan and a gentle arch in section, the glass bridge was a conscious attempt to evoke drama, contrast and mystery, tempting shoppers to explore the 35-metre long tunnel and emerge, at the far end, into an oasis of light and calm.

Rather than create a single 'wall', the full-height mirrors that line both ends of the shop were angled in sections towards the wall of windows, emphasising the brightness of the space and extending it endlessly in layers of alternative reality.

of providing shop windows. Furthermore, the only entrance from the street was via what seemed to be a rather gloomy tunnel.

Foster's reaction was characteristically unexpected: "It sounded like it might have amazing possibilities", he wrote later. Hamnett and her associates agreed. They acquired the garage and commissioned Foster Associates to carry out a full renovation.

Foster's first visit had "revealed a two-storey industrial slum through which occasional glances of a more graceful past could be discerned — a truncated piece of cast-iron column, a blocked-in circular window, anonymously traditional industrial glazing". It was split into two levels. The design team felt that the only way it could be fully appreciated was by carrying out a measured survey and by building a model of the shell without floors.

What emerged was a curious triangular space, the geometrical effect of which was to create an unusually long wall in relation to the space it enclosed. In a handwritten letter to Katherine Hamnett, early in the project, Foster

The only external wall overlooked a railway cutting on the District Line. In need of remedial repairs and new glazing, work was complicated by the fact that it could only take place at night and by arrangement with London Transport.

Below: mystery and surprise — the essence of the design concept was summed up in one of Foster's early sketches, though several options would be explored before the final design was realised.

posed certain questions over how this particular feature might be exploited. Perhaps a mezzanine level should be provided, in which case the long walls would allow a gentle ramp to be built? Perhaps the 'heart' of the space should be kept sacred, with all activity restricted to the perimeter? Or again, perhaps the perimeter was so dramatic that it should be left fully clear of extraneous clutter, and functions concentrated in the centre of the space?

Whatever the answer, Foster was determined to ensure that the integrity of the great space was retained. This meant finding some way in which the necessary cellular spaces — lavatories, staff room, kitchenette and, of course, changing rooms — would not detract from the main space.

In response to a spirit discerned in Hamnett's design work, Foster Associates' approach was almost puritan. They avoided unusually elaborate materials, concentrating attention

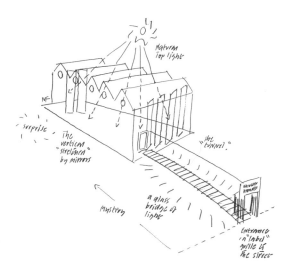

instead on how the existing resources and simple new elements could be set off to best effect. For instance, the removal of the existing intermediate floor would necessitate certain alterations to the structure: by fixing outriggers and tension cables, for example, the existing columns could be made to work harder. As it turned out, careful analysis was to show that the columns could, in fact, span the distance between floor and roof without intermediate support. The sides walls, however, required

During the first visit to the site, the 'noble space' which was to capture Norman Foster's imagination was all but lost beneath layers of neglect, a heavy mezzanine floor, a spray-paint tank and cars everywhere.

restraint, which was provided simply and directly with horizontal diagonal bracing.

To keep costs down, work to the existing enclosure was limited to replacing rainwater goods, reglazing the rooflights in Georgian wired glass and repointing one side wall — no mean feat as this was built on the edge of the District Line cutting. Internally, the smaller cellular spaces were accommodated at the edges of the site. Changing rooms lined the walls at each end, behind massive mirrors and curtains 20 feet high. Behind these, at the northern apex, were the other service rooms. In keeping with the overall approach, the floor finish was power-floated concrete — a basic material laid with the utmost care.

Of all the features of the original building, it was the entrance tunnel that represented the most fascinating challenge of all. It was essential to handle it skilfully and in such a way as to fully vindicate the choice of premises.

It was an awkward space, curving not only laterally, but also vertically as it lacked a consistent level floor. At one point, the design team considered using it as the starting point for a ramp which continued upwards as a browsing route. The eventual solution was far more subtle — and far more effective. In the final design, a gently curving bridge — glazed in etched glass and lit from below — floats effortlessly along the entire length of the corridor. (Though on a far smaller scale, it echoes, in many respects, the unbuilt scheme for an all-glass plaza floor at the Hongkong Bank.) Whatever its antecedents, it was a remarkable piece of theatre, transforming what was a dark tunnel into an elegant and enticing entrance.

The Katharine Hamnett shop was Foster Associates' most daring exercise in retail design — triangular, like Joseph, but radically different in the extent of its exposure to passing consumer traffic. Sadly, within a year the shop was closed. However, the design remains an ingenious architectural solution which, in its attempt to layer the new and the old, has paved the way for a series of subsequent projects which have explored the constraints and challenges of working in older or historic buildings.

Timothy Ostler

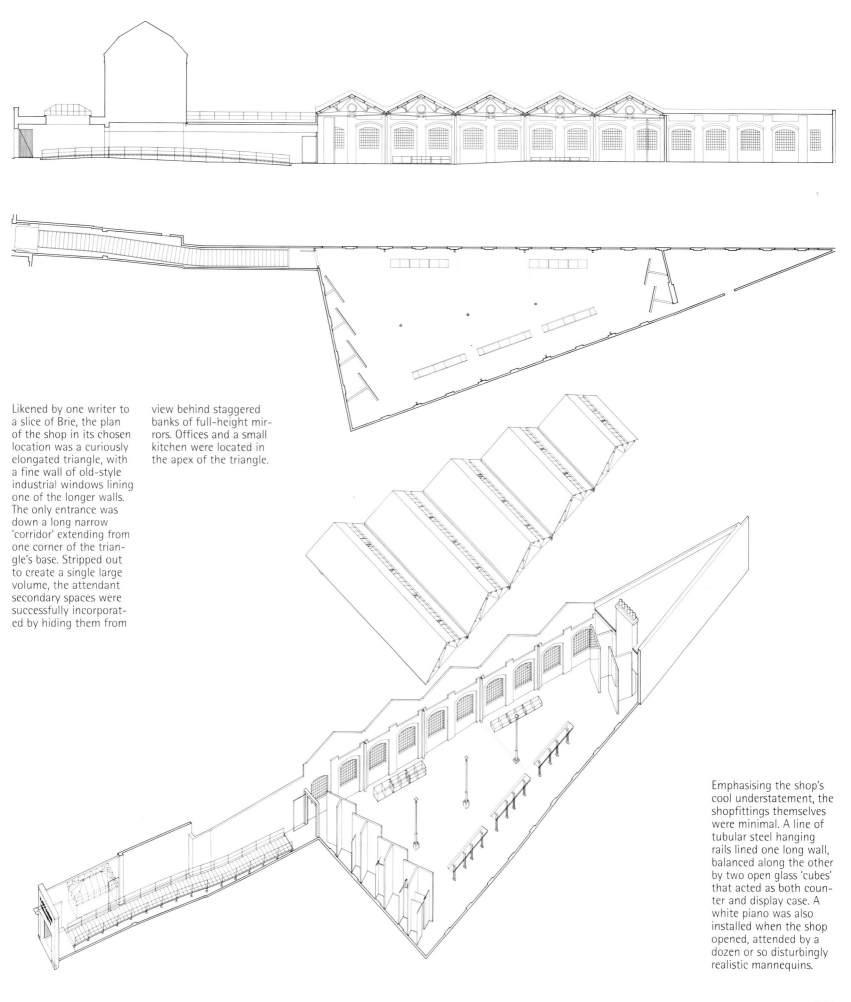

Likened by one writer to a slice of Brie, the plan of the shop in its chosen location was a curiously elongated triangle, with a fine wall of old-style industrial windows lining one of the longer walls. The only entrance was down a long narrow 'corridor' extending from one corner of the triangle's base. Stripped out to create a single large volume, the attendant secondary spaces were successfully incorporated by hiding them from view behind staggered banks of full-height mirrors. Offices and a small kitchen were located in the apex of the triangle.

Emphasising the shop's cool understatement, the shopfittings themselves were minimal. A line of tubular steel hanging rails lined one long wall, balanced along the other by two open glass 'cubes' that acted as both counter and display case. A white piano was also installed when the shop opened, attended by a dozen or so disturbingly realistic mannequins.

In one early sketch, Foster recreated the shop window in photographic form along the walls of the entrance corridor. Shops without shop windows are not the contradiction in terms they might seem — as demonstrated by Frank Lloyd Wright's celebrated jewellery store in San Francisco, still open after 40 years.

The entrance at night, the glowing bridge calling to mind the office's unbuilt proposal for an all-glass plaza floor at the Hongkong Bank.

Over six metres high and 3.6 metres wide, the great mirror panels — in fact six separate sheets butt-jointed together — expand the space both vertically and horizontally. Using a large-scale model, a number of options was carefully studied before the final disposition and angle of the panels was resolved.

Early proposals for lighting the space included suspended 'sails' of white fabric beneath the rooflights lit by uplighters cantilevered from the existing columns. Fitted with sensors, the lights would grow progressively brighter, as night fell, to maintain constant light levels within.

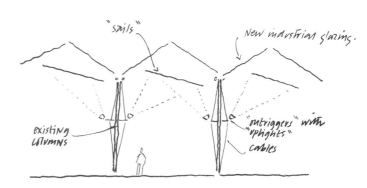

"sails"

New industrial glazing.

existing columns

"outriggers" with "uplights"

cables

During the day, the space was brought to life by the combination of side light — the old industrial windows reglazed with translucent white glass — and direct top-light from the rooflights overhead. Moveable spotlights mounted on tracks, which provided subtle accents and sparkle during daylight hours, were supplemented at night by wall 'washers' and downlights which cast pools of light on the floor. To avoid the effect of blank, black holes, the side windows were also illuminated at night, by lights fitted along the building's parapet.

Shop for Esprit
New York
USA

With a structure too heavy to contemplate any but the most minor of modifications, the lifts and stairs had to be installed in the building's existing shafts. Extensive use of glass in their refitting, however, transformed them into shafts of light rising the full height of the building.

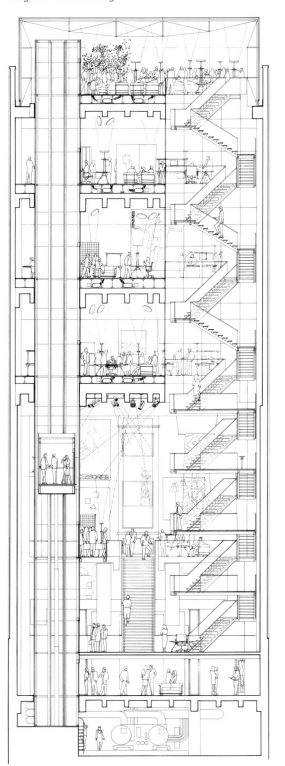

Foster Associates first started working with Doug Tomkins of Esprit in 1986. The young, San Francisco-based chain of shops was beginning to expand rapidly and Doug and Susie Tomkins were hoping to build a new Foster-designed headquarters in the Bay area. A trip was made to San Francisco to look at two possible sites, but the project remained a hypothetical one.

In 1987, Doug Tomkins bought an old Con-Edison power station on 39th Street in New York, to be Esprit's main showroom on the East Coast. The enormous building had a strong axial structure. Huge electrical batteries had been housed either side of a central aisle, sitting on massively strengthened concrete floor slabs. The office's proposal turned the aisle into a vast processional staircase leading slowly from the ground floor entrance to the first floor gallery. The power station was to become a veritable cathedral of merchandise. Access to the basement and to the four floors above the gallery was to be from lifts and triangular stairs placed on either side of the lofty entrance hall.

The shop would have been a glowing jewel in mid-town Manhattan. As designed, both the lifts and the stairs were made of glass, creating columns of light running the entire height of the building. The floors were glass blocks, lit from below to form a glittering crystalline carpet stretching the length of the building. The clothes themselves were to have been displayed using the 'Nomos' system, with glass shelves and table tops, and video screens between the racks of bright fabrics.

Apart from the new steel structure of the top floor, the ceiling of the power station was left bare, with deep reinforced beams dividing the space. Angled mirrors jutted out from the raw concrete, catching and reflecting the light from uplighters — also part of the 'Nomos' system — and flinging it throughout the space.

Surveys had been completed, the building stripped out, and the office with their New York architects were negotiating their way through the building codes, when work was abruptly stopped. With its significant market in the Far East, the growing currency crisis between the American dollar and the Japanese yen was beginning to take its toll on Esprit's financial arrangements. Plans for new shops were temporarily put on hold and the building was sold.

Diana Periton

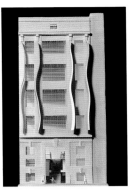

The proposed refurbishment of an existing industrial building for a quite different purpose at Esprit *(left)* was just the first of a sequence of similar projects that have continued to this day, the most recent being the installation of a design museum in an old steel foundry in Essen *(right)*.

Whatever problems may have been presented by the building's immoveable structure, they were more than offset by its dramatic double- and triple-height spaces. The most impressive of these were at the ground and first floors where, by chance, there was an existing narrow slot of lightweight structure just the right width for a connecting staircase. The floors above were to be enlivened with raised glass floors lit from below. In contrast, the roof level was designed as an all-glass pavilion with a solid floor.

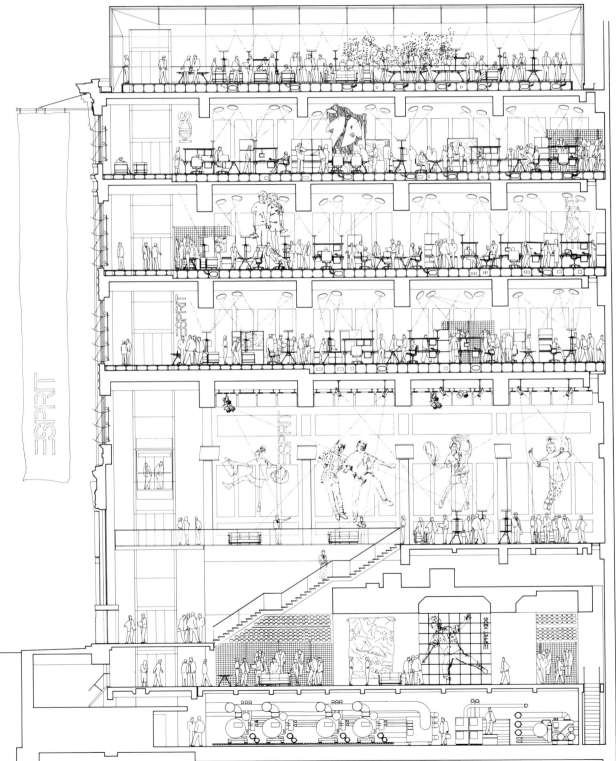

1987-1988 Shop for Esprit
Sloane Street
London

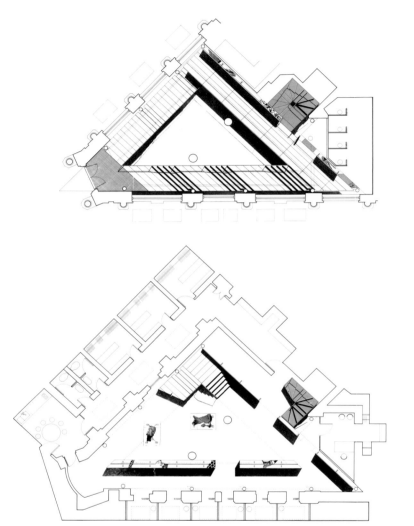

By the time Doug and Susie Tomkins first met Norman Foster, Esprit had become synonymous with a lifestyle – sporty, energetic, optimistic, unfussy. Esprit shops were being set up around the world to sell high-quality, reasonably priced clothes to a young and lively clientele.

The design of the company's shops was an integral part of Doug Tomkins' approach. Sotsass in Germany, Citterio in Belgium, Weil and Taylor in Australia; all had created shops which shared the bright, dynamic, high-quality image of the clothes Esprit aimed to sell. Foster Associates' shop for the company in London, however, was to have a different emphasis – a single spatial concept and tough, bare materials to set off the company's colourful fabrics.

Esprit's London agent was Joseph Ettedgui, so it was unsurprising when they proposed renovating the former Joseph shop on Sloane Street as their first shop in the capital. Where Joseph had used only the tall ground floor, however, Esprit preferred two floors of selling space, which meant descending into the previously unused basements.

From the outset, the design team's ideas were based on spatial solutions rather than stylistic dressing. The shop was to become a theatre, a place of procession, focusing on the clothes as the narrative of the drama. The first proposal involved removing the ground floor completely.

From the entrance, a glass staircase following the longer of the glazed external walls led gently up to a gallery that looked out over the space. A second staircase, hidden behind the clothes-rails and shelves that lined the back wall of the shop, then took customers down to the basement display area and counters. From here,

In the early design, the entire back wall of the shop, over its full two-storey height, became the display in the shop window. Proposals included front- or back-projected screens allowing an ever-changing montage of images to attract the passer-by, particularly at night.

The first design proposed removing the ground floor entirely, to create one dramatic space encircled by a processional staircase that led from the basement, via the entrance door, to a raised mezzanine level running across the back wall. Secondary spaces were hidden away in the pavement vaults.

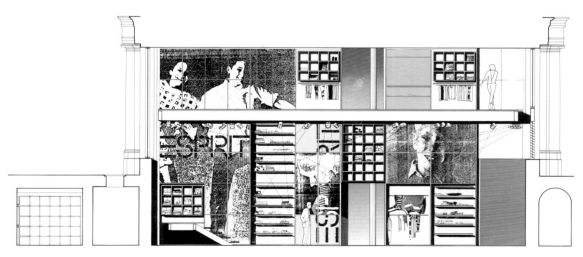

Resolving the geometry of the triangular staircase in its circular hole was complicated by the need to incorporate two existing structural columns that support the floors above.

From the outside, apart from a discreet sign over the door, it might easily be assumed that nothing of substance had changed since the building had first been converted in 1978, again by the office, as a shop for Joseph.

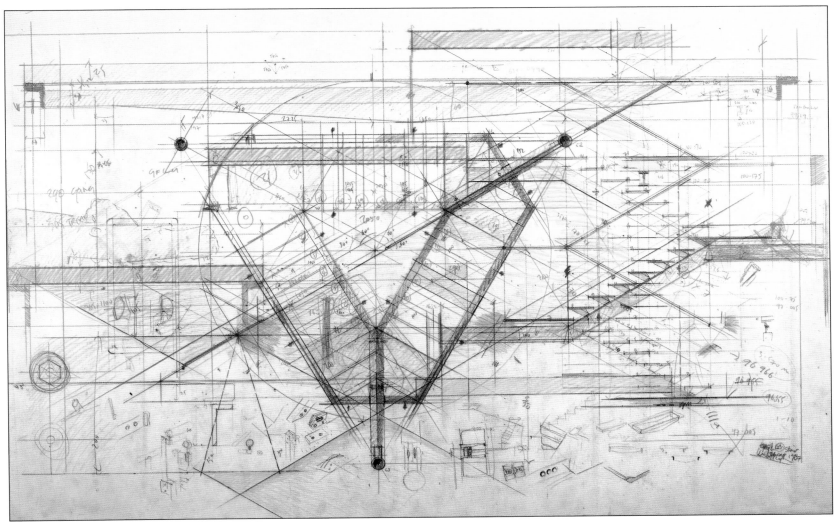

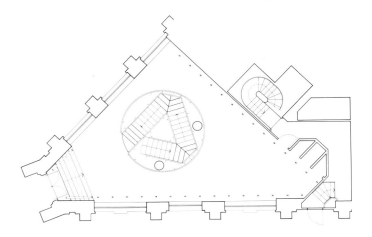

In the final design, the triangular staircase and the existing columns pass through the circular hole in such a way that no one element quite touches another. The rest of the shop is left open, with ancillary spaces and a secondary staircase hidden in the back wall.

the lower arm of the main staircase completed the processional route back to the entrance.

Work began and the floor had already been removed and the existing steel columns sheathed in concrete, when the freeholder insisted that the floor would have to be replaced at the end of the 18-year lease. Money would have to be set aside to guarantee this, and builders would have to be brought back on site to carry out the work before the lease expired.

To avoid this, the design team quickly put forward a second proposal as bold and simple as the first. The space was organised as a triangle within a circle within a triangle, with the floor reinstated at a slightly higher level, with a large circular hole cut into it containing a triangular

Stainless steel, polished concrete, sand-blasted glass and slim wooden shelves: the whole shop was finished in the simplest palette of materials, detailed to the highest standards.

Though not quite as dramatic as the first scheme, in which the entire ground floor was taken away, the removal of a circular section, five metres in diameter, had much the same effect, flooding the basement with light and creating one unified space.

staircase. The refurbished, concrete-sheathed columns shot up inside the circular hole, touching neither floor nor stair.

Storage space was tucked away under the pavement on Sloane Street, while the changing rooms received top-lighting from Basil Street's pavement lights. The changing rooms were hidden behind the display of clothes, hung from a light, flexible system of grit-blasted stainless-steel channels, steel rails and birch-faced panels. Steel ladders with timber treads, two per floor, were used to reach merchandise on the higher shelves. Running on rubber wheels, these were attached to a rail at high level, and became an integral part of the display system.

Both of the proposals for the Sloane Street shop aimed to open up the area below ground, dissolving the difference between the basement and the upper floor by using a staircase to create a single vertical space. In its final form, the staircase was supported by three slender steel columns, a separate piece of furniture within the circular hole. The main structure was made from mild-steel box sections, on to which grit-blasted stainless-steel frames were bolted, to carry the 25mm thick sand-blasted glass treads. Their edges were polished, to catch and reflect the light.

The lighting followed the triangular path of the staircase. In the basement, a triangle of lights was set into the smooth concrete and terrazzo floor below the stairs, acting like landing lights for the strange steel structure. A triangular cluster of spotlights also shone down on the staircase from above, creating a glittering tube of brightness at the heart of the space and transforming the descent to the basement into an exciting drama.

Diana Periton

Supported off a rail at the top and on rubber wheels at the bottom, the moveable stairs became an integral part of the display system, allowing the full height of the wall to be used for both storage and display.

Like the central staircase, the demountable display system employs simple materials, faultlessly finished and elegantly detailed. Standardised shelves of birch-faced plywood, some of which are fitted with clothes-rails below, are supported off vertical rails of grit-blasted stainless steel that span between floor and ceiling.

Prefabricated and with only bolted connections for fast and accurate on-site assembly, the central staircase was simply detailed in meticulously finished materials. Mild-steel box sections, coated in micaceous iron-oxide paint, support grit-blasted stainless steel handrails and tread frames. Bonded to the frames with silicon sealant, the 25mm-thick glass treads have polished edges and sand-blasted sides.

The Tate Gallery Lecture
by Norman Foster

The work in this volume forms just part of Foster Associates' output during the 1980s. It was a period of change and growth, that saw the office expand from a successful atelier of 40 or so designers into a major international office with over 120 employees in London, offices in Nîmes, Hong Kong and Tokyo, and projects in a dozen cities in between. The sheer scale and scope of the work undertaken during that period will be covered in three volumes, of which this is only the first. To talk about projects in isolation is a somewhat arbitrary way to discuss an architect's work; to separate those projects across three volumes can be positively misleading. This lecture, given by Norman Foster at the Tate Gallery on 20 February 1991, goes some way to redress the balance and provides a welcome overview of the thoughts and concerns that link all the projects of this period.

I want to talk this evening about my work as an architect and a planner, and the work of the hundred-strong, multi-disciplinary team to which I belong. I shall address the issue of the European Community and the coming of the single European market, but I want to try to do so by way of our own experience, gained through working on projects here and on the Continent.

I will start by describing two projects in Britain. One is a building, the recently completed passenger terminal at Stansted Airport; the other is the ongoing planning project for a new rail transport interchange and redevelopment at King's Cross. In their way, both these projects have a European dimension, but what they really have in common is the fact that they are dominated by the same issues. Each one has a history. Each one required a return to first principles. And each one forms part of a continuing search for more environmentally sensitive ways to build in the future.

To take history first. Surprisingly, the design of the new terminal at Stansted was strongly influenced by it, even though the history of air transport is short. Only 50 years ago, for example, Heathrow Airport was a military airfield surrounded by open countryside *(1,2)*. In the next decade it expanded its passenger operations and became London's principal airport, with the more distant Gatwick in a supporting role. Yet even then, as early as 1953, when a transatlantic flight from Heathrow in a piston-engined Lockheed Constellation was an ordeal lasting 17 to 20 hours *(3,4)*, the need for a third London airport had already been identified and Stansted had already been proposed as the site for it.

It is here that a European comparison first comes to mind. In France, Paris Charles de Gaulle, the third Paris airport, was not proposed until 1965, more than a decade after Stansted, and yet it began operations in 1974 after a delay of only nine years *(5)*. Stansted will finally begin operations next month after a delay of nearly 40 years — a delay compounded by three public enquiries, three reports and one false start at another site, Foulness.

1

2

3

4

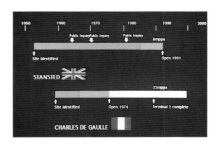

5

6

7

8

9

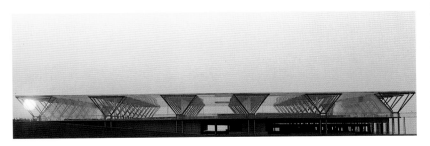

10

11

12

As I said, the history of air travel is very short. The first heavier than air flight took place in 1903 and the basic principles of the airport were established soon after. The aerial photograph of Candlas Field, Atlanta *(6)*, taken in 1925, shows a large area of grass where the aircraft landed and took off; a dirt road used by arriving and departing vehicles; and a shed between the two. There were no 'orientation problems'. The simplicity of the Atlanta layout makes an interesting comparison with contemporary Heathrow *(7)*, which looks more like a new town or shopping centre. It is not a place where orientation is obvious. Instead, visitors depend on announcements and a graphic sign language to help them move around. You almost need a guide dog.

One of the questions that we asked ourselves at the beginning of the design process was, notwithstanding the complexity of any modern international airport, how far we could get back to the simple logic of that early arrangement. That question informed the shape of our response.

Two images are of interest here. The first *(8)* shows a photomontage of our proposed terminal at a very early stage to demonstrate its environmental impact; the second *(9)* shows the actual building under construction from the same viewpoint. At Stansted, the tree planting programme has been enormous, but the principal means of diminishing its visual impact was not tree planting but earth movement, a technique which permitted what is actually a two-storey building to appear as a single-storey building from outside.

This model *(10)* was shown to the board of the British Airports Authority in 1982 and the principle it established has held good ever since. You approach the terminal walking towards the aircraft, which you can see, while your baggage is processed through the lower level. One advantage of the simplicity of this arrangement was the way in which direct rail access from Liverpool Street Station could be integrated into the building after construction had started, by using the subterranean floor. Over time, the flat roof started to undulate and it is now supported by a tree-like formation of columns, but it is still very close in spirit to the original idea. There is an airfield, a big shed, and an access road with car and coach parking in front of it.

The roof at Stansted is unique in its transparency as well as its single level. Its design is dedicated to natural light, with a proportion of the surface glazed to let sunlight in, and 'daylight reflectors' inside that bounce the light back up on to the sculptural shape of the ceiling *(12)*. At night, artificial light achieves the same effect. This arrangement is quite different to more conventional airport terminals of recent years, such as Terminal Four at Heathrow *(11)*, where the ductwork, suspended ceilings, roof-mounted air-conditioning units and fluorescent lighting involve a lot of structural and servicing redundancy and a great absence of natural light.

There is an interesting parallel here with the evolution of passenger aircraft. All the heavy servicing equipment mounted on the roofs of conventional airport buildings is actually in the wrong place for easy access. It has to be repaired and replaced frequently, yet the airport itself can never be closed down to facilitate this. In the same way, the engines of the first jet airliner, the de Havilland Comet, were buried inaccessibly in its wing roots. At Stansted we have located all the heavy equipment on the ground (13) where it can be most easily handled — just as the engines of the Boeing 747 are slung under its wings (14) to provide easy access for maintenance and removal. So the unobstructed roof at Stansted is not only about the poetry of natural light, it is also about logistical efficiency.

If Stansted is about space, light and calm in an airport context, I think it achieves these goals in the same way as did the great transport structures of the railway age. The clear spans at Stansted are 36 metres; at Lewis Cubitt's King's Cross station (15), built in 1852, they were 32 metres. Sixteen years later William Barlow's great train shed at St Pancras (16) spanned 74 metres, the largest single-span structure in the world at that time.

This comparison brings me to the second major project I wish to talk about, the proposed redevelopment of King's Cross. Image 17 shows the present state of this 134-acre stretch of railway land, created by the commercial rivalry between two railway companies in the nineteenth century and running north from their two stations. The adjacent image (18) shows our planning proposal for the same area, generated in its turn, if you like, by the railway renaissance that will come with the completion of the Channel Tunnel. Our project shows commercial development and a park as the central feature, but the driving force of the project is the new international rail terminal itself. An immense task separates these two images. As architects and planners we are only one of 100 consultancies working on this project, and the programme allows three-and-a-half years of design work before construction even begins.

It is easy to put up a sign saying: "It could be the only home they ever own" (19). It is even easier to say: "Let's build in the Green Belt because it's easier there than in the inner city". But that is not the answer to the problem. There are vast areas of derelict land in inner London, and King's Cross is typical of them in terms of the difficulties it presents. Our project attempts to tackle the issues of inner-city development without taking any of the easy options. It is an immense challenge. How did we approach it?

We began at King's Cross, as we began at Stansted, with a search for the roots of the development. We considered the history of the site, its heritage buildings, the listed gas holders (20) and the intractable canal and railway infrastructure. Then we considered the urban grain of the surrounding areas. London has its own urban tissue, quite distinct from that of other cities, whether Barcelona, Amsterdam, Washington, Paris or New York (21,22). London is permeated with green areas. A ride in a double-decker bus will show you: Islington

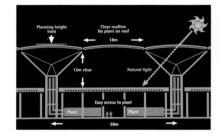

13

14

15

16

17

18

19

20

Green, Hampstead Heath, St James's Park, Primrose Hill, Shepherd's Bush — they are all green spaces: large, small, varied, different. Image *23* shows the pervasiveness and yet the dissimilarity of them all.

Then if you look at the original King's Cross site, with its canal winding across, and peel away the layers of subsequent railway development, you begin to see how you might bring back some of those freshwater basins in their original form; adapt them for leisure, or use them as a focus for housing. Then the housing could be integrated with offices and slowly a strategy emerges that might knit all these elements together to create a unified community around a 34-acre park, a new addition to London's historic green spaces and probably the first of such a size to be created in over 100 years.

The focus of the King's Cross development is the rail terminal at its southern tip *(24)*. In one sense it is the heart of the whole enterprise; in another, it is an entirely separate exercise with a different client — British Rail. The form of the terminal we have proposed was generated by the geometry of the two great nineteenth-century rail termini on the site *(25)*. It sits between them without touching either — respecting them as historic buildings in their own right. At the same time it opens up new vistas of both these buildings that have, for generations, been blocked by a kind of urban vandalism, typically the temporary structures that still obscure the principal facade of King's Cross.

There is, however, another reason for the transparency of the terminal. It reflects the fact that, like the two great nineteenth-century termini, it, too, is an iceberg, concealing an even larger complex of infrastructure beneath the ground. What happens beneath King's Cross is a virtual spaghetti junction — far more complex, in fact, and without reliable records of any kind. The first underground surveys are actually taking place at this moment.

It is interesting to digress for a moment on the subject of infrastructure. Image *26* makes a comparison between the percentage of gross domestic product invested in roads and railways in different European countries between 1982 and 1985. We trail miserably behind at less than half of one per cent. The average is about three-quarters of one per cent, and the best performance is West Germany, at over one per cent. Image *27* makes a direct comparison between investment in rail infrastructure in Britain and France between 1975 and 1989, and that, too, tells the same story.

I think it is instructive that, in general, the Continental European countries do not look at roads and railways in isolation; they take an overview of all means of transport and think in terms of integrated policies *(28)*. We, for example, have just over 1850 miles of motorway and plan a small increase that will take us to just over 2000 miles by the turn of the century. France already has 2900 miles of motorway and plans to have 14,000 miles by the year 2000! Now when

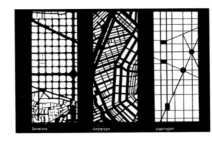
21

22

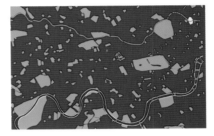

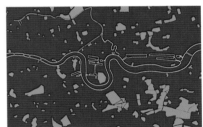
23

24

25

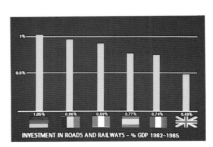
26

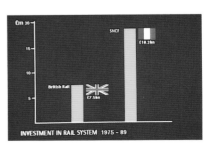
27

I constructed this graph *(29)*, people objected that such comparisons were unfair because of the difference in population, land area and so on. But even allowing for such factors, there is an enormous disparity.

It seems to me that investing in infrastructure is rather like building a building. You can't design a building without a client organisation to tell you what they want. In the same way, I do not believe you can design transport infrastructure without a political infrastructure to play the same supporting role. And this has nothing to do with the political leanings Left or Right. If you analyse investment in London's Underground system, for example, it has fluctuated quite independently of the political party in power.

The situation is quite different across the Channel. I will concentrate on France, but I could just as easily compare Britain with Spain, or a Scandinavian country. In France, the political infrastructure, so to speak, starts with the president of the Republic, who involves himself actively with architecture and planning at the level of the *Grands Projets*. Nor is this merely a nominal involvement, as I know from my own experience as a competition assessor. The president awards the commissions for the design of official buildings through a very well developed competition system dedicated to the achievement of quality. This pursuit of quality permeates French society. It reaches back through the French system of architectural education so that talented young designers are invited to compete for small-scale projects in local government competitions. In this way young talent is exercised and developed, and it is focused upon architecture centres.

Images *30* and *31* show the Centre Arsenal, one of the three architecture centres in Paris. There are other architecture centres in France, and throughout western Europe, although Britain thus far has none. The Centre Arsenal was opened in 1988 by the mayor of Paris, Jacques Chirac. Its construction was paid for by commercial developers and the City of Paris, and the city pays the wages of its employees and meets its running costs. In its first year this architecture centre attracted 60,000 visitors to 15 major exhibitions displaying the work of 570 architects. One of its most popular features is a large model of Paris where any major development project can be displayed and discussed, a process that reflects the intensely democratic nature of the whole process of patronage in France.

My personal insights into architecture in Europe are inevitably confined to those areas where we are currently active, and these are illustrated in image *32*. In a number of these places, such as Nîmes and Cannes in France, we are responsible for masterplans as well as buildings, but in all cases the main difference with the way things are done in England is that we are responsible to a single person in authority, frequently the mayor of the municipality. In Continental Europe a mayor is not a figurehead with no real power, as is the case here, but an active politician who can get things done. I would like to give an example of what

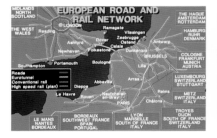

28

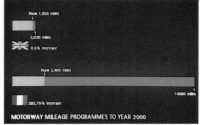

29

30

31

32

33

this means in the case of Barcelona, where we have designed a new communications tower at Tibidabo. The photograph here *(33)* shows the mayor at the ground-breaking ceremony.

Barcelona lies at the foot of a range of mountains which forms a backdrop to its whole urban development. In order to meet the enormous communications requirements of the 1992 Olympics, the expansion of local television and the Spanish telephone service, plans were being made for the erection of something like 30 individual transmission masts on the mountains *(34)*, with all the problems of electronic shadowing that such aerial 'farms' can lead to. It was the mayor of Barcelona who resolved the problem. He said: "This competitive approach won't work. You must form one company and together we will build one great communications tower. It will also be a public building, open to the citizens of Barcelona. And because this will be such a large project we will throw it open to international competition".

Now it is impossible to describe the potential for conflict when rival companies are ordered to co-operate in this way. The first thing they did was to try to sabotage the umbrella company by demonstrating that it couldn't work. There were resignations — I think there were 40 or so changes in the composition of the board in the first year — but the mayor would not be dissuaded. Somehow, he drove this great project through; it would not have happened without his drive and determination.

The outcome of the mayor's vision was the competition to design a single tower that we won. We won it with a design that, like our work at Stansted and King's Cross, started with a historical survey. We looked at the evolution of communications structures over time and discovered that they had almost always been modifications or additions to structures built for some other purpose *(35)*.

Our own approach to the design *(36)* broke new ground. We proposed a mast that was also a symbol of a new age in that it broke conclusively with the adapted structures of the past. Instead of cantilevering from a base with a diameter of 25 metres, our structure rested upon a central needle 2.4 metres in diameter. The fact that the tower was sited in a national park *(38)* meant that this tiny footprint was a great advantage. The tensile guys supporting this needle were anchored some distance away and the whole structure was conceptually no more complex than a suspension bridge, like the motorway bridge proposal for Rennes in France *(37)*. Interestingly though, in the Barcelona mast design, the tensile supports began as steel but then became Kevlar, a product which is electronically transparent and so does not interfere with signal transmission or reception.

Another unorthodoxy is the way the various decks for satellite and microwave communications, and the public viewing gallery, are confined to a glass tube in the central section *(39)*. This gives the Barcelona tower a unique appearance. It is, in effect, a piece of public sculpture as well as a complex of technical equipment *(40)*, but that does not mean that it

34

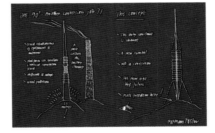

35

36

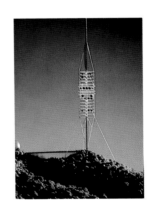

37

38

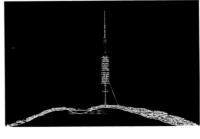

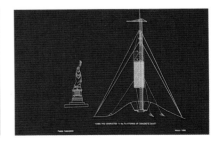

39

40

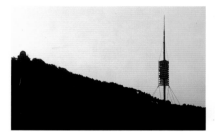

41

42

43

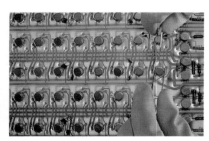

44

45

46

47

48

sacrificed any element of practicality. The British Telecom tower in London took eight years to move from conception to completion. The Eiffel Tower, that miracle of nineteenth-century fast-track construction, was conceived and erected in four years. The Barcelona tower *(41,42)* was conceived and authorised in one year, and built in the following two, a performance that I attribute in large measure to the tenacity and forward vision of the mayor, and to a structural concept which allowed the tower to erect itself, in much the same way that a car aerial does.

Another field we have been involved in recently, in Europe, concerns urban redevelopment. The city of Duisberg, in Germany, has about 26 per cent unemployment at the moment as a result of the withdrawal of heavy industry *(43)* from the Ruhr valley. Krupp, Mannesmann and Thyssen have all left, leaving a kind of industrial void and a community in decline. We have been working for a developer and local community groups to explore ways to encourage new micro-electronic industries *(44)* to relocate in the area. The site is presently an industrial wasteland, part of which is used as a bus park.

Our proposal in this case hinged on the way in which modern non-polluting electronic industries can be combined with residential development without any harmful effects. Thus we proposed linking an existing small park on the site with a business development, housing and a new area of parkland. In this project there is a historical element, as in the other schemes that I have talked about, because we discovered that such mixed-use urban areas were the norm in Germany and elsewhere until the intervention of heavy industry with its concomitant transportation problems which led to the era of separate zoning. We thought if we could knit together something like the old, pre-industrial zoning relationships, where working and living share the same environment, there would be some very exciting possibilities.

Apart from the mixed-use zoning principle, there were three small but important buildings at the heart of our proposal: a Telematic Centre *(45)*, a Business Promotion Centre and a new Micro-Technology Centre *(46)*. The Telematic Centre *(47)*, which is now under construction, is the brain of the whole development: it houses all the building management systems, but is also a major public concourse, so it is the focus of interaction between the new industries and the community. The Business Promotion Centre *(48)* will contain exhibition space, a bank on the ground floor, and offices for research institutions and the local authority to use.

Although these buildings could be described as symbols of a new urban fabric, they also reflect a good deal of environmental thinking. The Business Promotion Centre uses a new material with an extremely high U-value patented by the developer, who specialises in low-energy products. Combined with an extensive use of glass and computer-controlled blinds, it gives an excitingly translucent quality to the

49

50

51

52

53

54

building but, more than that, because of its excellent insulation properties, it also offers the prospect of a building that could be heated by ambient energy alone.

From northern Germany we now move to Nîmes in the south of France, where we won an international competition several years ago to design a public arts and media centre, the Carré d'Art, for a site adjacent to the Maison Carrée *(49)*, one of the best preserved Roman temples in Europe. Our response was, inevitably, historical again. We uncovered and analysed the ancient Roman planning grid, and respected the surprisingly uniform height and massing of the later buildings that surround the temple. To reassert the original street pattern we designed a very simple rectangular building for the site *(50)*.

This project has been a long time in gestation, but the time has not been wasted. Since that first project, the city of Nîmes has uncovered a great deal more of its Roman past and, in the area of the site, a lot of nineteenth-century additions have been removed to expose Roman paving and pedestrianise the area around it. Like the mayor of Barcelona and so many other enterprising mayors across Europe, Mayor Bousquet of Nîmes is a tremendous force for development and investment in the city. When the arts and media centre project finally received government funding, Mayor Bousquet printed hundreds of posters *(51)* celebrating the courage and determination of the city in pressing for the building. It shows, I think, the spirit that animates the city.

Nîmes is also advanced in its understanding of the needs of modern transport planning, and we have been able to help here too. An existing motorway curves around the south of the city but this is due to be replaced by a new motorway following a better route, as well as a new high-speed rail service, the TGV — a reflection perhaps of what I said earlier about French infrastructure investment and its enviable reputation for speed of implementation. Our role in the planning of the new infrastructure at Nîmes has been to study an eight-kilometre stretch of land along the new railway line *(52)* and explore the possibility of new public parks and lakes, residential areas, as well as a new transport interchange and an enlargement of the airport.

Coincidentally, just as our arts and media centre at Nîmes is now nearing completion, so is our much smaller addition to the Royal Academy *(54)* here in London. Both these projects began with the challenge posed by an existing historic building, in the case of the Royal Academy, Burlington House itself, together with its nineteenth-century additions. Now an art gallery may not be as complex a building as an airport, but it does impose the same discipline of being required to remain open while building works take place, and thus in some ways it poses similar problems.

Our task was to provide new galleries on the top floor, using the light well between the two existing buildings of the Academy both as a means of access and to provide extra accommodation. What was exciting here was the possibility of working within this light well — a space that would never normally be seen by visitors — and not only using it functionally but, in the process, exposing the garden façade of Burlington House (53) for the first time in more than 100 years.

As image 55 shows, the original windows of this façade still open on to the light well, while the lift and staircase that we have installed permit ease of movement between all levels in a way that does not detract from the function of the grand staircase of the Academy itself. Image 56 shows the new Sackler Galleries under construction. They, too, were designed to provide every advanced technology climate control and lighting modulation feature, but within the context of a traditional gallery shape appropriate to the age and status of the main building.

Environmental controls are increasingly important in all buildings, not only art galleries. We trace our interest in the subject back to the formation of the practice, and what we call our oldest thatched roof. It is the grassed roof of the Willis Faber & Dumas building in Ipswich (58), which is 7000 square metres in area yet acts as a kind of insulation quilt in much the same way as a traditional thatched roof (57).

This kind of approach can be seen at our new extension to the Sainsbury Centre for the Visual Arts at the University of East Anglia. The new Crescent Wing (59), as it is to be called, is effectively an underground building, and for this reason it achieves a rate of heat loss only about one third that of a conventional above-ground structure. Although the building is not quite complete, this progress image (60) conveys the extraordinary lightness it has been possible to gain by exploiting the slope of the land away from the original building towards the lake. The crescent of glass provides an uninterrupted view without itself constituting a visual obstruction, rather like the eighteenth-century device of the ha-ha wall.

The internal offices of this underground building will constitute an art conservation laboratory, entirely privately financed. Museology and lighting researchers will be able to examine objects under infinitely varied lighting conditions using special installations that do not exist anywhere else in the country. I am sure that nowhere on the Continent would such a project have to be privately funded if there was no equivalent national facility.

The subject of comparative Continental and British methods and achievements is fascinating and a whole talk could be devoted to it. Images 61 and 62 make some interesting comparisons. The National Gallery extension that is nearing completion now, for example, was first projected more than 40 years ago. The British Library, the Mappin & Webb site and the National Theatre, those too are all 40- to 50-year projects. In France they would all have been accomplished in five or six years, and that would include a competition phase — often an international competition — that we tend to omit over here.

Even if we ignore buildings — and there is still no building on the Mappin & Webb site in prospect after 30 years —

55

56

57

58

59

60

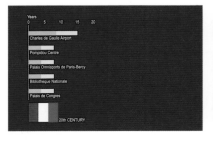

61

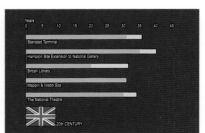

62

and concentrate on infrastructure alone, we discover that in Britain the average time needed for the passage of an Act of Parliament to build a railway line or a bridge is five years. Five years from now, in Spain, having won an international competition for a new Underground system in Bilbao, we will almost certainly be riding on the trains.

But just as disturbing as these international comparisons, are comparisons over time in our own country. Images *63* and *64* show the same sort of analysis relating nineteenth- and twentieth-century projects in Britain. In a most shameful way, the nineteenth century emerges as far more capable than our own. For example, our motorway network, which was late starting by Continental and United States' standards, only extends to 1850 miles after more than 30 years of desultory construction. Yet the Victorian railway system covered the 10,700 miles of the present Intercity network *(65)* only 20 years after the introduction of the first fare-paying passenger train service in 1829. Today, in Europe, they are introducing the TGV network *(66)* at a similar rate.

The currently much-discussed East London River Crossing, a totally non-contentious scheme, was first projected 45 years ago and still no bridge has been built. Even the London Crossrail route, which we are assured has the highest Government priority, will — if it proceeds according to plan — take as long to drive a seven-mile railway tunnel under London as it took the United States to develop an entirely new technology to place men on the moon. And coming back to that five-year lag for an enabling Act of Parliament: it was not always like that in Britain. In 1840, at the height of the Victorian railway boom, Acts of Parliament for new lines were being passed at the rate of one every 1.2 days. Over the whole of the first 20 years of railway construction in Britain, an Act was passed, on average, every eight days. We, in this country, have a great deal to learn from our own past.

I will finish with an image that has a certain abstract relationship to the theme of my talk this evening. The Vulcan bomber *(67)* is a transitional object — a jet aircraft that marked a quantum leap from the era of its propeller-driven predecessors, but also one that marked a less well-known transition from one system of navigation to another.

Prior to the jet age there was no difference between navigating aircraft or navigating ships, because aircraft were slow enough not to press the navigator to work faster than his methodology allowed. But when the speed of aircraft doubled and trebled, the old navigational system could no longer cope. By the time the navigator had worked out where he was, he was somewhere else. It is a fate that reminds me of today's planning enquiries, legal procedures that go on so long that those taking part forget what the original issues were because the circumstances have changed and a totally different set of issues has to be faced. So things move on.

Thank you.

63

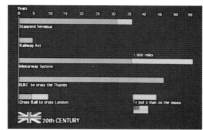

64

65

66

67

City of London Heliport
Allhallows Lane
London

CANNON STREET HELIPORT
AERIAL VIEW LOOKING WEST

Creating a heliport for the City of London has proved a perennially seductive idea. Such a facility would certainly offer exceptional connections between the capital's congested business district and its major airports — notably City Airport, just a few miles downstream, and Heathrow, a 15-minute flight to the west. From a location on the north bank of the Thames, between Cannon Street and London Bridges, a heliport would combine maximum passenger convenience with the least possible impact on the environment.

In 1987 this idea seemed to be near realisation when the City of London Heliport Group — a body comprising, among others, Hanson Trust, BAA, Trafalgar House and Midland Bank — brought the concept to Foster Associates. At this stage, the practice was simply asked to generate outline proposals intended to advance the feasibility of the idea.

The design team focused upon a cantilevered tubular steel structure projecting over the river. Essentially a straightforward platform, the structure's chief merits lay in its simplicity, its response to the practicalities of helicopter flight requirements and local planning restrictions, and the needs of river traffic.

Helicopter flights over London are carefully regulated, with access for single-engined machines restricted to a route that follows the line of the River Thames. Twin engined machines can overfly built-up areas while maintaining a height of 1500 feet or more but, again, can only descend to land over the river. Potential sites for a heliport are, therefore, very limited. Situated between Cannon Street and London Bridges, the location chosen for this proposal seemed to offer the best opportunities, with excellent links to the heart of the City and yet reasonably removed from any inhabited buildings.

A requirement to avoid obstruction of the operational shipping lanes determined a sectional form that cantilevered progressively out over the river. The first proposal reflected this with floor-plates of increased size that stepped out beneath the helipad proper, from a vertical service zone adjacent to the river-bank.

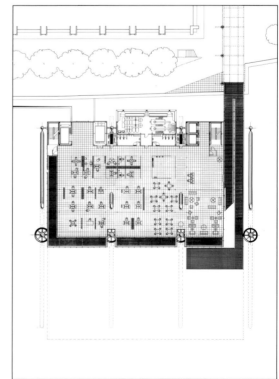

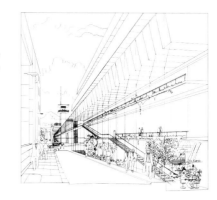

A covered pedestrian walkway was proposed, linking the new heliport with a suitable vehicular drop-off point in nearby Angel Passage.

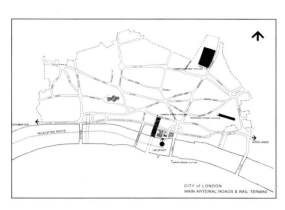

The proposed site offered excellent links to Underground and main line stations, and good traffic connections to both Westminster and Docklands. More importantly, it was within walking distance of many of the City's most prominent institutions.

A series of options was outlined for the space below the heliport deck, including offices in various permutations, and access to the facility from the river. Primarily though, the proposal's chief strengths lay in a particularly favourable confluence of local conditions and amenities. Sited in front of British Telecom's international telephone exchange, Mondial House, the heliport would be close to Cannon Street Station and easily accessible on foot from the riverside walkway, Angel Passage and Allhallows Lane. Underground access was also nearby and many City offices were within walking distance.

The single most obvious drawback — and one which had defeated all previous London heliport proposals — was that of noise pollution. Here the present bid appeared to have the strongest possible claim: the nearest building was an automated telephone exchange, totally enclosed and without windows, and none of the other neighbouring buildings was residential. A decision to use only twin-engined helicopters meant relatively quiet operation while at the same time offering high safety levels and a capacity for near-vertical take-off and landing.

Two years passed before the City of London Heliport Group returned to Foster Associates

with the go-ahead and a revised plan. There had been two major changes to the brief: no office space — except for that of the handling agents — was required beneath the platform; and a cut in budget, compounded by rising steel costs, meant that the original steel-based design of the structure would have to change. A third condition was that the office would work in partnership with structural engineers, Trafalgar House Technology.

In some ways this was an unlikely alliance since Trafalgar House Technology was aligned with a contractor, rather than an independent consultancy of the sort that the practice might normally have chosen. Having just finished the Queen Elizabeth Bridge at Dartford, Kent, Trafalgar House Technology joined the project essentially as bridge builders. This was not particularly illogical, since from the beginning the heliport's form had evoked the image of a half-completed bridge jutting out over the river.

The major change came with Trafalgar House Technology's recommendation to use a 50-metre concrete cantilever. Initial reservations from the Foster team soon evaporated in an unexpectedly rewarding partnership of skills, as robust structural engineering initiatives were

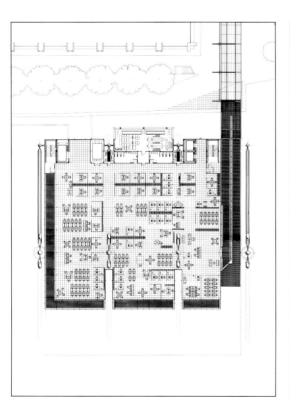

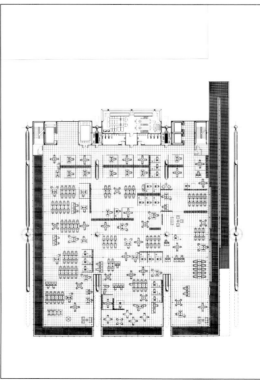

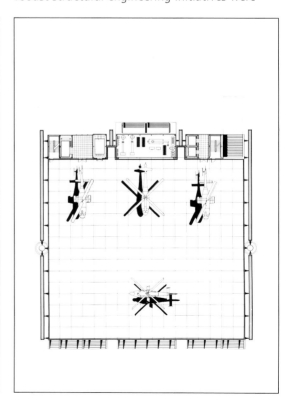

Below: measuring 48
metres square, the heli-
pad was of sufficient
size to accommodate a
clear landing and take-
off point for one heli-
copter, and a temporary
holding area for up to
three others.

A presentation model of
the first design proposal
was presented to the
client in September 1987.
Maximising the full potential of the site, this early
scheme included two
floors of lettable space
immediately below the
helipad, suitable for use
as offices or cafés and
restaurants. A third lower
floor, closest to the river
and with the potential to
serve river-bus services,

accommodated the heli-
port reception areas and
ancillary offices for the
heliport and helicopter
operators. A dedicated
lift provided access to
the helipad and control
tower above.

refined into an expressive and elegant architectural solution.

In this final proposal, the heliport deck is
formed from three parallel box beams which
together create its flat 48-metre square, 'table
top' surface. Precast and post-tensioned by
means of internal cables, the box beams offer
a durable and inherently sturdy method of cantilever support. Two rows of inclined support
columns took the form of concrete-filled steel
tubes with the front columns being founded
upon a substantial profiled pile-cap resting on
large-diameter bored piles.

The deck itself was subject to a number of
obligatory safety measures, including a perimeter safety net, automatic fire-fighting installations and an anti-skid surface that was imper-
vious to leaking hydraulic fluid or oil.

As an architectural solution, this revised
design expressed very clearly the degree of

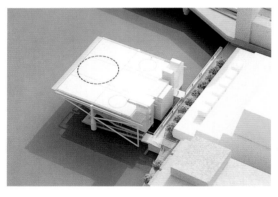

excellence that the City of London Heliport
Group was seeking to convey to those it had to
convince on many levels. Meanwhile, there was
no shortage of objectors, some of whom were
inclined to judge the enterprise, not so much on
its merits as on its assumed significance, as setting a precedent which would allow increased
air traffic to be gradually introduced into the
heart of the City.

In fact, every conceivable sensitivity had
been taken into account, not only in terms of
practicality and safety, but also in the heliport's
superior design quality and its response to the
neighbouring twin towers of Cannon Street
Bridge. There was strict adherence to the local
height planning restrictions that are intended
to preserve key views of St Paul's Cathedral.
Even day-to-day issues of security were diligent-
ly addressed in the design of the access route
into the heliport from the riverside walkway.

"As British business expands its interests in continental Europe ahead of 1992, it will become increasingly important that communications are improved between central London and, particularly, the City — where a majority of the leaders of British business are based — and the major continental centres of industry and commerce. Helicopters will undoubtedly play a key role in this."

Extract from the CBI report *Trade Routes to the Future*, London 1989

The main support piers for the steel superstructure were set into the river bed well outside the shipping lane, but were sized, nevertheless, to resist accidental impact in line with the Port of London Authority's requirements. The height of the helipad was also the subject of statutory regulations due to the proximity of St Paul's Cathedral.

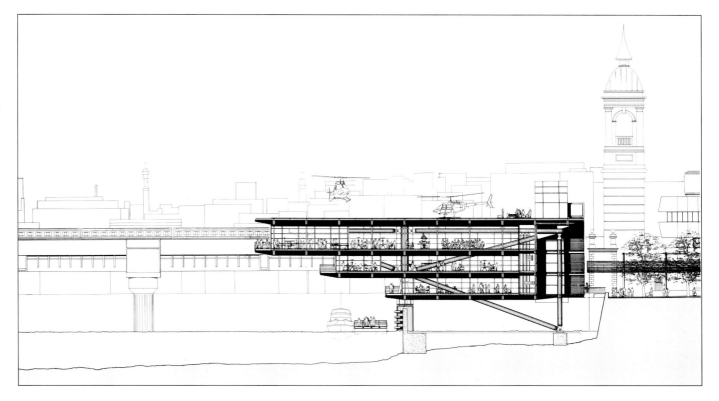

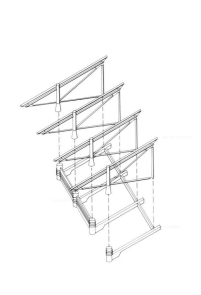

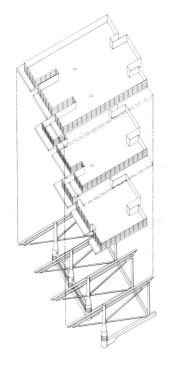

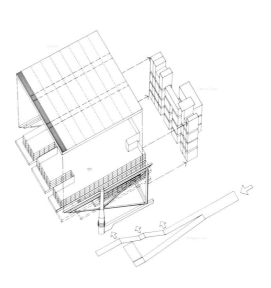

In the first scheme, the helipad was supported on a steel structure comprising four tubular steel frames set perpendicular to the river-bank at 18-metre centres. Each frame was supported at two points and the cantilever was triangulated. The helipad itself was a proprietary aluminium system, separated from the the floors below by a heavy concrete deck to ensure complete insulation from fire and noise.

199

Pedestrian routes were conserved and few doubted that the heliport itself would represent a beneficial feature for the area.

However, objections persisted. Residents in Southwark, on the opposite side of the river, railed, as did — somewhat less plausibly — representatives of the Tower of London who claimed that their yeoman tour-guides would be rendered inaudible by the passing helicopters.

Eventually the local authority referred the scheme to a planning inquiry where it was ultimately rejected on the same grounds that had defeated all earlier schemes: noise pollution.

If it was a regrettable conclusion to the project, there were several positive aspects. And the practice itself, today highly experienced at bridge design, enjoyed an unexpectedly creative introduction to some of that field's engineering principles through the alliance with Trafalgar House Technology.

The City of London Heliport Group, for its part, could at least be certain that its scheme had not been rejected because of the central structural solution — rather rejection had come despite architectural excellence.

Graham Vickers

As in the earlier scheme, a vertical service zone lined the building on the side closest to the river-bank, though this now catered for only two office floors at the lower levels and a larger service floor immediately below the helipad. This housed the necessary fire systems and other plant, plus two 'top-up' fuel tanks, each with a capacity of 1000 gallons.

Presented in November 1989, the second scheme was far simpler than the first, accommodating only enough office space for the heliport's own requirements and supported by a reinforced-concrete structure rather than the earlier steel.

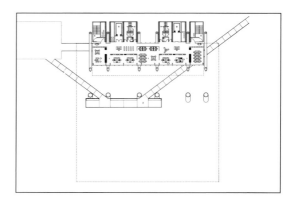

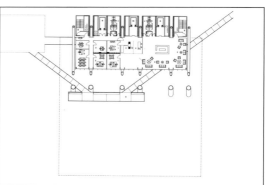

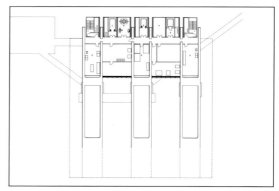

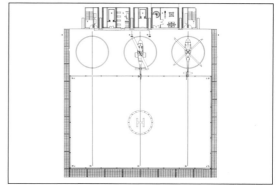

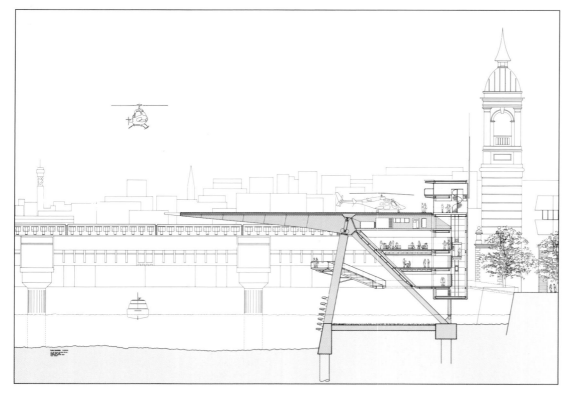

The dramatic helipad structure of the second scheme was formed by three linked reinforced-concrete box beams, each cantilevered off angled pairs of support columns, again of reinforced concrete but here cast in permanent steel shuttering.

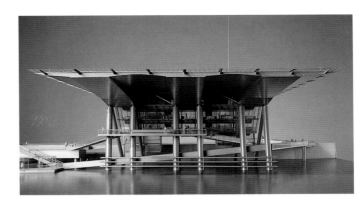

Several photomontages of the final scheme were prepared, showing views of the model set into its surroundings. This is the view from the riverside walkway linking London and Cannon Street Bridges. The bridge-like form of the final design was specifically chosen as one suitable for the river location, while its axial relationship to Mondial House helped tie it into its immediate setting. An elevated terrace was incorporated in the final design, cantilevered off the outer columns and providing spectacular views up and down the river.

Paternoster Square
The City
London

St Paul's Cathedral is not simply one of the best known and most widely admired buildings in Britain. Wren's masterpiece is equally a national icon and a symbol of the historic identity of London. The cathedral, which rose after its medieval predecessor burned in the Great Fire, survived the Second World War intact, but the area of the City around it was largely devastated by bombing. The streets to the north of St Paul's, around Paternoster Square, suffered particularly badly. The square itself was a Victorian creation, occupying the site of an old market. Paternoster Row, running east-west, however, was in origin an ancient street, traditionally the home of the book trade. At the end of 1940, a German air-raid razed the entire quarter, destroying or seriously damaging most of the buildings.

The provision of a more appropriate setting for the cathedral was seen as a high priority when it came to rebuilding the City after the war. The Royal Academy plan of 1942 had proposed a highly formal setting for St Paul's, somewhat at odds with the informal and unmonumental character of London. To the east of the cathedral, this approach produced the insipidly neo-Georgian New Change scheme. The Paternoster site itself, however, was entrusted, in 1955, to Lord Holford, who fought hard for a development which would be informal in layout and essentially modern in its architecture. Holford's proposals were eventually realised, faithfully but with a marked lack of distinction, by Trehearne & Norman between 1962 and 1967.

Widely disliked, the Paternoster development epitomised the 1960s. By the '80s, it was seen as technically obsolete. The so-called 'Big Bang' — the measure to deregulate financial trading in London which came into effect in 1986 — fuelled a property boom which eclipsed even that of the 1960s. The City, anxious to protect those old buildings and areas which had survived the war and earlier development campaigns, was happy to see unloved post-war office blocks replaced by new buildings more in tune with the fast-changing needs of business — raised floors, to accommodate electronic services, and large floorplates, adaptable for modern dealing rooms, were prerequisites. Competition from Docklands, fast becoming an alternative financial quarter, was also perceived as a threat, which encouraged developers to look at sites within the Square Mile.

The proposed demolition of the Holford development was generally welcomed and the objectives of the site's former owners, embodied in the brief for the 1987 design competition for the Paternoster area, were uncontentious. The Paternoster Consortium declared that it was looking for a masterplan, not detailed designs for a building or buildings. It was seeking "clarity and inspiration of concept rather than completeness, ideas rather than detail, a designer rather than a scheme".

Though the masterplan had to be commercially viable and maximise development opportunities — the City's planning policies allowed a plot ratio of 5:1 — it had equally to "create a recognisable identity for the site", making it "a memorable place", and provide amenities for tourists and City workers, as well as around one million square feet of offices. "Street patterns which attract pedestrian movement" were seen as desirable, and the history of the site and the dominance of St Paul's should be respected. The rigorously enforced St Paul's Heights policy provided for strict controls on height.

The competition addressed the future of two sites, the 4.3 acre 'core' owned by the consortium, and the wider seven-acre Paternoster site, including land in separate ownership — Juxon House, the high-rise Sudbury House and the small octagonal block at the eastern tip of the Holford development. It was hoped, and assumed, that the other owners, if they remained in possession, would develop their own proposals in tune with the selected masterplan.

Seven architectural practices — five of them, including Foster Associates, British-based, along with Arata Isozaki from Japan and Skidmore, Owings & Merrill from the USA — were invited to compete. Some competitors, for example James Stirling and SOM, conceived the rebuilt area as a mesh of buildings and public streets and squares. Isozaki and the Richard Rogers Partnership offered impressive internal public spaces on a scale unknown in Britain. In the event, the entry by Arup Associates was selected and subsequently developed in collaboration with several other practices.

The changing ownership of the site, however, and, more seriously, the intervention of the Prince of Wales, who supported counter-proposals by the Classicist, John Simpson, led to the eventual abandonment of the Arup scheme. A new tripartite, British/American/Japanese consortium launched a completely redesigned masterplan in 1991, the work of a team of largely Classicist architects, obtaining planning permission for it in 1993.

Paternoster Square as it was at the time of the competition, the dotted line indicating the extent of the 'core' site. It was hoped that the owners of buildings which completed the block would develop their sites in line with the masterplan.

From a distance, Wren's London was a city dominated by church spires and the soaring dome of St Paul's Cathedral, the only features which rose above a largely medieval city of dark and crowded uniformity.

Paternoster Square at the time of the competition. William Holford's arrangement of Modernist buildings and open spaces was not well liked and no longer met the needs of today's financial institutions.

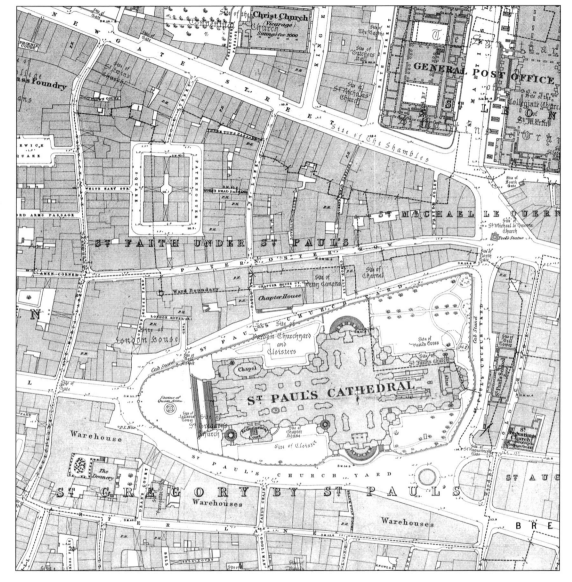

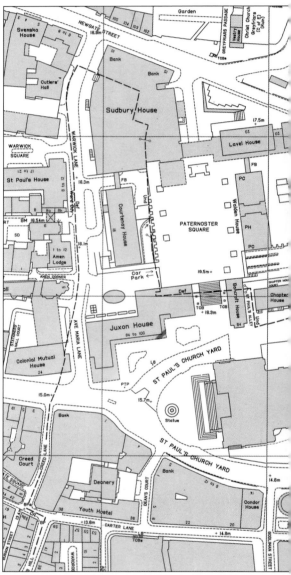

From an Ordnance Survey map of 1876. Until the end of the nineteenth century, the area around Paternoster Square was dominated by the old Newgate Market at its centre, and the needs of commerce and trade.

Creating a better setting for St Paul's has exercised architects' imaginations since the building's completion. Indeed, no sooner was the building finished than Hawksmoor proposed both this piazza encircling the cathedral and a new baptistry.

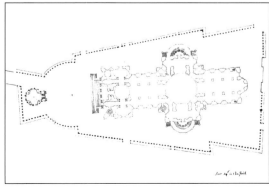

Right: occasional attempts towards a more formal symmetry have been put forward over the years, but have never adapted themselves well to the surrounding streetscape.

This aerial view of St Paul's in the 1930s shows an area of London little changed since Wren's time: a dense warren of medieval streets and buildings of uniform height, dominated by the great dome, church spires and the newer towers of corporate success.

Foster Associates' competition entry reintroduced a network of narrow alleys leading into St Paul's Churchyard at a slight angle, with the buildings cut short at the site boundary in a modern reinterpretation of an older asymmetry.

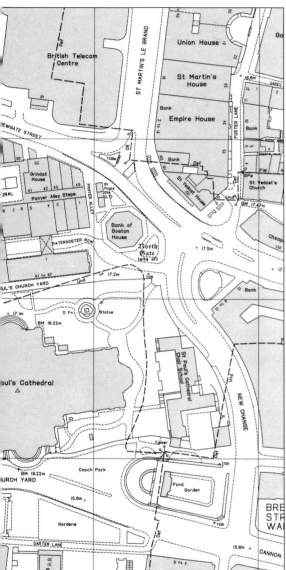

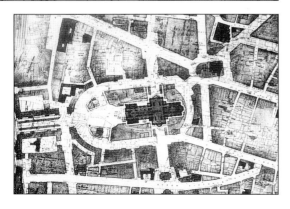

The Foster proposal sought inspiration from the spatial contrasts of earlier street plans, with an asymmetrical churchyard approached from a maze of narrow alleys and streets.

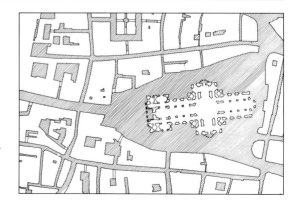

"On the one hand lay the irreducible fact of the great cathedral. On the other was the commercial reality of requirements for so much of the big, deep, highly serviced office space . . . and the mix of retailing which this wonderfully accessible site has so far failed to attract. Above, like a cloud, lies the constraint of St Paul's Heights. . . Below, existing footings which it was thought advisable not to disturb. This was the space within which the competitors were asked to generate an urban design concept which would be workable, look confident, and be complete at each stage of a phased development — and lead to interesting and varied architecture. In effect, the conditions forced each competitor to state his position about access, imagery, the accommodation of change, the relation of one building (and one century) to the next, all the stuff that the city is built of."

Francis Duffy, *The Architectural Review*, January 1988

A perennial feature of the long and often acrimonious debate which has focused on the Paternoster site has been the divergence between those, like the Prince, who argue for explicit continuity and deference, and others, including Norman Foster, who interpret those terms in a more radical light. The 1987 Paternoster masterplanning competition was, according to Frank Duffy — who was largely responsible for the competition brief — "urban rather than architectural in scope". Though consisting of a number of separate buildings around open spaces, the 1960s' development could be read as a self-contained megastructure, unconnected with adjacent parts of the City and responding only passively to St Paul's itself.

The development brief implied that Paternoster would be reintegrated into the City, yet to the east and north of the site were bleak areas of post-war development, while to the west the modest clerical residences around Amen Court provided an inappropriate point of reference for a late twentieth-century commercial complex. Where was the scope for continuity? Did deference to the cathedral imply, as some later players at Paternoster apparently believed, stylistic reference? Or could an entirely contemporary design address Wren's architecture with a confidence and assurance of its own?

Norman Foster had shown his ability to react incisively and sympathetically to historic context at Willis Faber in Ipswich. During the next decade, he emerged as an urbanist with a clear grasp of civic concerns which were coming to the fore as the planning prescriptions of the Modern Movement were effectively discarded.

Foster Associates' winning scheme for a new cultural centre opposite the Maison Carrée at Nîmes demonstrated a willingness to work with the scale and grain of an old city. The abortive BBC Radio Centre project was even more challenging and produced a design where public and private spaces — on an impressive scale — would have been boldly juxtaposed at the heart of London's West End. The very foundation of the scheme was its dynamic relationship to Nash's Portland Place and to the church of All Souls, on which that street — and the office's new pedestrian route — pivoted.

All Souls' is a modest landmark, St Paul's an overwhelming presence when seen at close range. Holford had successfully resisted attempts to make St Paul's a domineering, axially-perceived set-piece. Foster, similarly, recognised that

St Paul's Churchyard on the north side of the cathedral, a quiet oasis much appreciated by tourists and local office workers alike. The Foster proposal would have extended this green space to embrace the old Chapter House.

The Foster scheme was based on an alternating grid of public routes and private courtyards, separated by a series of 18-metre wide buildings with retail space at ground level and offices above. All service access and car parking was below ground.

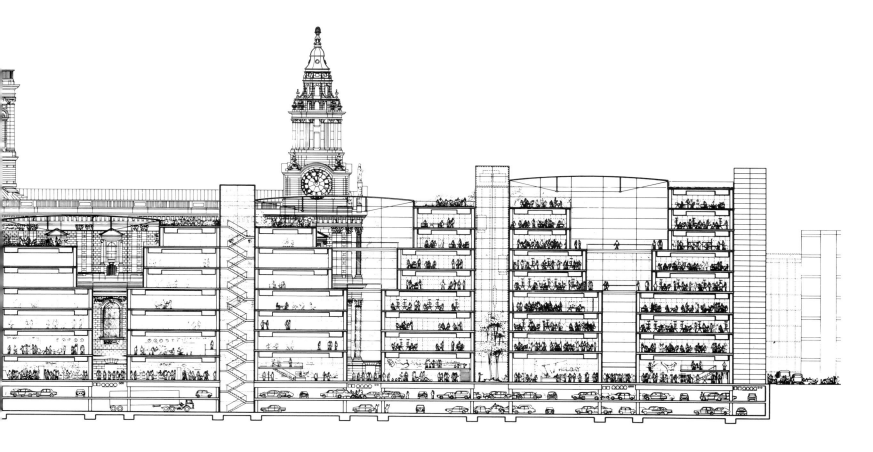

The design team drew on a variety of historical precedents to communicate the spirit of their design and the nature of the internal courtyards and alleys — including these photographs of the Inns of Court around Gray's Inn Gardens and Inner Temple.

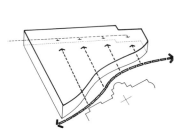

Generator: the urban context — routes, edges and surrounding building heights.

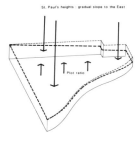

Generator: the St Paul's Heights regulations and the plot ratio.

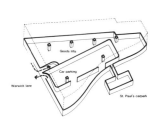

Generator: service access — a complete undercroft that will create a new platform at street level.

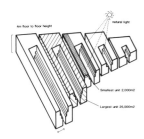

Generator: natural light and the optimum dimensions for office space — width, height and unit areas.

Generator: the appropriate mix of retail and commercial space — shops below, offices above.

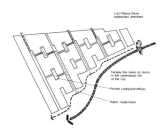

Generator: routes — the public and private, the major and minor, the ceremonial.

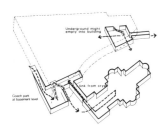

Generator: visitors and tourists.

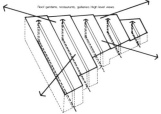

Generator: the roof — another level for leisure and recreation.

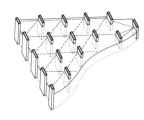

Generator: means of escape.

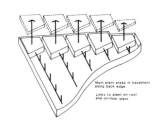

Generator: a co-ordinated servicing strategy covering the main plant and supply grid.

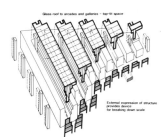

Generator: the external treatment of all elevations, including the roof.

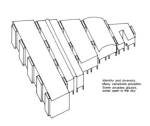

Generator: the masterplan — a sound basis for individual identities and separate design responsibilities.

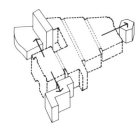

Generator: the consortium site and phased development.

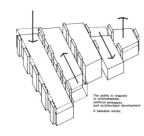

Generator: flexibility — vertical and horizontal growth and variability.

The Concept.

As part of the competition entry, a montage of supporting images drawn from around the world was compiled. This included photographs of the Galleria in Milan, a variety of nineteenth-century British arcades and, as shown here, the Gum department store in Moscow.

As the presentation model shows, the competition entry was conceived as a single composition, capable of extending over the entire site. The multi-layered planning and servicing grid, however, allowed considerable flexibility.

the visual dominance of the cathedral had been reinforced by its lost setting amid narrow streets and alleys which still survive, for example, in the ancient Inns of Court. His proposals for Paternoster sought to recreate a grid of pedestrian routes on the site, running north-south. Diving into one of these public arcades from the heavy traffic and noise of Newgate Street, the pedestrian would emerge in St Paul's Churchyard, with the cathedral, seen at an oblique angle, towering above. Disdaining any pretence of urban continuity, the design team produced a self-contained City quarter, far less megastructural in character that Holford's Paternoster, which addressed Wren's great building without deference or condescension.

The basic theme of the Paternoster proposal — an alternating grid of public routes and private courtyards — can be found in the unrealised Televisa project, designed for a radically different context. Yet the format is profoundly urban. Critical references to the Foster proposal as a *souk* or *casbah* suggest exotic influences, yet a more apposite reference can be found in the markets of London itself. Half a mile from the Paternoster site is Leadenhall Market, with glazed streets providing a refuge from weather and traffic. The nineteenth-century shopping arcades found in many cities — most imposingly at the Galleria Vittorio Emanuele in Milan — are clearly a further source of inspiration.

The starting point for the project is the site, sandwiched between Newgate Street and the churchyard, the latter itself a much-frequented pedestrian route as well as a place for tourists to linger and office workers to picnic. The office assumed the need for a substructure to provide parking and servicing; it was implicit, indeed, in the brief. Over this was placed the offices, increasing in height from east to west — in line with the St Paul's Heights policy — and terraced in form to provide both views out and generous external rooftop courts and gardens: a by-product of the planning restrictions dictating a spreading, relatively low-rise development. The office buildings are 18 metres wide, with shops at ground level.

The offices had their 'front doors' on Newgate Street, but could also be entered from private courtyards, themselves accessible from the public arcades. The latter were full-height, daylit spaces, either glazed or open to the sky, into which many of the offices had a view. The office space was designed to be highly adaptable. The courtyard plan allowed for it to be extensively

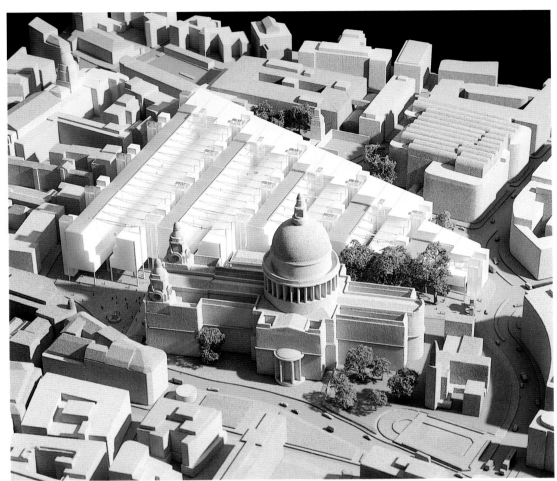

subdivided, with each tenant — or division of a larger organisation — able to give a particular identity to his domain. Alternatively, the system provided for the space to be let, at the other extreme, to a single tenant. The buildings could be divided into cellular offices, or used as large, open-plan floors. Identity and diversity were the key to the Foster masterplan and they underpinned a highly flexible programme.

The competition brief recognised the uncertainties resulting from the divided ownership of the masterplan site. The office's great piano-shaped 'grouping' of buildings was designed to occupy the entire seven-acre site, but the plan also provided for the three 'fringe' buildings to remain indefinitely or to be incorporated into the scheme at some later date. The servicing strategy was designed both to allow for phased

construction and to give tenants a considerable degree of choice and control over plant and environmental conditions. The principal chiller and boiler installations were centralised on the edge of the site, along Newgate Street, where a rooftop 'spine' contained further plant.

This very clearly expressed servicing grid was in accord with the overall strategy, with flexibility supported by a highly defined organisation of elements. 'Composite' construction — *in situ* concrete slabs on a steel frame — allowed for rapid assembly, while the 18 x 9-metre structural grid provided the potential for large, column-free floor spaces.

The masterplan provided a sheltered, arcaded frontage to St Paul's Churchyard, the focal point of the pedestrian arcades. The design team eschewed any formal urban statement here, yet the generous, if irregular, square proposed along

"(Foster's) approach allows an organisational order, certainly, but is organisation a sufficient principle of art, as Hannes Meyer proposed. It is interesting that among the architect's analytical sketches there is one that shows a diversity of character among the pieces, suggesting that the layout is a masterplan, or structure plan, capable of providing 'a basis for individual identities and separate design responsibilities'. In that admission there is a whole world of adjustment still to be made."

Robert Maxwell, *Casabella*, no 557, May 1989

the north side of the cathedral echoed Wren's preference for a tight enclosure of the building, in contrast to the more relaxed approach of Holford. Wren's Chapter House, compromised by 1960s development, was allowed to stand apart as a free-standing structure in the Cathedral Close. The historic Temple Bar was brought back to the City and used to close the eastern end of the public space. By extending the square around the west front of St Paul's, to claw back road and coach-parking space on the south side, the office enhanced the setting of the cathedral and created a buffer zone against the traffic, which had been identified as a cause of potentially serious structural damage to the fabric.

The Paternoster masterplan was, on the one hand, an expression of the office's rational, universal and formal approach to urban architecture. The plan was devoid of gestures designed to appeal to nostalgic, hierarchical or explicitly historicist views of the City of London, in general, and the area around St Paul's in particular. The programme underlying the development was rigorously and unashamedly expressed in a built form which was both boldly dramatic and entirely contemporary — in stark contrast to a number of other proposals for the site. The masterplan was an expression of a late twentieth-century response to place and history, respectful to both but motivated by a conviction that respect for the past should inspire the best efforts of the present.

Kenneth Powell

The individual buildings terraced downwards from west to east, responding to the St Paul's Heights regulations and creating a sequence of generous roof courts and gardens, both inside and outside the glazed atrium roofs.

The internal courts encompassed a number of uses, from private gardens for the benefit of larger corporations, as shown here, to shared reception areas providing access to the smaller office units.

As Foster proved at the Willis Faber project in Ipswich, it is a relatively simple task to turn an office roof into a beneficial amenity. With their unprecedented views and ready public access, the roof terraces of the Paternoster scheme offered an unrivalled opportunity to create spaces for the enjoyment of all.

The network of public alleys running right through the site, each offering a tantalising glimpse of St Paul's at one end, allowed retail units to be integrated into the entire fabric of the scheme, dedicated to neither tourist nor office worker exclusively, but shared equally between the two.

1987-1989 Riverside Housing
Hammersmith
London

Foster Associates' projected housing and office development at Hammersmith, west of central London, represented an attempt to identify an appropriate architectural and urban response to the River Thames and, within the context of a privately-financed development package, to contribute to the public's perception and enjoyment of the river. The office was already addressing these issues on a smaller scale at the Riverside project close to Battersea Bridge, but the site at Winslow Road, Hammersmith was far larger and more problematic.

The 9.26 acre site was occupied by an undistinguished and unsightly sprawl of factory sheds, partly disused and increasingly seen by the local authority and local residents as an undesirable intrusion. Just yards to the east, a similar site had recently been redeveloped for mixed use to designs by Richard Rogers, who had retained the best of the old buildings and converted them to contain offices, including his own. Reluctant to see further job opportunities lost, this was seen as a clear public gain and was declared a planning objective for any future development.

Adjacent housing — an area of modest, two-storey Edwardian terraced houses extending to

the Fulham Palace Road — offered no obvious point of reference for the new residential development. The mansion blocks and the vast bulk of the depository owned by Harrods' store, on the other side of the Thames, however, had a scale more in keeping with their location.

The office's first instinct was to develop the required housing around a generous square, rising in height away from the river. Commercial space would be provided as a low-rise buffer between the new housing and the existing Edwardian streets. Light manufacturing and studio-type offices were envisaged as an environmentally friendly alternative to the existing operations on the site.

The idea of using the centre of the square as a marina for small boats reflected the success of marinas recently developed at Brentford, Chiswick and Chelsea Harbour, all nearby, while reinforcing the fact that more and more Londoners were turning to the river as a place for recreation. The marina idea was technically viable, but costly, and after due consideration the square of housing appeared too introspective, in danger of becoming a private preserve forming a barrier between the river and the nearby streets. Given that the site was to be

Having outgrown their river-bank location, the old industrial buildings *(top)* were no longer viable. Foster Associates proposed replacing them with a square of residential buildings *(bottom)*, at the centre of which was a new marina.

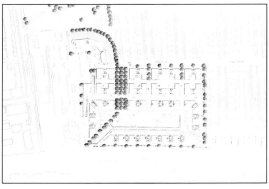

The first scheme was adapted into a series of T-shaped apartment buildings which were set at right angles to the river, with inlets of water between them, creating a new marina in place of the muddy river-bank.

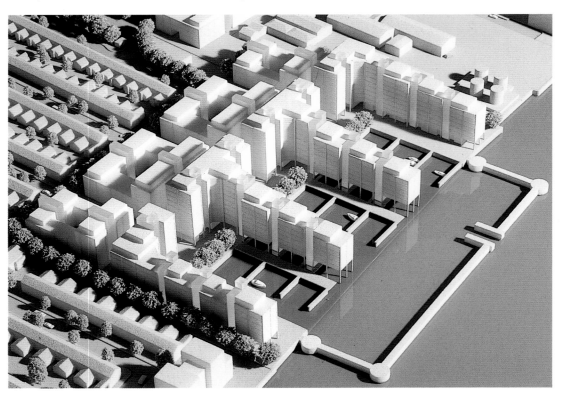

212

In the final proposal, the apartment buildings became L-shaped blocks separated by communal gardens. Behind these, lettable studio space was provided around open courtyards, and as before the individual buildings are separated to maintain open 'viewing corridors' to the river.

Situated just a few hundred metres downstream from Hammersmith Bridge, the apartment buildings were aligned to enjoy unprecedented views of the river. By raising the buildings well above ground level, access to the riverside marina remained open to everyone, while lockgates at its entrance ensured water levels remained at the correct height even at low tide.

Public access to the site was improved by a series of new footpaths, running along the riverbank and between the individual buildings. The buildings themselves were carefully positioned to ensure uninterrupted views of the river from the neighbouring streets.

comprehensively redeveloped, there was an obvious opportunity to create a more expansive public space.

A new approach produced a fundamental rethinking of the project. With the marina now relocated to the river — formed by digging out the muddy bank of the Thames — it was possible to dispose the apartment blocks in 'T' shapes at right angles to the river, with inlets of water and boat moorings between them. The advantages of this approach included the opening up of views through to the River Thames, with more convenient pedestrian routes through the site, and the generally greater sense of openness achieved by keeping the buildings back from the river front.

The final planning submission for the site — presented in March 1989 — developed this theme, but now with 'L'-shaped blocks set end on to the river. The marina had been dropped and the spaces between the blocks were laid out as communal gardens. Containing 268 apartments, the four blocks stepped up in height away from the river, where a varied series of public spaces replaced the relatively confined walkway featured in the office's first scheme.

Behind was 300,000 square feet of commercial space — 'B1' space in the jargon of contemporary British planning regulations, containing office studios and workshops for new-style industry — organised around courtyards to accord with protected 'view corridors' to the river. Most of the car parking for the development was to be below ground, while deliveries would be handled within the internal courts, minimising noise and disruption. The employment potential of the project — up to 1600 jobs — was presented as a major gain to the borough.

The Hammersmith scheme was never realised: by 1989, the residential property market in London was beginning to falter. The project remains of interest, however, more for the ideas it contained than for its relevance to an uncertain development scene. As a highly disciplined approach to the vital issue of mixed-use urban regeneration, designed to respect the character of London and to meet local needs as well as those of developers and incomers, it remains worthy of close study.

Kenneth Powell

213

Docklands Square
Canary Wharf
London

In plan and in section, the proposed towers for Docklands Square embodied a cool elegance based on the simplest of planning diagrams and straightforward detailing.

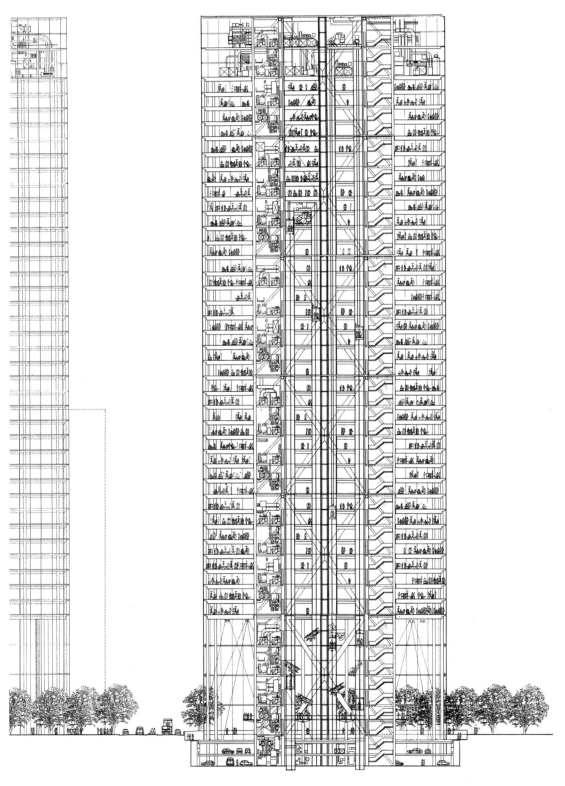

When Canadian developers Olympia & Yorke took over the massive Canary Wharf project in London's Docklands in 1987, they brought with them decades of experience of skyscraper building in North America, including the famous Battery Park City in downtown Manhattan. Canary Wharf was going to be built the American way: fast, simple and — by American standards — traditional. Not surprisingly, the architects they chose were mainly American: Skidmore, Owings & Merrill, Pei Cobb Freed & Partners, and Kohn Pedersen Fox for the 'low-rise', 20-storey buildings, and Cesar Pelli for the 50-storey tower, the tallest in Europe.

But the client was also keen to involve the local architectural community. The London practice of Troughton McAslan designed one of the buildings at the foot of Pelli's tower in a straight Modernist style quite unlike its brash neighbours and, in 1989, as Pelli's tower began its ascent, Foster Associates and the Richard Rogers Partnership were invited to submit designs for a pair of towers that would almost match it in height.

The Foster office knew something about tall buildings. After all, the Hongkong Bank had been finished only three years earlier. But that was a special building, tailor-made for a special

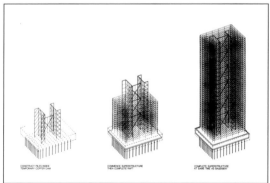

client. The Canary Wharf towers, by contrast, were to be regular, commercial, lettable office blocks — a building type new to the office.

Olympia & Yorke were expert clients and they knew what they wanted. They would not be relying on their architects for innovative ideas, whether architectural or technical, and they were not interested in reinventing the skyscraper. But they reckoned without the Foster design ethos, which demands that every brief be questioned and every project be thought through from first principles.

The east tower in elevation. The design team's first proposal was totally uncompromising: an all-glass tower with minimal external detailing, rising sheer from pavement level to rooftop.

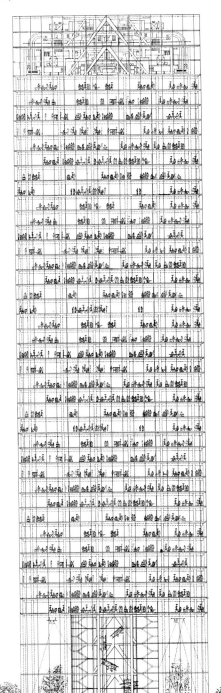

Olympia & Yorke's brief located two new towers symmetrically on either side of a new square in front of Cesar Pelli's existing tower, as shown here. Foster Associates proposed an alternative arrangement, moving one of the towers to the end of the square and so opening the square to the river.

The planning of the towers was quite traditional, with offices arranged around a central services and lift core. The lifts were separated into four groups which stopped off in stages over the height of the building, releasing more lettable space on the upper floors.

At ground floor, a magnificent eight-storey high lobby was created, separated from its surroundings by a minimal wall of suspended clear glass. Early proposals indicated glazed service cores and lift-shafts.

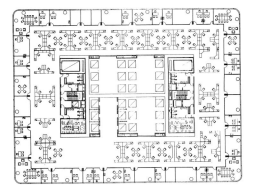

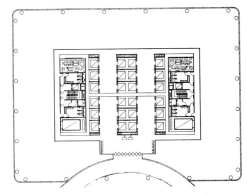

The first radical proposal was to change the site plan. The client envisaged a symmetrical arrangement with a new public square to the east of Pelli's tower, flanked by the new buildings on the north and south sides. The office's proposal was more subtle, placing one of the new towers on the east side of the square, leaving the south side open to the sun and water.

The form of the proposed towers was also rather different from that envisaged by the client. Like most developers, they believed in what they thought of as simple, traditional urban forms. In their philosophy, cities should consist of ordinary streets and squares 'at grade', surrounded by buildings with front doors.

But this eminently sensible principle carried with it an aesthetic prejudice: that buildings ought also to be traditional in form, with beginnings, middles and ends, or, in Classical terms, bases, shafts and capitals. Pelli's tower had already compromised these expectations to some extent. It had no projecting base, but it did have slender 'add-on' colonnades at ground level, and at the top it sported a pyramid for a hat, which hid the mechanical plant and gave it a traditional obelisk form.

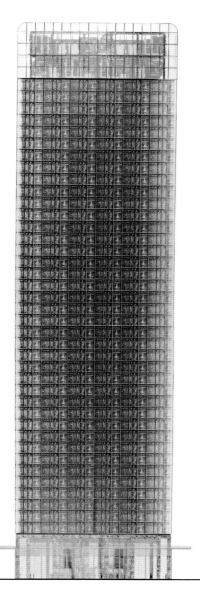

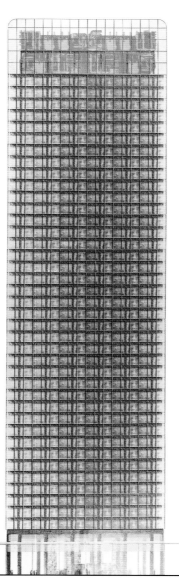

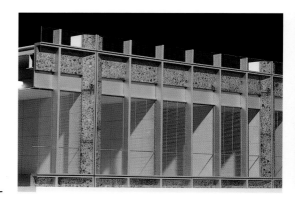

Below: the new façade, with its granite facings and storey-high glass panels, was studied in a series of detailed models.

In the first designs, the Foster Associates towers made no such compromise. They rose sheer from the pavement and were cut off straight at the top, with no embellishment except the open framework of the plant enclosure. At ground level the expected solid plinth was replaced by its opposite — an eight-storey-high lobby like an internal garden, separated from the surrounding urban space only by a transparent curtain of glass. Even the service core was to be glazed.

Some aspects of the brief, however, were not negotiable. There was no question of Hongkong Bank-style escalator circulation systems or atria in the sky. The net-to-gross ratio was paramount and each office floor would take the traditional 'doughnut' form, the offices around a vertical circulation and service core.

Here, there were a few tricks of the trade for the office to learn. Making the optimum use of space at each level turned out to be a complex three-dimensional game as the lift-shafts successively 'dropped off' at the higher levels, to be replaced by usable floor area. The structure too was traditional — a steel frame for rapid erection, supporting concrete slabs on permanent metal shuttering, with raised floors and suspended ceiling voids for services distribution.

It was, however, the cladding that absorbed most of the detail design effort. Low emissivity insulating glass was the main material, in enormous storey-height panes, mechanically fixed to a structural subframe which showed on the façade only as a grid of narrow grooves. Curved glass panels dealt neatly with the potentially awkward corner detail. The ITN building was the immediate precedent for this minimally detailed external skin, though this recurring theme in the practice's work can be traced back to the Willis Faber & Dumas building of 1974.

The client was not convinced by the austere elegance of the first design and requested the use of more opulent materials. The office resolved the problem in its own way, proposing granite facings to the floor edges and columns, not as a formal cladding but layered behind the original glass wall.

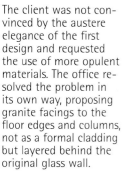

Drawings were prepared to study the effects of using different coloured marble or granite for the facings, including this bold example in red. At ground level, the lobby was reduced to four storeys in height and a canopy was included.

Despite the success of the revised cladding system, the office retains a fondness for the simplicity of the first scheme which is still shown in lectures today.

Shortly before the project was cancelled, a full-size mock-up of the proposed cladding system was prepared to ensure that the granite cladding remained visible in normal lighting conditions.

Below: granite facings or not, the main rooftop plant remained open to view behind the clear-glazed cladding.

The Foster towers relied for their architectural effect on utter simplicity, extreme refinement and maximum transparency — the very opposite of the solid, heavily modelled forms of most of the buildings on Canary Wharf. Not surprisingly, the early designs met with some

resistance from the client, who believed that future tenants would demand more obvious signs of quality and opulence — some granite cladding, perhaps, and some kind of articulation of the base. In later versions of the design, the office was to meet these requirements without compromising its own aesthetic preferences. The lobby space was reduced to the equivalent of only four storeys and a sheltering canopy appeared, surrounding the base of each tower.

The breakthrough came when the design team proposed an extraordinary answer to the client's repeated request for some form of stone cladding. Why not, argued the team, have both glass and stone, not side by side on the façade in the conventional way, but layered one behind the other, stone behind glass. Columns and floor edges would be clad in green Italian marble, emphasising the solidity and permanence of the main structure, but would be screened by a delicate glass skin. A full-size mock-up was made which proved the idea would work.

Both client and architect were satisfied by the clever compromise and the project looked set to proceed. It was then that the design team received the letter telling them to stop work. The Canary Wharf project was running into financial difficulties and the eastern half of the development was to be put on hold for the foreseeable future.

Colin Davies

217

During 1986 and 1987 Foster Associates found themselves experiencing an almost inevitable period of adjustment following their all-consuming involvement in the Hongkong Bank. If not exactly a hiatus, this was still a period that seemed to demand a certain shift of gear. Stockley Park had just been completed, Stansted, the next major job, was due to start on site and, in the meantime, a proliferation of small developer-driven London projects served as a reminder that this century-old method of realising buildings in the capital still flourished. Indeed, such projects were now starting to look like a legitimate source of work for a firm which had, at the time, with the notable exception of Stockley Park, surprisingly little experience of developer-led projects.

Typical of this kind of work, where costs are under the microscope at all times and land-swapping practices may derail building design considerations at any moment, was the project known as the Royal Thames Yacht Club.

The office had been approached by the developer Chelsfield to design a replacement for this 20-year-old building situated on a wedge-shaped site in Knightsbridge. The appeal of the project is not hard to see: overlooking Hyde Park

Located in one of central London's most fashionable districts, just minutes away from Harrods, to the west, and Hyde Park Corner to the east, the redevelopment of the Royal Thames Yacht Club site presented an exciting opportunity for the office, particularly as the client was interested in developing a mixed-use building that would accommodate the club, as well as provide potential space for offices or an exclusive hotel or, indeed, a combination of the two. A model of the immediate area was prepared so that the site, and its potential, could be studied in detail.

The site was bounded on one side by the Brompton Road, one of central London's busiest arteries, and on the other by Hyde Park. The new building would have to mediate between the two.

Various elevation treatments were tried out on the early study models, some with plain façades and others that expressed the building's structure. Every option, however, favoured an understated simplicity.

The view along Brompton Road from the west. The existing building, a rather nondescript 1960s office block, was somewhat lost among its more articulated neighbours. The new scheme would benefit from a more dynamic presence.

and adjoining a major hotel, this prestigious site posed a series of fascinating design challenges in a very high-profile location.

The new premises were mooted by the client as needing to be adaptable to mixed use – residential, office space or even hotel accommodation – in various permutations. One floor would have to be retained for the yacht club that gave the building its popular name. The plot also included a small branch of the National Westminster Bank, first thought to be eligible for demolition but soon excluded when it was given listed status.

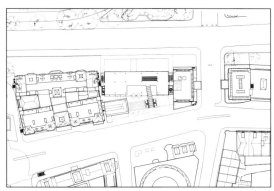

Left: what was already an awkwardly-shaped site was further complicated by the need to retain the building at its south-west corner, previously a branch of the National Westminster Bank and recently listed.

The practice's initial role was to suggest how this tight urban plot might be flexibly treated to accommodate the proposed mixed-use elements. This task struck a particular chord with Norman Foster's continuing concern about the negative social effects of London's regulatory bias towards single-use occupancy. In this respect it is interesting to note that the Royal Thames Yacht Club project was an almost exact contemporary of the Riverside project, part of which was to become the office's new home.

However, the most demanding part of the brief was how to insert a new building into such an awkward site, while making it engage positively with its contrasting neighbours.

To the north it would have to address Hyde Park while holding the line of the other buildings on South Carriage Drive. On the south side it needed not only to accommodate the newly listed bank building – itself an out-of-scale insertion among the much taller façades of Knightsbridge – but also to respond to the powerful vertical modulation of the street's predominantly nineteenth-century buildings where cornices, turrets and detailing combine to create a very strong upright gridding.

Site and model studies made it clear that views of the new building from the south were only possible at an oblique angle. As the existing building demonstrated, a plain façade would be difficult to pick out from among its more animated neighbours. The projecting towers of the adjacent Edwardian building offered a clue as to how an appropriate presence might be established. By pulling the lift-shaft out of the new building and setting it on the pavement line, the vertical dynamic of the street would be reinforced and a new 'event' created.

Drawing on experience gained from the design of the ITN building and the Riverside project, the elevational studies for the revised 1990 scheme were proceeding well when the project was suddenly cancelled.

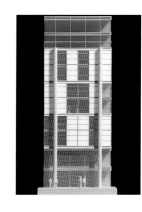

The design team's initial proposal sought to solve the problem of mixed-use interior space by placing lavatories, stairs and plant rooms at either end of the new structure. These were the points at which the new building would meet its neighbours: the hotel to the west and, to the east, a smaller nineteenth-century stucco building that formed the apex of the site.

The immediate effect was to achieve a minimum of clutter internally, an effect aided further by pulling the lifts out of the main body of the building and using them, in effect, to reclaim the street line on the Knightsbridge side. Since the bulk of the building had necessarily been pushed back from the street by the need to run behind the bank, the 'projecting' lifts became the building's link with the pavement. This siting also solved two other design issues.

Instead of being an awkward monolith, knocked out of its natural alignment by the bank, the new building had instead made a virtue out of a necessity and acquired an inviting public square, defined by the lift towers to the east and the bank to the west. This would draw people towards the building's entrance where revolving doors would give on to a reception area sited at the foot of a full-height atrium.

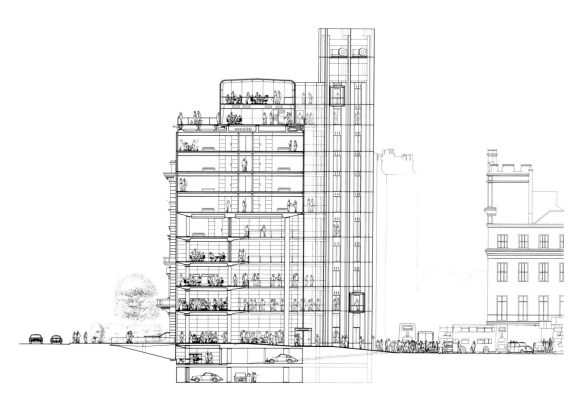

A cross-section through the first scheme. The main building was a straight-forward rectangle in plan, nine storeys high if the upper floors were given over to hotel accommodation, or eight if offices. Unified around a full-height atrium, the first five floors were dedicated to the club that gave the building its name, with extra offices placed in a semi-basement if required. The rest of the basement was given over to car parking. A separate pavilion on the roof was set aside for leisure and restaurant facilities, to be shared by the club and the hotel, with an extensive roof terrace giving views over Hyde Park.

The simple rectangular plan, 18 metres wide, of the main building passed comfortably behind the old National Westminster Bank building. The upper floors could be planned either as offices or hotel rooms.

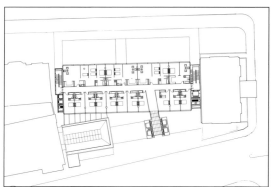

Provisional facilities for the first floor. Incorporating the refurbished bank building, the club floors could be laid out in a variety of ways, depending on the final brief.

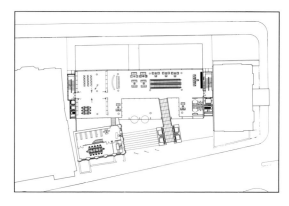

Redesigned in 1990, to a brief that now incorporated the Edwardian building at the apex of the site, it was soon established that nearly all the design principles put forward for the first scheme held true for the second. At first glance, the new proposal is all but indistinguishable from its predecessor.

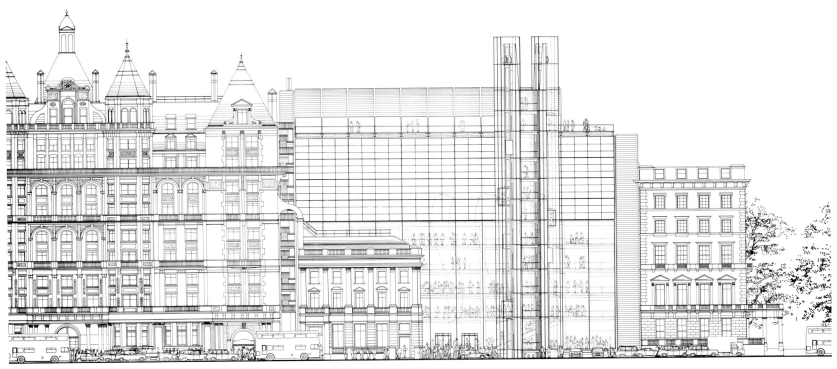

Behind the animation of the clear-glazed lift-shafts, the elevations of the main building were calm and understated. At the lower levels, the club floors were clad in clear glass, allowing uninterrupted views through the building to Hyde Park beyond.

At the same time, the extra height of the lift towers could be used to make the Knightsbridge aspect of the building achieve a vertical scale pitched halfway between those of its two adjacent buildings. At a single stroke, the lifts — so often seen as a necessary evil or at least an architectural inconvenience — had been strategically deployed to confer three positive design advantages upon the building they would serve.

In addition, the lift tower acted as a useful barrier between pedestrians and vehicles arriving at the building. As pedestrians arrived to the left, vehicles entered to the right where a ramp would lead them down to two levels of subterranean parking.

This, then, was the essence of the design, although some variables were included. If the residential or hotel scheme were to be adopted, the building would have nine storeys; if office space predominated, the deeper floors would translate into eight storeys. Either way, there was an intention to define the elevation of the building with banded glazing that would respond to the differing internal usages.

This design solution, which has since been described as "a very complex piece of urban dentistry", was distinguished by a coherence

that looks very logical in the plans and models but which was far from obvious at the outset. Its implementation was prevented when the site was sold to Mountleigh, although, interestingly, a revised version was commissioned from the office by the new owner in 1990. The new proposal adhered to the essentials of the original, although by this time various other factors had changed. The stucco building at the apex of the site was now incorporated, and the atrium was no longer included.

This version was never built either, the vicissitudes of property development having once more overtaken the design process.

However, what the Royal Thames Yacht Club project succeeded in demonstrating very clearly was that good building design is not automatically negated by the volatile market pressures under which the property developer operates. Rather, it simply has to work that much harder to satisfy the shifting economic equations while still doing justice to its central concerns of form, space and context.

Graham Vickers

1986-1990   The Riverside Development
Battersea
London

'Riverside' is a unique example of a modern British building which reintroduces the idea of mixed-use development. By helping to create a new network of pedestrian routes, the project has also played a major role in regenerating the local neighbourhood. Finally, the building's completion marked a watershed in the evolution of Foster & Partners, as the practice is now known.

Although it has recently become fashionable to advocate the virtues of mixing uses such as living and working in one location, there are, at the time of writing, still no contemporary examples of these ideas in Britain. It is easy to cite examples of such coexistence in the Middle Ages or the Renaissance, and even in more recent times the tenement buildings of Glasgow combined shops and pubs at ground level, offices immediately above, and then several levels of residential accommodation over that — rising between five and seven storeys in all.

Such compact communities, however, are in direct contrast to most of today's planning guidelines, which specify separate zones for residential, commercial or industrial use, or for leisure and culture. The consequent problems of this approach to urban planning — the social alienation, the need for extensive commuting

with all its associated traffic and pollution, and the ecological impact of low-density sprawl — are only now beginning to be fully appreciated.

In the past, it was the blighting nature of heavy industry that was responsible for many of these zoning policies. Today, however, the 'clean' industries — such as micro-electronics — and the new service-sector offices and studios are totally compatible with residential areas. In our recent work in Duisburg, we have demonstrated that the inner city can be revitalised by introducing these newer industries and locating them alongside housing and schools — even creating more green spaces in the process. Furthermore, we have shown that such buildings can be ecologically sensitive and strive towards sustainability.

Riverside was an early example of applying this philosophy to the way that we, as an office, might live and work — a version of trying to practise what we preached. Foster Associates, as it then was, had occupied a variety of office locations in central London. But the word 'office' has always been inappropriate for the way that we design. More than any practice I know we develop models, full-size mock-ups and prototypes as an integral part of the design process.

The entrance to the site from Hester Road — into what is now the courtyard — as it was in 1986. In reality, it was a collection of small lots, some of which included access to a run-down dock that gave on to the river. The entire site would have to be cleared before redevelopment could begin.

The north side of the river, looking towards Battersea Bridge and, beyond it, the site. Although less than 10 minutes' stroll from Cheyne Walk, one of Chelsea's most fashionable addresses, in 1986 both sides of the river quickly deteriorated into areas of seedy dereliction, lined with ageing and redundant industrial buildings.

Until the introduction of heavy industry during the eighteenth century, a city's workshops, houses and commercial establishments co-existed at all levels. A number of the office's recent projects have sought to reintroduce similar diversity into modern urban life.

But the modern property market cannot accommodate these realities, with the result that we were forever splitting these activities, one from the other. Even the studio in Great Portland Street, where we were before the move to Riverside, was split, with model-makers on a separate level. Eventually, they overflowed to a warehouse several miles away. It was then that a vision for the future emerged where all of these activities would be integrated, as far as possible, in one space and on one site. Ideally, too, this would be combined with urban living and a riverside perspective.

The search for a suitable location was long and drawn out. In the mid-1980s, however, a site was identified on the south side of the River Thames between Albert and Battersea Bridges, opposite Cheyne Walk in Chelsea. In reality, the site was made up of many separate lots, most with decaying industrial structures on them, creating an area of seedy dereliction which extended up to the edge of the river. On one side was a dock, filled with rotting debris and stagnant water. Working with an enterprising estate agent, a site was finally assembled and then secured with the help of a bank loan.

The next task was to turn the site into a project and, in particular, a home for the practice. So conversations started in earnest with potential developers who might buy the site and create space for the practice to rent. In parallel we were exploring design options. As architects, with an eye on the potential of the site, it seemed obvious that in a mixed development the flats and offices should share the best views on to the river.

It also seemed inevitable that the work places would be close to the ground with the living spaces elevated above, where they would enjoy privacy and the best views, as well as command a higher price — which would help the development equation. With the creation of a private courtyard we were able to show that it was possible to provide separate access and security to both those who would work in the building and those who would live there.

However, we were soon to discover an apparently irresolvable conflict. All the financial institutions behind the developers insisted that, for funding purposes, there should be two separate buildings: one for offices, the other for apartments. Worse still, it was argued that the higher-value residential spaces should overlook the Thames and a separate office block should

One of the many new approaches to the site today; this one is from the south along the side of the old dock. Since the completion of 'Riverside', the entire neighbourhood has gradually been transformed, with the best of the existing industrial buildings refurbished as apartments, studios or restaurants, and others redeveloped.

overlook the dock. All our arguments for an integrated mixed-use building were to no avail.

By contrast, the planners and the local authority of Wandsworth were totally supportive. There was a shared enthusiasm to see the dock cleaned up and brought back to life, and European Community funds were pursued for its rehabilitation. In the negotiations that followed, we worked with Wandsworth's chief planner to develop a network of pedestrian routes which would open up the river and the dock to the public with good connections through to the surrounding streets. It was this early planning decision that was to prove so important to the future regeneration of the river and the areas which extended beyond the site.

At this time , quite by chance, I happened to meet David Gabbay, who was one of the developers for the site on the other side of the dock. We agreed to have lunch together. His group was just about to submit a relatively conventional scheme of apartments for planning consent. We got on extremely well together and shared an excellent meal. Over dessert I explained the seemingly impossible dilemma that we faced with our site. To my surprise, he was immediately sympathetic and agreed to help.

The early scheme from Albert Bridge. The adjacent site, nearer the bridge, was also being developed at this time as luxury apartments. Unexpectedly, the developer for this block was sympathetic to the idea of a mixed-use building and became actively involved.

Early attempts to design a single mixed-use building for the site were initially thwarted by financial institutions that preferred a clear separation of domestic and commercial functions. This option was explored in an early scheme which placed the offices in a single-volume, barrel-vaulted enclosure running parallel to the old dock, with only the residential building looking out over the river.

David and his then partners eventually became the developer, client and builder of the project. We worked to a very simple formula, which was shaking hands on whatever was agreed. It drove the flocks of lawyers and accountants to despair but it worked. The project went through upheavals — one caused by the collapse of a major subcontractor halfway through the job. Also, David's company exercised the right to change details such as the kitchen and bathroom fittings, or the internal finishes, door furniture and staircase detailing. Given that he was taking the financial risk for the apartments — as opposed to the offices that we would fit-out and rent from him — it was difficult to argue the point. The reality was that the project was being realised against all the odds and the main priorities were still intact.

The apartments were generously planned with virtually no waste circulation or corridors. Sliding windows maximised the view and, according to David, most people would do their own fit-out anyway. It is easy to look back now, in the light of experience, and demonstrate from conversations with many of the present owners of the apartments that the interiors as originally planned would have commanded a tangible value. But it also has to be conceded that a significant proportion of the flats have been stripped out and rebuilt — one owner bought three and joined them together to make one huge unit. More recently, another has purchased two with the same intention. There is also a delightfully 'extreme' conversion by Claudio Silvestrin, who removed just about everything except the supporting columns!

Commercially, the apartments have been extremely successful; not only selling at a period when the market experienced a downturn, but much sought after since and still continuing to change hands at high values. The group, of which David Gabbay was a part, has since split but we remain good friends and still enjoy excellent lunches together.

During the early stages of construction, the developer secured an option on a site which backed on to the rear of the project. Plans were hurriedly redrawn and permissions secured to add a two-storey pavilion and a gallery entrance which extended to create a gateway to the private courtyard.

A grand staircase in the gallery ascends to the main studio space, at first-floor level, a two-storey high volume with good connections to other secondary spaces on a mezzanine level and on the ground floor. The total space offered opportunities for subletting as well as scope for future expansion, which has since proved to be a lifeline for the practice.

More important than anything else was the opportunity to create a properly integrated studio which could be tailored to our own special needs. Not surprisingly, it is unlike any other space that I know. Even so, if economic pressures demanded, the main space can be easily converted — by inserting the missing floor — into two storeys of conventional offices, or 12 apartments, or a combination of the two kinds of space, each capable of being served by a separate entrance.

The period leading up to the fitting out of our new spaces was one of intense debate back in the Great Portland Street office. The

"Architects' offices (like architects' houses) are a permanent and conspicuous expression of a practice's philosophy, organisation and day-to-day working methods, which will be judged by clients, critics and *cognoscenti* alike."

Catherine Slessor, *The Architects' Journal*, October 1990

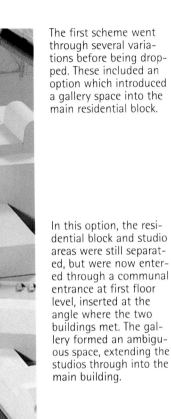

A sketch model of the interim scheme. Far from convincing the architects that this was the way forward, the unresolved areas of the design only served to remind them that a single, mixed-use building was the better option.

The first scheme went through several variations before being dropped. These included an option which introduced a gallery space into the main residential block.

In this option, the residential block and studio areas were still separated, but were now entered through a communal entrance at first floor level, inserted at the angle where the two buildings met. The gallery formed an ambiguous space, extending the studios through into the main building.

The roof of the studio block was designed as an extensive terrace, overlooking the adjacent dock and river beyond, and open to residents and office workers alike. The possibility of including a rooftop swimming pool, enclosed in a free-standing pavilion, was also explored.

design team, headed by Ken Shuttleworth and Howard Gilbey, assumed that everyone would want some degree of privacy in the open space and many versions of carrels were mocked-up at full size for comment. The reactions were as positive as they were unexpected — nearly everyone wanted less privacy and more openness. By way of explanation they pointed to the central wall in the existing office, which despite its openings was a substantial division and undermined the concept of optimum communication. The process of consultation continued and it was from this dialogue that the present rows of big benches were to evolve.

Riverside was realised at a time when the practice faced some of its most difficult challenges. This was in the aftermath of the Hongkong Bank project, which was opened to the public towards the end of 1985. There was great

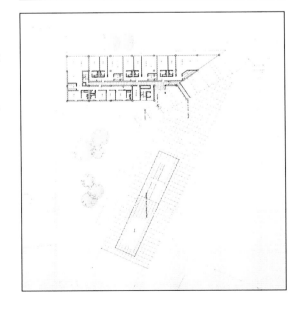

"From the outside at least, the new building fails to betray any hint of the soul-baring and stylistic argument that played such a fundamental role in its conception. As ever, the point of departure for the overall design is an innate conceptual simplicity, which aims to eliminate the superfluous. As a result, the rectangular eight-storey building squares up to the riverfront with a display of understatement and coolness that verges on the glacial."

Catherine Slessor, *The Architects' Journal*, October 1990

With active support from the local planning authority and the developer of the adjacent site, the design for a single mixed-use building — including a small two-storey pavilion at the rear of the site — quickly fell into place. A presentation model was produced to explain the concept more fully.

pressure on the practice to move to Hong Kong in its entirety during this period, especially when the office there was peaking at 120 employees, while the London office had dropped to a mere 16. One of the present partners, Spencer de Grey, had made the initial move to Hong Kong to open our start-up office there in 1980. On his return, at the end of 1982, virtually all the other key individuals had to leave *en masse* for Hong Kong to follow through the design which had been developed in London. I was torn between commuting to Hong Kong, Japan, America and Europe — all the places where the Bank was being made — and having to start a new practice with Spencer, virtually from scratch.

While the Hongkong Bank was on site — growing simultaneously up into the sky and down into the ground — the London office was completing projects like the Renault Distribution Centre; winning international competitions such as the Frankfurt athletics stadium, the BBC Radio Centre and the Carré d'Art in Nîmes; and competitively securing projects like Stansted Airport and the new headquarters for Televisa in Mexico City. The mental and physical stresses pushed us to the limits. Although we were unaware of it at the time, we were laying the foundations for a better way of working and it is impossible to separate the practice now, in Riverside, from that collective experience which forged very personal bonds.

In 1985 the remainder of my present partners — Graham Phillips, David Nelson and Ken Shuttleworth — returned from Hong Kong, and nearly all the other directors in the practice today are from that critical period in Hong Kong and London.

The regrouping in London could have been an unsettling anticlimax after the triumph of the Bank. Instead, it was the reverse. There was a collective energy and experience eager to tackle new projects and to move forward. It was that same drive which later enabled us to fight off a domestic recession and successfully go out and compete for work internationally.

Started at the end of 1986, the Riverside project was an opportunity to question everything about the way that we designed but with a renewed enthusiasm. Nothing was too important or trivial to merit discussion. Many of the changes that the move achieved were, in retrospect, radical — although we now take them for granted. For example, some of us thought it would be better to have a 'no-smoking' office. The idea was floated, but we never expected it to happen because we assumed one group would feel alienated. To our surprise, however, it was the heaviest smokers, who saw it as an opportunity to help curb their habit, who were the strongest supporters. This hardly seems radical today, but then attitudes have changed since the late 1980s.

Some of the later alterations to the project mentioned earlier, such as the addition of the gallery entrance, were also turned to social advantage. For example, most places of work ensure that the visitor is carefully shielded from the activities within. From the very beginning, our office has been open to scrutiny. Meetings, whether formal or informal, take place in the midst of the creative process itself. The essence of the spaces has always been about lifestyle and communication. In that spirit, the revised entrance dispensed with the traditional waiting area and, instead, the visitor can enjoy the bar, which is the social focus of the office, and drink a coffee, read a newspaper or make a phone call if there is any need to wait.

The double-height glass façade of the main studio space overlooks the river — in terms of shading and solar gain, it was helpful that it

As the early model *(opposite)* shows, nearly all the main features of the final design were present from the very beginning, not least the double-height studio that occupies the entire first floor – a space so large that it would accommodate Norman Foster's Caproni glider with ease. At the time the model was made, it was assumed that the ground floor would be given over to car parking, hidden from the riverside walk by screens of glass blocks.

Site surveys indicated that a basement car park was viable, allowing the ground floor to be re-planned as lettable office space to complement the lettable studio space proposed for the small pavilion at the rear of the site.

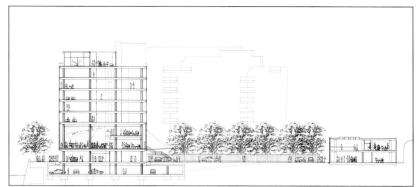

In the final design, a narrow two-storey 'gallery' was added along the west side of the site. This provides covered access to the main studio and creates a visual barrier shielding the courtyard from the light-industrial development on the adjacent site.

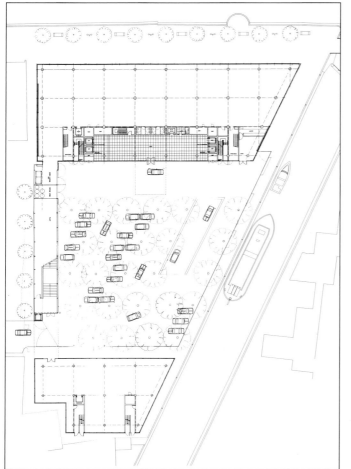

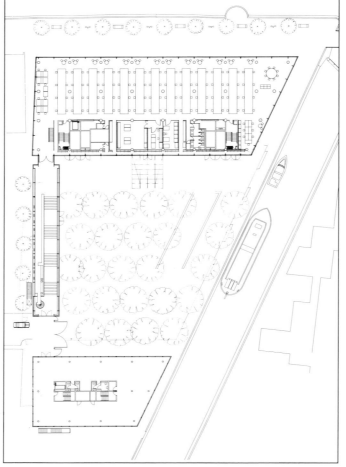

The presentation plans of the final design, including *(from left to right)* the ground floor, the main studio at first-floor level, a typical apartment floor, and the penthouse on the roof. Just as the project went on site, a small plot at the rear corner of the site became available, allowing the pavilion to be replanned in the simpler rectangular form, indicated here only on the first-floor plan *(left)*.

Unlike earlier proposals, in the final design the apartments and ground-floor offices were given separate entrances from the central courtyard. The main building has two full-height service cores, located at the rear of the building and linked, at the lower levels, by a secondary service zone.

A cross-section through the final design, along the line of the entrance gallery. Though designed as separate lettable space, the offices on the ground floor and in the pavilion have since provided a lifeline for the practice during its rapid growth of recent years.

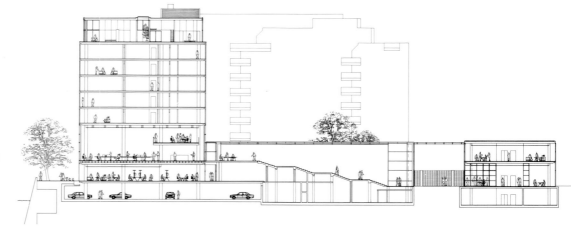

The glazed curtain walling, which wraps round the whole building, is modulated with translucent and fritted panes of glass where privacy or protection from solar gain or glare is required.

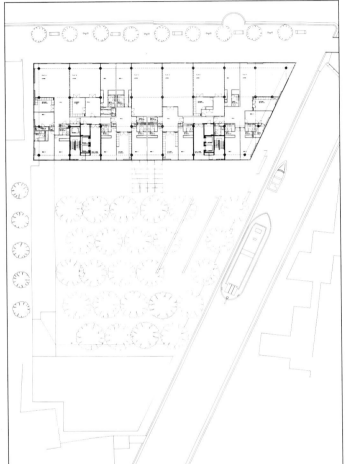

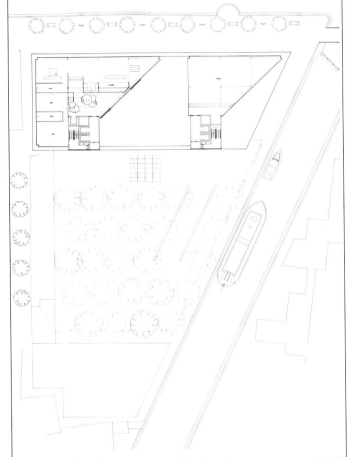

The north elevation, overlooking the River Thames. Like the studio below, the apartments enjoy floor-to-ceiling glazing on this façade to make the most of the views over the river and Chelsea. Full-height sliding panels allow the living rooms to become their own balconies.

was north facing. Along this edge, interspersed with whatever models and mock-ups might be under current review, are small tables. All day long they are in use, for random meetings or by individuals working quietly on solitary tasks.

On the opposite side of the space is a mezzanine which contains the three main meeting and presentation spaces, as well as our library — all open and visually connected. Underneath are the model shop and back-up areas — enclosed behind glass where the processes are noisy or have special needs, such as dust or fume extraction. Otherwise, almost everyone else has a place at a bench — directors, students, partners, modelmakers, computer operators, secretaries and architects. The only exceptions are those people working on competition projects which might require special security, or small overflow groups concerned with accounts and finance.

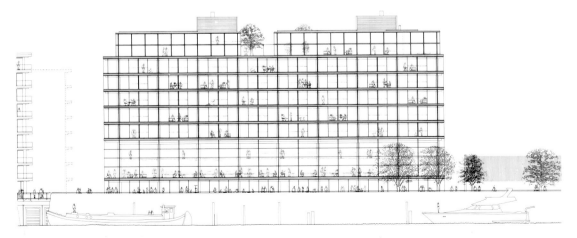

"It is the view forward that grips your attention. Like some gigantic species of car windscreen it offers an unbroken panorama of the River Thames, with Battersea and Albert Bridges and the traffic on Cheyne Walk so near you could reach out and touch them. No 'interior' could match the kaleidoscopic detail of this view of the outside world. In a flash you realise again what the 'glass architecture' of 60 years ago was all about. And now you can have it in gigantic single sheets with the insulation of triple glazing."

Martin Pawley, *Building*, 16 March 1990

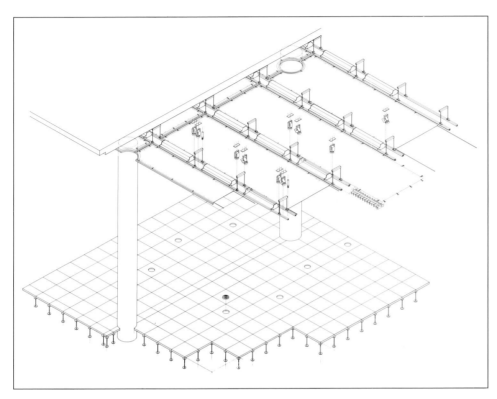

The materials which enclose this main space are simple — painted concrete, stretched fabric and carpet tiles to the full access floor, which is essential to cope with the frequent changes in layout of computer and communications hardware. It is the calm ambience which surprises most visitors. This is, in part, due to the carefully designed acoustic environment, which can easily cope with up to 250 people, including visitors for meetings, and still ensure privacy.

The tempo of the office changes by the week, the day and the hour. The bar is a lively meeting place from early breakfast-time, through lunch to evening drinks. Smaller groups might gather in the early hours, as the office is open 24 hours a day, seven days a week. There are no pressures or rewards for working antisocial hours; preferences and attitudes vary between individuals and this is reflected in a degree of choice — the important thing is that people are together when they need to be. Riverside is virtually a self-contained world with its own printing shop and photographic studio.

Although design is centralised in London and management flows out from there, it is impossible to think of the practice in isolation from the network of project offices around the

Services are concealed under a 'traditional' raised floor of calcium silicate tiles, with bonded carpet tiles, or above a suspended ceiling. The ceiling itself is constructed of a grid of Unistrut metal channels which support lighting 'strips', incorporating fluorescent and spotlights, and rectangular panels of stretched cotton fabric. Metal rods, which pass through seams along each edge of the cotton sheet, are clipped back to an angled steel frame using small stainless-steel springs to ensure the panels remain rigid.

The main space is divided by 13 double-sided drawing tables seating up to four people along each side, their places delineated by panels of sand-blasted glass.

world. The dynamic of Riverside owes much to the interaction and movement between these different places and cultures.

Communication is at the heart of our work as architects. A building must communicate to those who will use it, live in it and look at it. But it must be born out of their needs. There is no substitute for discussion and debate about the issues which will inform the design — this is an essential part of the creative process. Much of that research and exploration has to take

A deliberately large tolerance gap was created around the columns to emphasise the suspended nature of the stretched cotton panels. Two sets of panels were fabricated, allowing them to be changed every six months for cleaning.

During the summer, the late afternoon sun floods the studio — and Albert Bridge nearby —with its warm light.

231

The main drawing tables stop short of the glazed north wall, allowing the insertion of a narrow band of informal meeting tables interspersed with the latest study and presentation models.

Below: the great tables are supported by monumental four-legged steel frames. Finished in white linoleum, the tables incorporate an aluminium 'tube' along each edge into which larger drawings can be rolled for safe-keeping.

place on the home ground of the client and the building users — the two may not necessarily share the same point of view. Often, some of the most important exchanges need neutral space, or the kind of venue where people can interact with models or full-size mock-ups. It would not be unusual, at the start of such a meeting in Riverside, to preview a prototype and suggest changes that the model-makers can implement before the end of the same meeting.

Ultimately, the quality of thinking transcends these practical benefits. The art of architecture can be practised just as successfully out

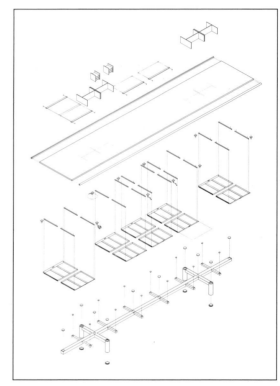

As well as its ceremonial granite staircase, the entrance gallery accommodates a narrow black-laminated bar, a communal meeting place where employees and visitors alike can enjoy coffee and meals throughout the day.

of a bed-sit in Hampstead, but the shift from that environment to the present one is not only more pleasurable, it has made it possible to contemplate far wider ranges of scale — from large-scale infrastructure projects to individual product design studies for door handles or bath taps. There is also an issue of principle. It is self-evident that if we suggest that an environment can influence the quality of our lives then it is inevitable that we should try to set an example in the environment that we create for ourselves as architects.

A directors' meeting takes place every Monday morning at the large round table located in the far corner of the studio nearest Albert Bridge.

The office's technical library is slotted into the narrow double-height zone between the edge of the rear external wall and the first line of structural columns. Fritted glass and stretched cotton panels protect against excessive heat build-up.

The east wall of the main building, alongside Ransome's Dock. The restoration of the riverside walk included the construction of a new bridge over the entrance to the dock and the refurbishment of the old lock-gates.

Right: the view from Cheyne Walk. The shift in rhythm of the external glazing module reflects the different uses within, from the studio and office space at the lower levels, through the upper apartment levels, to the penthouse on the roof.

The small pavilion on the southern edge of the site, seen here from the bridge over Ransome's Dock, employs the same glazing system as that lining the main studio. The regeneration of the area since the building's completion has included a thorough cleaning of the dock itself, which is now home to several houseboats.

The main building from Albert Bridge. Facing almost due north over the river, both the studio and the apartments have been able to enjoy the benefits of full-height clear glazing without recourse to any form of solar protection.

If Riverside demonstrates the value of good communication and a sharing of the main space by everyone on an equal basis, this should not be confused with an absence of hierarchy. Every Monday morning at 9 o'clock there is a directors' meeting which takes place at the round table in the far corner of the studio. This regular forum reviews every aspect of the practice and makes the critical decisions, such as which projects to accept or compete for. But there is also an interaction with other meetings which take place and involve a wider body of the practice.

For me, Riverside is a rare combination of a wonderful team and a great place to work. So much so that I contemplate the start of each day with eager anticipation. But the ultimate luxury is being able to live and work in the same location. I am not alone in that respect. For several people in the building it is a place to live as well as a place to work. Two individuals that I know of lease office space in the building and commute by lift from their apartments above — others have used the flexibility of their domestic spaces to blur the edges between their private and professional lives.

I have emphasised the importance of communication in the creative process and I have hinted at the link between creativity and sustained endeavour. The counterpoint to this is the physical communication that Riverside has created locally and how that relates to the wider context of London. For all of us there is contrast and stimulation in being able to move out through the network of pedestrian routes that we have helped to create. Sometimes these generate their own focus of social and commercial activity. For example, at the junction between the local road and the pedestrian path which leads down from the river, a lively shopping and café life has developed which spills out on to terraces overlooking the dock.

There is no road between Riverside and the Thames, unlike the Embankment opposite which is always busy with traffic. The result for those of us who live in the apartments is the luxury of a surprisingly calm style of urban living. This is particularly true at weekends when I often equate the experience to that of a rural retreat. From the apartments, whether they be on the third or eighth storey, you look out across London and not down on it. The skyline is constantly fascinating and punctuated by a surprising amount of greenery. London is an essentially

low-rise city and the area of Chelsea and Kensington that the building overlooks is, by European standards, quite dense. But the contact with the sky and the weather is sublime. Another unexpected surprise is the bird-life — for a wide variety of species the Thames seems like a play-space and aerial highway. Although there is no doubt that one is in the midst of a city, the proximity of Battersea Park and the ease of being able to walk everywhere gives this place a village-like quality.

I find intuitively that the most pleasant routes always take precedence over the others — even though they might be longer. For example, it is a shorter distance to walk to and from the local cinema via Battersea Bridge, but the journey is not as pleasant as using Albert Bridge, and the walk along the edge of the river is much more interesting than by the road which is a part of the other route.

I think most designers would welcome a second chance with any project — whether it is a building or an artefact. I know I would. But, more than any project, I would like other opportunities to explore the integration of spaces for living and working, particularly in an urban environment. Perhaps that is, in part, because I have learnt so much from the personal experience of Riverside and because I believe that it offers so many optimistic lessons for the future of cities. But, more than anything, it is because of the sheer pleasure, proximity and privacy that this way of life offers.

Norman Foster

Riverside, by day *(above)* and reflecting the setting sun *(left)*. As Martin Pawley has written, the building is "testimony to a renewed enthusiasm for Modern light, height and transparency."

1982-1989 Foster Associates

Directors

Anthony Beeley
Loren Butt
Chubby Chhabra
Barry Cooke
Spencer de Grey
Norman Foster
Wendy Foster
Martin Francis
Gordon Graham
David Morley
David Nelson
Richard Paul
Graham Phillips
Chris Seddon
Ken Shuttleworth
Mark Sutcliffe
Richard Wade

Project Directors

Howard Gilby
Richard Holyoak
Valerie Lark
Andy Miller
Robin Partington
John Silver
Rodney Uren

Associates

Ram Ahronov
Arthur Branthwaite
Hans Brouwer
Chris Eisner
Nick Eldridge
Roy Fleetwood
Katy Harris
Brandon Haw
Birkin Haward
Richard Hawkins
Neil Holt
Edward Hutchison
Paul Kalkhoven
James Meller
Tom Politowicz
Alex Reid
Charles Rich
Mark Robertson
Winston Shu
John Small
Chris Windsor

The Team

Chris Abell
Steve Abbott
Sue Allen
Ken Armstrong
David Arnett
James Attree
Nic Bailey
Gerry Baker
Keri Balding
Ralph Ball
Julia Barfield
Stephen Barrett
Vicky Bartlett
Nigel Batchelor
Eike Becker
Stefan Behling
Gabrielle Beier
Serge Belet
Dennis Berry
Charlotte Best
Andrew Birds *
Chris Blencowe
Camilla Blois
Susan Blyth
Etienne Borgos
Michael Borinski
Guiseppe Boscherini
Barbara Bouza
Manuel Bouza
Simon Bowden
Mary Bowman
Mark Bramhall
David Brindle
Grant Brooker
Claudine Brown
Nicola Brown
Peter Busby
Angus Campbell
Ben Campbell
Kevin Carrucan
Howard Carter
Paula Cassady
Colin Catchpole
Lesley Cauty
Hing Chan
Gillian Charman
Susie Chauveau
David Chipperfield
Sarah Christodolo

This book is the first of three volumes covering the work of Foster Associates during the 1980s. These were years of dramatic change and growth for the practice, during which time it moved from its offices in Fitzroy Street, first to Great Portland Street and then, in the spring of 1990, to its new home in Battersea. A great many people worked in the office during this period, some for a few months and more than a few for the entire decade. For reasons of organisation, the list given here includes all of those who worked either in London or in the Nîmes project office during the years 1982 to 1989. Those who worked only in the Nîmes office are marked with an asterisk. Those who worked in the Hong Kong project office, which also operated during this period, are listed in volume 3.

Chris Clarke
Lynette Clarke
Miriam Cohen
Sophie Cole
Simon Colebrook
Mark Collins
Chris Connell
Sarah Conrado
Ruth Conroy *
Alistair Cook
Martin Cook
Tony Cooke
Diane Copeland
Jo Crawshaw
Jonathan Crinion
Jane Cunningham
Neena Davé
Ian Davidson
Kim Davis
Susy Davison
Rudy De Boer
Arnauld de Bussière
Katherine Delpino *
Ian Dempsie
Cliff Denn
Pascal Desplanques *
Serena Doxford
John Drew
Shayne Drury
Alex Duckworth
Andy Duncan
Bryn Dyer
Shaun Earle *
Helen Eastick
Phil Edwards
Chris Eisner
Mike Elkan
Philippe Faure
Bertrante Feinte *
Georgina Fenton
Jacques Ferrier
Lulie Fisher *
Jason Flanagan
Johannes Flugel
Connie Flynn
Dawn Ford
Paul Fredericks
Juliette Freedman

Tobias Fusban
David Galbraith
Maria Gannon
Anna Garreau
Gareth Gaterson
Garnet Geissler
Jean-Pierre Genevois *
Ken Gomez
Carol Goodsman
Graham Goymour
Bruce Graham
Gilly Graham
Karen Grant-Hanlon
Carsten Granz
Christopher Grech
Robert Greenhalgh
Nigel Greenhill
Margot Griffin
Keith Griffiths
Armund Grüntuch
Gerold Haas
Pedro Haberbosch
Anthony Hackett
David Hale
Pauline Hanna
Catherine Harris
Leonie Harris
Jane Harrison
Bernard Harte
Philip Hartstein
Michael Haste
Chris Hennessey
Paul Heritage
Henk Hermans
Hans Heubeck
Paul Higgins
Lucy Highton
Serina Hijjas
Thomas Hoeger
Andreas Hofmann
Eric Holt
Richard Horden
Susan Horrocks
Alison Howard
Lyn Howell
Christian Huber
Sheila Jack
Lara Jayawardena
Syd Jeffers
Glenys Jones
Iwan Jones
Michael Jones
Paul Jones
Sally Jones

Declan Kaffrey
Jan Kaplicky
Joachim Kappeler
Julie Kellett
Ben Kern
Lisette Khalastchi
Melissa Koch
Jan Krarup
Peter Krepsi
Christine Kurpiel
Nicola Kutapen
Simon Lambert
Alexander Lamboley
Ian Lambot
Eddie Lamptey
David Langston-Jones
Katrina Laurino
Annette LeCuyer
Paul Lewis
Li Wen Tze
Alex Lifschutz
Huat Lim
Maria Loizou
Heiko Lukas
Gerry MacCreanor
Mike McColl
John McFarland
Wendy Mace
Philip Magee
Mouzhan Majidi
Michael Mak
Nick Marks
Frances Martin
Steve Martin
Naonori Matsuda
Caroline Matthews
Paul Matthews
Will Matthysen
Fiona Maxwell
Sophie Mears *
Clair Medhurst
James Mellor
Bobbie Michael
Tonia Michael
Stig Mikkelson

Nick Morgan
Steve Moxon
Colin Muir
Sachiko Murai-Ellison
Max Neal
Jesper Neilson
Clare Nelson
Michael Ng
Cordula Nies
Ian Norbury
John O'Donoghue
Anthony O'Donovan
Alex Oliver
Camille Olsen
Judy Paine
Heidi Palmer
Adele Pascale
Divya Patel
Gareth Paterson
Polly Paton
Gregoris Patsalosavvis
Rob Peebles
Irene Pham *
Victoria Pike *
Graham Potinger
Mark Presland
Theresa Pritchard
Janet Procter
Justus Pysall
Tim Quick
Mark Raymond
Lois Reich
Victoria Reis
Etienne Renault *
Goy Roper
Nina Rossides
Joel Rutten *
Thomas Scheel
Hartwig Schneider
Lucinda Schwerdt
Alf Seeling
Kriti Siderakis *
Ian Simpson
Lucy Skinner
Piers Smerin
Gabriel Smith
Mark Smith
Tony Smith
Oliver Sorg
Mark Sparrowhawk
Mike Stacey

Keith Stanton
Joachim Staudt
Steven Staughton
Seth Stein
Howard Stephens
Chris Stewart
Kenji Sugimura
Dawn Sutherland
Samantha Taffinder
Peter Terbüchte
Huw Thomas
Andrew Thomson
Mary Thum
James Tillman
Danielle Tinero
Paul Voysey
Ken Wai *
Abby Walker
Jeremy Wallis
Cindy Walters *
Kath Ward
Ann Watson
Maxine Webb
Martin Webler
Christian Wendt
Scott White
Melior Whitear
Jurgen Willen
Louisa Williams *
Chris Windsor
Anna Wood
Arek Wozniak
Armstrong Yakubu
Angie Young

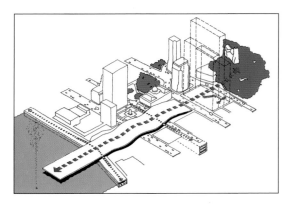  

Statue Square

Client
The Hongkong and Shanghai Banking
Corporation

Project Team
Spencer de Grey, Norman Foster, Birkin Haward,
Richard Horden, Jan Kaplicky, Winston Shu

Consultants
Structural Engineer: Ove Arup & Partners
Quantity Surveyor: Northcroft Neighbour &
    Nicholson

Hongkong Bank Annexe

Client
The Hongkong and Shanghai Banking
Corporation

Project Team
Peter Busby, Peter Clash, Spencer de Grey,
Norman Foster, Wendy Foster, Graham Phillips,
Thomas Leung, Winston Shu

Consultants
Structural Engineer: Ove Arup & Partners
Lighting: Claude R. Engle

BBC Radio Centre

Client
The British Broadcasting Corporation

Project Team
Ken Armstrong, Nic Bailey, David Chipperfield,
Spencer de Grey, Nick Eldridge, Norman Foster,
Wendy Foster, Annette LeCuyer, David Morley,
Max Neal, Robin Partington, Tom Politowicz,
Mark Sutcliffe, Martin Webler

Consultants
Structural Engineer: Ove Arup & Partners
Mechanical and Electrical Engineer: YRM
    Engineers
Quantity Surveyor: Davis Belfield & Everest
Acoustics: Tim Smith Acoustics

Autonomous House

Client
R. Buckminster Fuller

Project Team
Norman Foster, Wendy Foster, Buckminster
Fuller, Paul Matthews

Consultants
Structural Engineer: Fuller & Sadao Inc

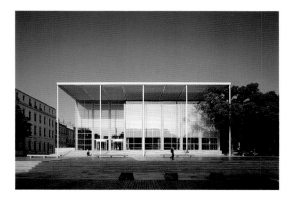

The Carré d'Art
Place de la Maison Carrée
Nîmes

Client
Ville de Nîmes

Project Team
Concept: Nic Bailey, Andrew Birds, Nick Eldridge, Norman Foster, Wendy Foster, Martin Francis, Paul Jones, Max Neal, Robin Partington

Development: Nic Bailey, Serge Belet, Arnauld de Bussière, Norman Foster, Martin Francis, Garnet Geissler, Michael Haste, Richard Hawkins, Edward Hutchison, Huat Lim, David Morley, Max Neal, Hartwig Schneider, Martin Webler

Construction: Chris Abell, Nic Bailey, Serge Belet, Arthur Branthwaite, Arnauld de Bussière, Ruth Conroy, Katherine Delpino, Pascal Desplanques, Shaun Earle, Chris Eisner, Nick Eldridge, Bertrante Feinte, Lulie Fisher, Norman Foster, Sabiha Foster, Martin Francis, Jean-Pierre Genevois, Bruce Graham, Michael Haste, Edward Hutchison, Michael Jones, Paul Kalkhoven, Alexander Lamboley, Eddie Lamptey, Huat Lim, John McFarland, Sophie Mears, Max Neal, David Nelson, Jesper Neilson, Robin Partington, Irene Pham, Graham Phillips, Victoria Pike, Tim Quick, Alex Reid, Etienne Renault, Joel Rutten, Ken Shuttleworth, Kriti Siderakis, John Small, Rodney Uren, Ken Wai, Cindy Walters, Louisa Williams

Consultants
Structural Engineer: Ove Arup & Partners/OTH Mediterranée
Mechanical and Electrical Engineer: OTH Mechanical
Financial Advisors: Thorne Wheatley Associés
Lighting: Claude R. Engle
Acoustics: Daniel Commins
Maintenance Systems: Jolyon Drury Consultancy

Principal Awards
1993 Interiors (USA) Award

Pavilion Cafeteria

Client
Ville de Nîmes

Project Team
Nic Bailey, Serge Belet, Norman Foster, Michael Haste, Huat Lim, Max Neal

Salle de Spectacles

Client
Ville de Nancy

Project Team
Nick Eldridge, Norman Foster, Martin Francis, Edward Hutchison, Paul Jones, David Morley

Consultants
Structural Engineer: Ove Arup & Partners/OTH Bureau d'Etude
Mechanical and Electrical Engineer: J. Roger Preston and Partners/OTH Bureau d'Etude
Quantitiy Surveyor: OTH Bureau d'Etude
Acoustics: Daniel Commins
Programming: Interconsult Culture

Urban Furniture

Client
JCDecaux

Project Team
Spencer de Grey, Norman Foster, Edward Hutchison, David Nelson, John Small

The Sackler Galleries
Royal Academy of Arts
Piccadilly
London

Client
The Royal Academy of Arts

Project Team
Julia Barfield, Spencer de Grey, Michael Elkan, Norman Foster, Tim Quick, John Silver, John Small

Consultants
Structural Engineer: YRM Anthony Hunt
Associates
Mechanical and Electrical Engineer: James R.
Briggs Associates
Quantity Surveyor: Davis Langdon & Everest
Lighting: George Sexton Associates
Conservation: Julian Harrap Architects

Principal Awards
1992 Mansell Refurbishment Award
1992 The Royal Fine Art Commission and
Sunday Times Building of the Year Award
1992 Institution of Civil Engineers Merit Award
1992 National Dryline Wall Award
1992 Design Review Minerva Award –
Commendation
1992 RIBA Regional Architecture Award 1992
1992 Interiors (USA) Award
1992 British Construction Industry Award –
High Commendation
1992 Structural Steel Award
1992 RIBA National Architecture Award
1993 RIBA Best Building of the Year Award
1993 Marble Architectural Award – Special
Mention
1993 Minerva Design Award

The Sackler Gallery

Client
Arthur M. Sackler Foundation

Project Team
Norman Foster, Wendy Foster, Serina Hijjas, Ken Shuttleworth, Rodney Uren

Consultants
Structural Engineer: Ove Arup & Partners
Quantity Surveyor: Davis Langdon & Everest

The Crescent Wing
University of East Anglia
Norwich

Client
The University of East Anglia

Project Team
Chubby Chhabra, Chris Connell, Norman Foster,
Carsten Granz, Richard Hawkins, Heiko Lukas,
Graham Phillips

Consultants
Structural Engineer: YRM Anthony Hunt
Associates
Electrical and Mechanical Engineers: J. Roger
Preston & Partners
Quantity Surveyor: Henry Riley & Son
Lighting: George Sexton Associates
Acoustics: Acoustic Design

Principal Awards
1992 Design Review Minerva Award –
     Commendation
1992 RIBA Regional Architecture Award 1992
1992 Civic Trust Award
1993 Citation Award from the International
     Association of Lighting Designers

Katharine Hamnett

Client
Katharine Hamnett/Aguecheeck

Project Team
Chubby Chhabra, Norman Foster, Wendy Foster,
Richard Holyoak, Paul Kalkhoven, Colin Muir,
Max Neal, Ken Shuttleworth, Mark Sutcliffe

Consultants
Structural Engineer: Buro Happold
Quantity Surveyor: Monk Dunstone & Associates
Lighting: Yates Associates

Shop for Esprit
Sloane Street
London

Client
Esprit (UK) Limited

Project Team
Chubby Chhabra, Norman Foster, Wendy Foster,
Colin Muir, David Nelson, Cordula Nies-
Friedlander, Robin Partington, Ken Shuttleworth,
Seth Stein, Rodney Uren

Consultants
Structural Engineer: Ove Arup & Partners
Mechanical and Electrical Engineer: Anthony
     Ross Limited
Quantity Surveyor: Davis Belfield & Everest

Principal Awards
1988 Annual Interiors (USA) Award

Shop for Esprit New York

Client
Esprit de Corps

Project Team: Nic Bailey, Norman Foster,
Wendy Foster, Colin Muir, Ken Shuttleworth,
James Tillman

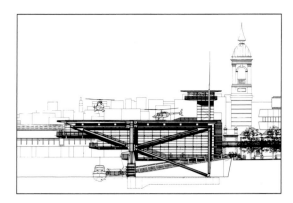

City of London Heliport

Client
City of London Heliport Consortium

Project Team
Simon Bowden, Spencer de Grey, Norman Foster, Joachim Kappeler, Richard Paul, John Silver

Consultants
Structural Engineer: Trafalgar House Engineering Services Ltd
Mechanical and Electrical Engineer: Trafalgar House Engineering Services Ltd
Costs: Cementation Construction Ltd
Project Liaison: British Airport Services Ltd
Advisors: British Helicopter Advisory Board/ Jolyon Drury Consultancy/London Scientific Services

Paternoster Square

Client
Paternoster Square Consortium

Project Team
Loren Butt, Spencer de Grey, Norman Foster, Wendy Foster, Gordon Graham, David Nelson, Graham Phillips, Ken Shuttleworth, John Silver, Rodney Uren

Consultants
Structural Engineer: Ove Arup & Partners
Civil and Traffic Engineer: Ove Arup & Partners
Mechanical and Electrical Engineer: J. Roger Preston & Partners
Quantity Surveyor: Davis Belfield & Everest
Acoustics: Tim Smith Acoustics
Environmental Impact: Tom Lawson
Goods Handling: Jolyon Drury Consultancy
Finance and Tourism: Coopers & Lybrand
Retail and Catering: The Piper Trust
Statutory Authority Requirements: XDS Consultants
Rights of Light: Wilkes, Head & Eve
Historical Consultant: Bob Crayford

Riverside Housing

Client
Petmoor Developments/Barclays Nominees (George Yard) Ltd

Project Team
Grant Brooker, Carsten Granz, Brandon Haw, Thomas Scheel, Ken Shuttleworth

Consultants
Structural Engineer: Ove Arup & Partners
Traffic Engineer: Halcrow Fox Associates

  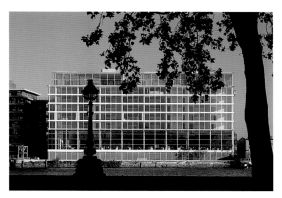

Docklands Square

Client
Olympia & Yorke

Project Team
Chris Abell, Mark Bramhall, Angus Campbell, Hing Chan, John Drew, Norman Foster, Brandon Haw, Iwan Jones, Stig Mikkelson, Robin Partington, Tom Politowicz, Mark Raymond, Ken Shuttleworth, Armstrong Yakubu

Consultants
Structural Engineer: Ove Arup & Partners/ Yolles/Cantor Seinuk
Mechanical and Electrical Engineer: J. Roger Preston & Partners/Flack & Kurtz/Cosentini

The Royal Thames Yacht Club

Client
The Royal Thames Yacht Club/Leigh Estates Ltd

Project Team
Chris Abell, Mark Brown, Eike Becker, Norman Foster, Jesper Neilson, Ken Shuttleworth, Danielle Tinero

Consultants
Quantity Surveyor: Monk Dunstone & Associates
Hotel Advisor: Pannell Kerr Forster

The Riverside Development
22 Hester Road
London

Client
Petmoor Developments

Project Team
Chubby Chhabra, Barry Cooke, Spencer de Grey, Norman Foster, Wendy Foster, Howard Gilby , Nigel Greenhill, David Langston-Jones, Valerie Lark, Heiko Lukas, Michael Mak, David Nelson, Cordula Nies-Friedlander, Michael Ng, Graham Phillips, Ken Shuttleworth

Consultants
Structural Engineer: Ove Arup & Partners
Mechanical and Electrical Engineer: J. Roger Preston & Partners
Quantity Surveyor: Schumann Smith
Acoustics: Tim Smith Acoustics
Lighting: Claude R. Engle
Graphics: Otl Aicher
Catering: Lorna Wing

Bibliography

Banham, Reyner, ed., *Design by Choice*,
 Academy Editions 1982
Benedetti, Aldo, *Norman Foster*,
 Zanichelli Editore Bologna 1987
Blaser, Werner, ed., *Norman Foster Sketches*,
 Birkhäuser Verlag 1992
Chaslin, François, *Norman Foster: Une Volonté
 du Fer*, Electa Moniteur 1986
Foster Associates, eds., *Foster Associates*,
 RIBA Publications 1978
Foster Associates, eds., *Selected Works 1964-
 1984*, Whitworth Art Gallery 1984
Foster Associates, eds., *Six Architectural Projects*,
 Sainsbury Centre for Visual Arts 1985
Foster Associates, eds., *Tre Temi, Sei Progetti*,
 Electa Firenze 1988
Foster Associates: *Buildings and Projects 1991*,
 Sainsbury Centre for Visual Arts 1991
Foster Associates: Recent Works, Architectural
 Monograph No 20, Academy Editions/St
 Martin's Press 1992
Jencks, Charles, *Current Architecture*,
 Academy Editions 1982
Lambot, Ian, *The New Headquarters for The
 Hongkong and Shanghai Banking Corpo-
 ration*, Ian Lambot 1986
Lambot, Ian, ed., *Norman Foster: Buildings and
 Projects 1964-1973*, volume 1, Watermark
 Publications 1991
Lambot, Ian, ed., *Norman Foster: Buildings and
 Projects 1971-1978*, volume 2, Watermark
 Publications 1990
Lambot, Ian, ed., *Norman Foster: Buildings and
 Projects 1978-1985*, volume 3, Watermark
 Publications 1990
Lasdun, Denys, ed., *Architecture in an Age of
 Scepticism*, Heinemann 1984
Nakamura, Toshio, ed., *Norman Foster*,
 A+U Special Edition 1988
Norman Foster, Monograph No 3, International
 Academy of Architecture 1991
Norman Foster, Quaderns Monografia (Spain),
 Editorial Gustavo Gili 1988
Suckle, Abby, ed., *By Their Own Design*,
 Whitney 1980
Sudjic, Deyan, *New British Architecture: Foster,
 Rogers, Stirling*, Thames & Hudson 1986
Treiber, Daniel, *Norman Foster*, Birkhäuser Verlag
 1992
Williams, Stephanie, *Hongkong Bank: The
 Building of Norman Foster's Masterpiece*,
 Jonathan Cape 1989

BBC Radio Headquarters
Architects' Journal, 10 November 1982, *Peak
 Viewing* by Gordon Cullen
Architects' Journal, 5 January 1983, *BBC Success
 Story* by Deyan Sudjic
Architects' Journal, 11/18 December 1991,
 Capital Ideas by Dan Cruickshank
Architectural Design, August 1986, *BBC Radio
 Centre*
Architectural Review, May 1987, *Foster at the
 BBC: A New Glasnost* by E. M. Farrelly
L'Architecture d'Aujourd'hui, December 1987,
 BBC Project by Peter Murray
Ariel, 8 March 1983, *Why Norman Foster is
 Looking for Imprints* by Andrea Michell
Casabella, No 557, May 1989
Financial Times, 24 June 1985, *The BBC Needs
 Foster's Foresight* by Colin Amery
Listener, 17 February 1983, *The Village Image
 Appears to be Central* by Stephen Gardiner
Observer, 18 July 1982, *Beeb on the Move*
 by Stephen Gardiner
Observer, 27 February 1983, *The Architect Comes
 of Age as Superstar*
Radio 3 Magazine, March 1983, *Langham Space*
 by Stephen Games
Sunday Times, 14 November 1982, *BBC versus
 the Gothic Monster* by Deyan Sudjic

House for Buckminster Fuller
Architecture and Urbanism, Special Edition, 1986
L'Architecture d'Aujourd'hui, February 1986

The Carré d'Art
Abitare, October 1991, *Interview with Jean
 Bousquet* by Claude Vuillermet
Archis, October 1993, *Norman Foster's Carré
 d'Art in Nîmes* by Geert Bekaert
Architecture, September 1993, *Portfolio of Three
 Buildings* by Colin Davies
Architectural Record, October 1993,
 Mediterranean Light by David Cohn
Architectural Review, May 1985, *Nîmes' Schemes*
 by Jonathan Glancey
Architectural Review, July 1993, *Carré Culturel*
 by Colin Davies
L'Architecture d'Aujourd'hui, December 1984,
 The Nîmes Centre Competition by Patrice
 Goulet
L'Architecture d'Aujourd'hui, February 1986,
 Médiathèque et Centre d'Art Contemporain
L'Architecture d'Aujourd'hui, June 1993, *Foster
 à Nîmes* by Michèle Champenois
Architecture Intérieure Créé, June/July 1993,
 Le Carré d'Art

Architecture Today, June 1993, *Gentle Giant:
 Foster's Carré d'Art in Nîmes* by Elisabeth
 Allain Dupré
Architektur Aktuell, June/July 1993, *Ein Tempel
 für die Kunst*
Art Monthly, June 1993, *The Exploded Museum*
 by Sarah Wilson
Blueprint, 5 November 1984, *Foster Wins in
 France*
Blueprint, May 1993, *The Beaubourg of the
 South*
Building Design, 9 November 1984, *Foster's
 Winner* by Ian Latham
Casabella, No 557, May 1989
Connaissance des Arts, *Nîmes Carré d'Art*,
 Special Issue 1993
Diseñointerior, September 1993, *El Carré d'Art*
 by Daniel Gomez Valcarcel
Domus, July/August 1993, *Norman Foster:
 Le Carré d'Art Nîmes* by Yehuda Safran
Independent, 24 March 1993, *A British Design at
 Home in France* by Jonathan Glancey
Libération, 16 November 1984, *Nîmes Upside
 Down*
Lotus 79, December 1993, *The Foster of Nîmes
 and the Carré d'Art* by Mario Lupano
Le Midi Libre, 20 October 1984, *Foster. . . avec
 les colonnades*
Le Midi Libre, 28 November 1984, *Ces archi-
 tectes venus d'ailleurs*
Le Moniteur, 2 November 1984, *Highflying
 International Competition for a Demanding
 and Determined Client*
Le Moniteur, 18 January 1985, *Nîmes: le Projet
 Foster, Nouvelle Version*
New York Times, 8 June 1993, *90's Minimalism
 Clashes with Ancient Rome* by Marlise
 Simons
Progressive Architecture, February 1985,
 The Beaubourg of Southern France
Space Design, September 1993, *Toward the
 Integration of New and Old* by Norman
 Foster
Sunday Times Magazine, 20 June 1993,
 A Thoroughly Modern Mayor by E. Jane
 Dickson
Techniques et Architecture, September 1993,
 Un Carré d'Art à Nîmes
Times, 2 April 1993, *Sun and Sympathy in the
 South* by Marcus Binney
World Architecture, April 1989, *Before and After
 the Flood*
World Architecture, No 24, 1993, *Contributing
 to a City* by Adrian Gale

The Sackler Galleries
Abitare, October 1991, *Sainsbury Wing, Sackler Galleries* by Fulvio Ivace
L'Arca, No 65, November 1992, *La Transizione Trasparente* by Paolo Righetti
Architects' Journal, 19 June 1991, *Foster on Show* by Alastair Blyth
Architectural Design, March/April 1989, *Foster at the Academy* by Marcus Binney
Architectural Design, November/December 1991, *Sir Norman Foster – Inaugural Academy Architecture Lecture*
Architectural Record, October 1991, *Royal Wedding* by Colin Amery
Architectural Review, December 1991, *Up into the Light* by Peter Buchanan
Architektur Aktuell, October 1991
Blueprint Extra 04, 1994, *The Sackler Galleries* by Rowan Moore
Daily Telegraph, 15 June 1991, *How to Fill a Gap with Art* by Kenneth Powell
Detail, December 1991/January 1992, *RA Sackler Galleries* by Karl Kauper
Financial Times, 17 June 1991, *And Then There Was Light* by Colin Amery
Independent, 12 June 1991, *Pavilioned in Appropriate Splendour* by Jonathan Glancey
Independent on Sunday, 9 June 1991, *Space, Light and Poetry Bridge the Gap* by Tanya Harrod
Journal of Architectural Conservation, March 1995, *Restoration of Burlington House* by Julian Harrap
New Builder, 26 March 1992, *The Subtle Art* by Dave Parker
New York Times, 31 May 1992, *A Priest of High-Tech in a Classical Temple* by Paul Goldberger
Perspectives, June 1994, *Bridging the Gap* by Martin Pawley
RIBA Journal, August 1991, *Ps* by Martin Pawley
RIBA Journal, September 1991, *An Academic Exercise* by Carl Gardner
RIBA Journal, February 1993, *New Buildings in Historic Contexts* by Norman Foster
Royal Academy Magazine, No 31, Summer 1991, *Breathing Freely* by Rowan Moore
Sunday Telegraph, 21 April 1991, *With Respect, Foster Does It His Way* by Kenneth Powell
Sunday Times, 9 June 1991, *Designed to Steal the Show* by Hugh Pearman
Time Out, 26 June/3 July 1991, *Wings of Desire* by Sarah Kent
Times, 30 June 1989, *All Change in Piccadilly* by Simon Tait

The Crescent Wing
Architects' Journal, 8 May 1991, *Second Generation* by David Jenkins
L'Architecture d'Aujourd'hui, September 1991, *New Crescent Wing*
Architecture Intérieure Créé, August/September 1991, *Extension du Centre Sainsbury*
Artscribe, September 1991, *Madam, Do You Know How Much Your House Weighs?* by Brian Hatton
Arts Review, 12 July 1991, *Norman Foster* by Tony Warner
Building, 24 May 1991, *Knight Light* by Matthew Coomber
Daily Telegraph, 16 May 1991, *Sir Norman Foster's Buried Treasure* by Kenneth Powell
Deutsche Bauzeitung, July 1991, *Adel Verpflichtet* by Falk Jaeger
Domus, December 1992, *The Crescent Wing*
GA Document, No 31, November 1991
Independent, 8 May 1991, *An Extension with More to it Than Meets the Eye* by Alastair Best
Lichtbericht 39, February 1992, *Crescent Wing* by Monika Salzmann
RIBA Journal, July 1991, *The Crescent Wing* by Richard Wilcock

Katharine Hamnett
Abitare, March 1987, *Remodelling: Space, Light and Fashion* by Norman Foster
Architecture and Urbanism, Special Edition, June 1986
Arena Homme Plus, Spring/Summer 1995
Art and Design, December 1986, *Katharine Hamnett Interview*
Blueprint, No 32, November 1986, *Hamnett in SW3* by Lisa Freedman
Designers' Journal, March 1987, *Foster's Entrance Bridge*
i-D, November 1986, *Katharine Hamnett*
Lichtbericht, No 26, March 1987, *Shop Design für Katharine Hamnett*
RIBAJ Interiors, January 1987, *Katharine Hamnett* by José Manser

Esprit
Architecture and Urbanism, Special Edition, June 1986
Architecture Intérieure Créé, October/November 1988

Bauwelt, No 34, 2 September 1988, *Foster Steels the Show* by Mattias Horx
Designers' Journal, September 1988, *Esprit de l'Escalier* by Rowan Moore
Domus, August 1988, *Negozio Esprit* by Lance Knobel
Principle, 1989, *Esprit: The Comprehensive Design* by Douglas Tompkins
World Architecture, No 6, 1990, *Communicate Don't Decorate* by Lewis Blackwell

City of London Heliport
Architecture Today, May 1990, *City of London Heliport on the Thames* by Dr Mark Swenarton
Building Design, 20 October 1989, *Foster's City of London Helipad*

Paternoster Square
Architectural Review, January 1988, *Power to the City* by Francis Duffy
Architecture and Urbanism, Special Issue, June 1986
Casabella, No 557, May 1989, *The Urban Dimension in Recent Work by Norman Foster* by Robert Maxwell
Quaderns, No 191 October-December 1991

Royal Thames Yacht Club
Architecture and Urbanism, Special Issue, June 1986
Casabella, No 557, May 1989

The Riverside Development
Abitare, October 1990, *Houses with a View*
AJ Focus, July/August 1990, *Great Fabrications*
Architects' Journal, 3 October 1990, *Office Politics* by Catherine Slessor
Architecture Intérieure Créé, August/September 1990, *Sur la Tamise*
Architektur Aktuell, October 1990
Baumeister, February 1991, *Architektbüro in London*
Bauwelt, 7 September 1990, *Metropolitan Sophistication* by Mattias Saverbruch
Building, March 1990, *Modern Perspectives Bring a Return to Glass-Consciousness* by Martin Pawley
Designers' Journal, September 1990, *Tales of the Riverbank* by Fay Sweet
Diseñointerior, 2 March 1991, *Nuevas Oficinas de Foster Frente al Tamesis* by Juan Herreros and Inaki Abalos

Credits

The editor extends his thanks to all those who helped in compiling and preparing the material used in this volume: the clients, consultants, contractors and members of Foster Associates, past and present, who gave freely of their time and knowledge, and the writers who gave shape and meaning to the considerable amount of information that was gathered in the process.

Special mention must also be made of those whose contribution to the production of this book has proved equally invaluable. At Foster and Partners, Katy Harris for all her help in tracking down key images and articles, ably assisted by Duncan Bainbridge, Lois Carleton, Marta Badia-Marin and Jo Olsen. Julia Dawson, Lesley Chisholm and Sally Welford worked tirelessly to proofread the text, and Lucy Chisholm helped with the layouts.

My thanks to one and all.

Drawings and Photographs

For the sake of simplicity, the drawings and photographs have not been individually credited; on those pages where the work of more than one draftsman or photographer is shown, the number in brackets indicates only how many images on that page can be assigned to each contributor. All attempts have been made to credit each picture correctly. Where this has proved impossible, credit has been given under the general heading of Foster and Partners, from whose extensive library the majority of this material was selected.

Drawings

Andrew Birds 66
Nick Eldridge 46(3) 47
Foster and Partners 13 15 16 21 23(1) 24(1) 25(1) 26/27 27 29 34(3) 35(3) 36 37 40 42 48 50 51 52 53 56 57 59 60 61(1) 64/65 67 70(1) 70/71 71 88 89 96 97 98 99 102 103 112 119 122 123 125 128 129 137 140 142(1) 144 146 147 160/161 162(1) 164 165 166(2) 177 180 181 182 183(1) 186 188 189 190 191 193 194 195 196 197 199 200 204(2) 205 206/207 208 212 213(1) 214 215 219 220 221 223 225 227 228 229 230 232 244
Norman Foster 20 28 30(1) 31 34(3) 35(2) 38 39 46(1) 61(1) 80 81 82 83 84 85 86 87 92 92/93 93   95 96/97 142(1) 156 157 161 162(1) 174 176 178 179
Buckminster Fuller 75
Russell Gray 143
Birkin Haward 22(1) 23(1) 24(1) 25(1) 30(1) 43 45 46(1) 70(1) 210 211 240(1)
Julian Harrap Architects 141
Helmut Jacoby 11 58 240(1)
Jan Kaplicky 22(1) 23(1)
Ordnance Survey 204(1) 204/205
Graham Phillips 160 162(1) 166(2)
Tom Politowicz 216
Ken Shuttleworth 158 183(1) 202/203 213(2)

Photographs

Architectural Press 95(1)
Clive Boursnell 158 159(1) 167(1) 242(1)
Richard Bryant/Arcaid 12(1) 13 135(1) 152/153 174 175 178 179 184 184/185 185 192(1) 230/231 231 232(2) 233(1) 237 238/239 243(1)
Peter Cook 170/171
Richard Davies 12(1) 15 16(1) 17(1) 22 25 26 31 32(6) 33(9) 36 37 41(2) 42(2) 44 45 47 48 49 51 54/55 55(1) 56 57 58 60 62 63 68 69 72 72/73 73 75(1) 76 76/77 83 85 87 88 90 91 94 95(3) 100 100/101 102 103 122 123(1) 126(2) 127(2) 129 130(1) 132 136 139 140 143 144 145(1) 146(1) 147 159(3) 163(2) 164 166 168/169 171(1) 172/173 181 187(3) 188(2) 189 191(2) 192(4) 193(1) 194(2) 198 201(1) 209(1) 210 212(1) 213 215 216 216/217 217(1) 218 219 220 221 224 225 226 227 228 229 230 234(1) 236/237 240 241(2) 243(1) 244 245(2)

JCDecaux 130/131 132/133 133(1)
Spencer de Grey 105 114(1)
John Donat 14(1) 163(1)
Richard Dudley-Smith 169(1)
Richard Einzig 11(1)
Neil Farrin 29
Fitzroy Robinson 135(1)
Foster and Partners 11(1) 20 21 32(1) 33(1) 41(2) 42(2) 55(1) 78(1) 79(4) 86 98 124(1) 126(1) 127(1) 133(1) 137 142 154 155 161 176 186 187(3) 188(2) 190(2) 191(1) 192(2) 193(2) 194(1) 195 196 203 205 207 208 209(1) 212(1) 217(1) 222(1) 242(1)
Norman Foster 10 18 32(1) 75(1) 78(2) 79(1) 80 81 84 123(1) 124(1) 125 128 223
Tai Foster 222(1)
Fuller & Sadao Inc 74
Dennis Gilbert 17(1) 109 110(1) 110/111 111 114(1) 116/117 119(1) 120/121 138/139 141 145(1) 146(1) 148 148/149 149 150 150/151 151 167(2) 168 169(1) 170 171(2) 173 187(1) 194(2) 242(1)
Hunting Aerofilms 40
Ken Kirkwood 14(1) 130(1) 131 162
Ian Lambot 16(1) 18/19
David Levenson/Telegraph Colour Library 134
Heiko Lukas 165 167(1)
Rudi Meisel 17(1) 112(2) 113(1) 114(1) 115(1) 118(1) 119(1) 232(2) 233(7)
Tom Miller 201(1) 245(1)
James H. Morris 107(1) 112(1) 113(1) 115(1) 117 118(1) 234(2) 235
John Nye 12(1) 28
Robin Partington 190(1)
Sharon Risedorf 183 243(1)
Tim Soar 106 106/107 107(1) 108 110(2) 113(2) 115(1) 116 118(1) 241(1)
Tim Street-Porter 194(1)
Tecno 14(1)
Xavier Basiana Vers 192(1)